SPIRIT OF THE SON

SPIRIT OF THE SON

The George Yoshino Story

Leroy Ledeboer

LEROY LEDEBOER

Spirit of the Son
Copyright ©2002 Leroy Ledeboer
All rights reserved

Cover design by Terri Jackson-Fuller and Pine Hill Graphics
Packaged by Pine Hill Graphics

ISBN 0-9714103-3-X

Printed in the United States of America.

Dedication

This book is dedicated to Kazuhi and Frank Yoshino, the Mom and Pop who George loved and admired so much and who were pioneering Americans, in the finest sense of those words.

It is also dedicated to every Japanese-American who emerged from the injustices of the internment camps, put those injustices behind them and once again emerged an integral part of this nation, as well as to the good men and women of all ethnic backgrounds who rose above the fears and prejudices of that era and helped reunite us.

Acknowledgments

First, a very special thanks to Marguerite Yoshino, who encouraged her husband to go forward with this project and then saw it through to completion. Early on George found it very difficult to revisit and talk about the more painful episodes in his life. Without his wife's constant support, as well as her probing questions, this may have proved impossible.

I would also like to thank Barbara Wilson, my wife Lois, and my son Lanny for their help in editing and proofreading, as well as their encouragement. Thanks also to Stephanie and Jeff Woerner for creating the fine cover art.

A Remembrance

As proofreader for this book I had the great privilege of reading about the extraordinary life of George Yoshino. I am still haunted by some of the passages, some of the insights, some of the tragedy and triumph of a life earnestly lived. I was George's friend; by the time I had read his life story, I was also his great, great admirer. Before I read this book, I knew him only as a trusted friend, the husband of my dearest friend, Marguerite, and always a source of very good company. After I had read of his life, his character and personality took on a more profound dimension. George was a quiet, courteous, generous soul; though he had great power, he carried that power lightly. And though he accomplished great things and possessed the material rewards such accomplishments sometimes bring, he had no need or desire to impress others with his importance. This quite elegant man, so soft-spoken, had a kind of gentle grace. There was nothing small about George-not his success, not his setbacks, not his triumphs, and certainly not his heart. And because he agreed to have his story told, others will be able to read of a life well lived, well loved, and well done.

Barbara Wilson

One

A FATHER'S
EARLY LEGACY

I had to pass sixty before I'd understand just how much I am my father's son," George Yoshino muses, reflecting back on his own life as a Japanese-American farmer, innovator and business man. "Oh, I ended up moving comfortably in a world of financial deals, new machinery, even politics, that had left Pop far behind, but the essence of what he was, I became.

"His work ethic, his dream of building a thriving family business, his constant search for new and better ways of doing things, these were the good things he passed on to me. The bad, well, maybe I took on too much of Pop's Old World reserve, his unwillingness to show much emotion, especially outward displays of affection, even for those he really loved. That, and far too often, just like my father, I'd end up putting my work before my personal relationships with my own family. Yeah, Pop definitely did that, and I have to admit, I followed suit."

Though this father he is describing, Frank Yoshino, was to have a profound effect on all four of his children's lives, only George would become a true reflection. Undoubtedly it was that

11

intricate combination of temperament, training and circumstance that lead to the defining moments in everyone's life, not just when key decisions are made, but more importantly when essential character traits are formed, that molded this youngest son into the man he became, his father's son.

Until he was thirteen, George knew little except the satisfying life of being one of four children in a highly successful Japanese-American farm family. Yes, the work was hard, but there was also the camaraderie of his older brother Vic and a host of friends, as well as recognition as a budding athlete and a first rate student. Then suddenly he and his family were shuffled off to a bizarre and painful life within two different World War II internment camps, to emerge a year later, his parents almost penniless and reduced to farm laborers. From that point on, growing up had to be done in a hurry.

"Actually, the hours and hours of hard farm labor in my pre-camp years had already given me a big step up toward taking on responsibility," he now explains. "But, yeah, the camps were definitely a real turning point. Without them I was heading into pretty normal high school years and maybe a college career. Instead I turned into a fifteen-year-old who had to step into a family void and take on a huge new role.

"Why could I do this?" George now asks, remembering those teen years when he took on the long hours and significant responsibilities of an Idaho row crop and mint farmer, and his twenties when he not only farmed in Washington's Columbia Basin but expanded into packing and marketing onions and potatoes. "Well, I'm not exactly sure, but I do know this: It was all about family, something else my father instilled in me."

"That void was there because Pop was almost sixty-three when he came out of the internment camp, and way too much had been taken away from him to make a significant new start. Oh, he could still work harder than most men half his age, and because we'd lost everything when we were hauled off to the camps, he had to, at first on other people's farms. He did whatever it took, pruning orchards, putting up hay, topping beets, anything to put bread on our table and hopefully to get a few bucks in the bank. We all worked, even Mom, who helped with the pruning and was out topping beets that first fall.

"No, camp life didn't destroy Pop's physical abilities. In fact he'd keep working, tending a small orchard and a huge garden, even after I was pretty successful and more than willing to take care of all his and Mom's financial needs. Internment destroyed something more internal and much more significant. It destroyed who he was. It destroyed his dignity.

"One day he was a prosperous truck farmer, our bread winner, a major employer in our valley, an authority figure not only to his family but to the whole community. Then suddenly he was stripped of his property and shuffled off to a make-shift prison where he was no longer our bread winner, where he constantly had to take orders, not give them. Pop had lost his authority and, in his eyes, without authority or respect a man was nothing.

"Sure, he could still put in a twelve-hour day of stoop labor if he had to, and when his family's welfare was at stake, he knew he had to. But Pop came out of those camps a different man, far less confident in his own abilities. Long before I was out of high school, I understood that if we were ever going to really have anything again, if we were to become anything but laborers working for other farmers, it was up to me. Maybe I was still six years shy of legal voting age, but I had no time to wait. I had to become my family's main decision-maker. Figuring out new ways to get ahead, putting in long hours sitting on a piece of farm machinery even when that meant giving up most of my social life and later too much of my family life as well, those weren't things I spent hours fretting over or even thinking about too much. They were tasks that were there, what had to be done to take care of my family."

This father that teenaged George believed he had to step in and replace was indeed a remarkable man, an Issei, or first generation Japanese-American, the epitome of the capable, industrious immigrant. In 1907 he came to this country as Heizo Yoshino, later Americanizing his first name. But unlike so many of his fellow immigrants, it wasn't poverty or a lack of opportunity in his homeland that drove this young man to America.

In fact, Frank was twenty-six when he set sail, the recent recipient of a Japanese law degree. His own prosperous and prestigious family, as well as an excellent position with an established

Tokyo law firm, awaited his return. Apparently he came to the new country with no intention of finding a new home. He simply wanted to further his legal studies and sojourn in a very different culture before settling into his life's work. Landing in Seattle, Frank quickly made friends among the established Japanese immigrants that had settled there.

None of his children ever knew what changed his mind, why he decided to give up everything that awaited him back home and stay in this new land, or why he hired on as a laborer with the Northern Pacific Railroad. This certainly wasn't a great position, but it did enable this inquisitive newcomer to explore the West.

"During the late forties Pop and I took a trip to Phoenix together," George now recalls, "and all through Eastern Oregon, Nevada and Arizona he'd point out the tiny towns where he'd been with the railroad, sometimes just traveling through, other times working there for a week or maybe a month. Even after the war I'd look at those towns and see little but desolation. What they must have looked like right after the turn of the century is hard to imagine. To this day I'm amazed that Pop didn't take one quick look and immediately head for the coast to catch the next boat back to Japan. Instead, he somehow envisioned a future in this country, dusty and undeveloped as it was way back then."

No doubt few young men with Frank's education and high expectations of a comfortable life in their homeland would have viewed the still rugged American west of 1907 as a place to build their future, but somehow he looked out at all that raw land and saw nothing but possibilities. Despite the fact that he came to this country with no agricultural background, farming had tremendous appeal. Yes, raw land was everywhere in the arid expanses east of Washington and Oregon's Cascade Mountains, but only a small fraction was close enough to a reliable water source to be irrigable. Pick the right place, Frank apparently believed, and vision, dedication, plus years of hard labor, could all add up to an American estate, his legacy to his future family. Growing and marketing his own crops, land ownership on a scale not possible in Japan, these became his goals.

Even when his adopted homeland passed the fantastically discriminatory law of 1924, limiting naturalization to 'free white

persons and to persons of African descent,' in effect excluding all
Asian immigrants from both citizenship and land ownership,
Frank wasn't deterred. He may have held out hope that this still
young democratic nation, which was rapidly emerging as the
leader of the free world, would soon come to its senses and remove
this absurd ruling. Unfortunately he'd have to wait until 1954, at
a time when his personal farming career was over. A year later he
and his wife proudly went through the ceremony, pledged their
allegiance, and became citizens.

But Frank also knew that the exclusion rule could only be
applied to him and his fellow Issei. His children, the Nisei, or second generation, would be born into U.S. citizenship. A time
would come when his family could own farm land in their names.
If he was going to farm, though, Frank had to start somewhere.
When railroading took him to Ringold, a tiny farming community
on Washington's Columbia River, roughly sixteen miles above the
larger town of Pasco, he made his move, quitting his railroad job
to work for a man named Rudkin, a row crop farmer who drew
water out of the river to flood-irrigate his fields.

Today the few urbanites who follow the paved but winding
roads to the Ringold area tend to see this place as a desolate back-
water, okay for the occasional hunting or fishing trip, but definitely not a place where they'd put down roots. In 1908 this land
was far more forbidding. For years it had been deemed suitable
only as a place to graze sheep, not a haven for row cropping. Arid
sagebrush and cheat grass hills rose up on both sides of the
Columbia. Winter brought icy winds and in the worst years deep
snow as well. The summer sun scorched the landscape, quickly
turning freshly plowed fields into dust magnets for the daily winds.
Rutted wagon tracks made up the region's meager road system.
Somehow, though, Frank decided this was the place to learn about
farming, and apparently Rudkin was a good teacher. His acreages
were small by today's standards, but the land was fertile. With a
steady supply of pumped-in river water, his vegetable plots were
highly productive. It was a system his new employee was destined
to emulate.

Two

THE IMMIGRANT'S AMERICAN DREAM

By 1910 Frank had learned enough about irrigation and raising vegetables to branch out on his own. Just as importantly, he'd gained the respect and confidence of his employer. That spring Rudkin helped him move twenty miles down river to Kennewick, to rent sixty raw acres with a rough house on it and get his first crops in the ground. Before a seed could be planted, all this raw land had to be cleared of sagebrush, then leveled. Frank started the process by using his new team of horses to drag a heavy logging chain across the ground, a horse attached to each end of this lengthy chain, entangling sagebrush limbs as they went, then ripping the sturdy plants out of the ground.

"When I had to do the same job forty years later, we used a pair of tractors to drag our chain," George reflects, shaking his head at the memory and the vision of his father. "And even then it was a tedious job because you sure weren't going to get all the sagebrush out in just one pass. We'd go over and over the same piece of ground before it was cleared enough to do anything else. With horses this must have seemed like an endless task."

Next Frank's new land had to be leveled, again entirely with horses. The team dragged a Fresno, a simple machine with a five-foot-wide metal blade. Besides controlling his horses, the driver had to continually raise and lower that blade, slicing the tops off the high knolls and dragging soil into the low spots.

"I only tried operating a Fresno once," George says, flinching slightly at the memory. "If you dropped that blade even an inch too much, it would dig in, catch in the dirt, the horses would lurch forward, flipping the whole machine, slamming the handles or maybe even the blade right into you. A square hit could do some serious damage. When I was growing up, I heard horror stories about farmers who'd been crippled for life by a Fresno. Luckily, when I upended mine, I was able to jump back fast enough to avoid a hard slam and only ended up with bruised forearms."

Despite this primitive equipment and having to do almost everything for himself, by the second season Frank had his new farm turning out strawberries, potatoes, carrots, and onions, all destined for the big Seattle and Portland markets. Fortunately, his land was in the Kennewick West Highlands, a rocky region that the spring sun warmed early. Then the long, hot summer days and moderate fall weather created a lengthy growing season.

It didn't take this industrious young farmer long to figure out that there was absolutely no reason to follow the local convention. Instead of harvesting a single crop and then letting his land lie fallow for the rest of the year, Frank was soon double and even triple-cropping everything except the perennials, his strawberry and asparagus patches. He'd rotate onions, cucumbers, radishes, carrots, potatoes and rutabagas.

In just a few years Frank became one of the Kennewick Valley's major employers, hiring dozens of seasonal pickers and retaining a fair-sized year-around crew to wash, sort and pack his produce. Before long he had two packing sheds, one for strawberries, one for vegetables. Strawberries, his biggest cash crop, had to be picked, washed and packed into boxes. Asparagus had to be hand-cut, sorted, bunched, crated. At peak times he employed as many as fifty pickers and packers. During major harvests his entire farm became a beehive of activity, with workers busy in the fields, produce trucks coming and going from early morning to late night. Buyers from Seattle, Portland and Spokane arrived to make purchases or pick up their produce.

If Frank Yoshino ever had to face the overt racism or the anti-Asian sentiment that ran rampant in many other parts of the west during the first half of the twentieth century, he never let his children hear about it. His white neighbors, many of whom would become his life-long friends, were more than willing to judge this hardworking insightful newcomer on his personal character, as well as his achievements. Frank soon earned a reputation for unwavering honesty, a reputation that would follow him throughout his life.

"Yeah, Pop did well in Kennewick, and it turned out to be a great place for me and the other kids to spend our childhood," George says, "but I guess I'll never understand why he chose to settle there. It seems his language problems alone would have pushed him toward a place like Wapato, not that far away and with an established Japanese community. Or at least he could have gone just across the river to Pasco, where there were a fair number of Japanese families. And I have no idea how he blended in with everyone in Kennewick so quickly. The town had a long history of other racism. For years blacks were essentially barred, even escorted across the bridge into Pasco by the local police if they tried to spend the night, and discriminatory real estate practices didn't end until after the civil rights uproar of the sixties, when government mandates forced changes."

Frank was not simply tolerated by his Caucasian neighbors. He was admired. Besides his reputation for honesty, his agricultural achievements and his early marketing were little short of remarkable. Not only would he become the region's biggest truck garden farmer, but despite the language barrier he'd struggle with all during his years in his adopted country, he'd play a key role in developing the Kennewick Irrigation District, an entity that turned a dusty semi-desert into a green oasis and exists to this day.

In so many ways this young Issei farmer and his adopted country were a perfect fit. From his native land Frank brought an incredible work ethic and a practical intelligence that enabled him to make a quick study of farming and marketing practices. For its part, the less tradition-bound young nation gave him plenty of latitude to innovate. Perhaps the words 'Yankee ingenuity' best describe Frank's entire farming venture. Not only was he a pioneer in multiple cropping, but early on he saw that the future of vegetable farming lay in quick transportation to major cities. He was among the first in that valley to purchase trucks, ton and a half Maxwells, his earliest ones sporting the old solid rubber tires. In the thirties Frank moved up to bigger Chevy truck and trailer rigs and started weekly produce runs to both the Seattle and Portland terminals.

"By that time Pop had way too much going on with his farming operation and his packing sheds to make these trips himself," George recalls, "so he hired a fellow who happened to be Chinese, a guy named Frank Wong Howe. Howe was a fine man, dependable as they come, but as a kid the thing that impressed me was that he was James Wong Howe's brother. James was probably the most famous Hollywood cameraman of his era, filming all the top movies, even the classic 'Gone With the Wind.'

"Pop would naturally have turned to those big over-the-road trucks because he was always ready to take the next step, anything he thought could expand his farming and turn a profit. He was always experimenting with new crops, trying to add variety to his arsenal, but he quickly discarded anything that didn't pay out. Before I'd come on the scene, Pop figured out that he could raise hogs on the beet and carrot tops, as well as all the other refuse you end up with on a vegetable farm. Then he made deals with local restaurants and grocery stores to pick up their food wastes so he could feed even more hogs. By the time I had to take part in this, we were fattening up to 500 hogs at a time and sending a truckload or two to market almost every month.

"As a kid one of my nastier jobs was to round up any pig that broke out of its pen and get it back where it belonged. But if a two hundred pound hog decides he doesn't want to be driven, it's pretty hard for a skinny eight-year-old lad to change its mind. Finally my older brother Vic taught me how to subdue these stubborn beasts. All I had to do was grab a handy two-by-four and give an ornery old boar a sharp crack right across his spine. This buckles any pig's back legs, temporarily paralyzing them.

"After that a hog's easy to control, and his hind-legs still work well enough for him to hobble back to his lockup. It sounds cruel, but my folks didn't accept excuses when they gave me a job to do, and that whack across the back was the only thing that worked for me. Plus, every hog I struck made a quick recovery. In fact, it was the same half-dozen pigs that always busted out, so getting smacked might have stung for a while, but it sure didn't intimidate them or improve their memories.

"Our farm prices were always going to be a roller coaster ride, but Pop's strategy of planting a variety of crops was a good one, and he had a few tremendous early successes. I once came across a Kennewick Courier newspaper printed in 1944 that told about Frank Yoshino's amazing potato crop twenty-five years earlier. It said Pop had sold that crop for $120 a ton right out of the field! To put that in real perspective, consider the fact that today's potato contracts call for eighty dollars a ton. Oh, Pop didn't have a huge potato acreage, but even so, what a windfall that must have been way back in 1919."

A YOUNG BRIDE'S
HARSH NEW WORLD

efore any of this could happen, Frank Yoshino had to take that next vital step toward becoming a family patriarch. He had to get married. In early 1915 it was time to emulate a pattern that had been established by earlier twentieth-century Issei bachelors. Finally prosperous enough to support a wife and family, Frank returned to his homeland to take a bride. Kazuye Hada, the cultured and charming teenaged daughter of his former employer in the law office, was the young woman he chose. She had grown up in Tokyo, in a family dominated by prominent lawyers and, a generation later, two federal court judges.

"We never talked about this at home," George reflects, "but I have to believe it was an arranged marriage. That was real common back then, especially for the Issei bachelors. Oh, this wasn't on the level of the 'Picture Brides,' where marriages were arranged after an exchange of photos and a few letters and maybe some assurances on the groom's part of financial security. No, given the station of her family, Mom's parents must have held Pop in high regard to accept him as a son-in-law and then watch their daughter go off to America.

"Mom was seventeen years younger than Pop, and he wasn't in Japan long enough for any real courtship. He went there in the winter, married her and quickly returned to the U.S., probably to get his fields ready for spring planting. I guess because Pop needed more time to get established, she didn't join him for a couple of years.

"Yeah, I'm sure it was arranged, but by their standards and values, I'd say they had a very good marriage. At least by the time I was aware of my surroundings, they'd settled into a warm, comfortable relationship, where Pop was the man of the house, Mom his willing helpmate, and they were definitely proud of each other.

"But I don't want to give the impression that my mother was a little shrinking housewife, hanging on her husband's every command. No, she was far from that. In fact, for her era she was an incredibly strong woman, well educated, always willing to vigorously state her opinion. When she was convinced she was right, she'd fight hard to get her way, sometimes for days, even weeks. She was still traditional enough to let her husband have the last word, to make that final important decision, but far more often than not, Pop gave in, accepting her judgment. Unless he was adamant on a subject, Mom could use just the right mix of persistence and cleverly worded arguments to bring him around.

"It sure helped that Pop had the highest regard for Mom's opinions. Yes, he demanded the final authority that husbands back then assumed was their God-given right, but he wasn't stupid about it. Early in their marriage he must have realized that Mom was an intelligent woman with real common sense because he always carefully listened to what she had to say."

George's word 'strong' may be an inadequate adjective to describe the seventeen-year-old bride who made that long-ago solo trip to America. Raised in a comfortable upper class home where she was surrounded by the refinements of a centuries-old culture and given perhaps the best education a Japanese girl could receive in her day, Kazuye married a man she could have only known for a short while, then embarked on a journey from Tokyo to early twentieth-century Kennewick that was much more than a matter of miles.

This journey started with a two-week boat trip to Seattle, fourteen miserable days, enduring endless rolling swales and daily bouts of sea sickness. Then a long slow train ride on a local took Kazuye to her new home where she'd have to face the dry, dusty life of an early Columbia Basin farm wife. Kennewick's country roads were little better than cattle trails or well established wagon ruts. By early June only her husband's irrigated fields and her own carefully nurtured flower plots near her little home broke the brown monotony of the sunburned landscape. In the evening coyotes serenaded her from the breaks of the river. As the sun warmed the morning, rattlesnakes slithered from their scab-rock dens into the farm's irrigated fields, in search of rodents and fresh water.

"When we'd ask about those early years, Mom would just shake her head," George recounts, still in awe of what his mother had to face. "She'd tell us how for that whole first year she cried every single day, partly because she missed her family so much, but mainly because her new home and that entire country was so dismal. The house they lived in was little more than a shack. Whenever a wind kicked up, which was almost every day in the Columbia River Basin, dust blew in through the cracks around the window sills and under the door jambs. Comparing what she now endured day after day to her former life would have made any young woman cry.

"But like I said, Mom was a remarkable woman. Despite the language barrier and everything else, it wasn't long before she had plenty of friends among the neighboring farm wives. These women were really good to her when she was starting out, and over the years several of them helped our family in dozens of ways. At first, though, Mom must have felt totally cut off, totally isolated. She'd never say anything bad about Pop, but she'd come thousands of miles to make a new life with a man she hardly knew and then was thrown into a world of daily dirt and toil. It's a real tribute to both her and Pop that they not only endured those early years, but built a strong, loving relationship."

As if the young bride didn't already have enough to deal with, sometime during their second year of marriage Frank's older brother, Takejiro, came to America and moved into the little house with them. Takejiro wasn't yet forty, but he already had a very complicated and troubled past. He'd left Japan after a military career that to a point was brilliant but then somehow went awry. More troubling, he'd gone through an incredible four marriages and divorces, which in that country and during that era had to be nearly a record, not one his family and friends were going to admire.

"Yeah, Uncle Takejiro not only moved in with the newly-weds, but he'd end up living with us from then on," George recalls, "right up to internment and then again afterwards. If Mom ever resented him or all the extra work he must have created for her, she never let on, never breathed a single complaint, at least when I was around. She cooked Uncle's food, washed his clothes, treating him as another member of her household."

Today this all sounds pretty incredible, especially to young people who have always enjoyed their own space, but in the early twentieth-century it was simply one more of those strong old-country traditions that were so ingrained in Kazuye and Frank. They held firmly to the belief that you take care of a family member, no matter what, and you never complain or do anything to make him feel unwanted.

Then, as if farm life and an extra man in her home weren't enough, her husband always had one or two young men from Japan employed, workers she had to feed. Like other established Issei men, Frank would sponsor a young fellow so he could come to America, then hire him until he was ready to strike out on his own.

"At least a couple of these guys didn't work out for Pop," George remembers, "probably because they'd fled Japan with criminal tendencies. I never knew any of the details, but before long they'd run afoul of this country's laws, too. As their sponsor Pop was responsible for their actions, but what really made him furious was that he'd given them a real opportunity to better themselves, and they'd blown it. Pop did everything in his power to make sure these criminals were deported. The two or three bad apples were a tiny minority, though. Most of these young fellows were honest and dedicated workers. They'd live in a separate small house we had on our farm, but they ate their meals with us. Some would go on after a single season, getting their own little piece of ground or finding steady work in a big city, but others stayed on with us, one for at least ten years.

"Well, for a young man who was a good worker but who had no great desire to be out farming on his own or maybe starting a business, life with us was a pretty good deal. Pop paid them fair wages for that time, and with no expenses for food and shelter, they'd always end up with plenty of spending money. But, yeah, this meant Mom was faced with forever having an extra man or two at her table."

Just when it would seem that this young woman had more than enough to endure, a pair of heart-breaking tragedies struck. Kazuye's first two babies died shortly after their birth, a little over a year apart, no doubt victims of the primitive prenatal and pediatric medical care of that time and place. In fact, Takejiro always maintained that her first child had died of exposure to the extreme cold that invaded the hospital nursery.

"Neither Mom nor Pop ever said a word to any of us kids about this," George soberly reflects, "maybe because if it was true, the memories were too sad, too painful, and there was nothing they could do about it anyway. But my uncle was adamant. Throughout his life he blamed the hospital for that baby's death, getting angry all over again whenever he told the story."

It was 1921 before Kazuye gave birth to a son, Elmer, her first child who would live beyond infancy. He was followed at approximately two year intervals by her only daughter, Louise, then a second son, Victor. Three years later George came along, completing her family. Somehow the mature, capable woman her children knew and admired emerged out of all this, a devoted wife and mother, thought highly of throughout her community, and a key figure in her family's always expanding farming enterprise.

Like most men of his generation, Frank Yoshino wasn't demonstrative nor lavish with his praise, though he understood how fortunate he was to have selected a bride who not only took care of his home and raised his children, but also spent long hours laboring in his fields, handled his finances, at times scratching desperately to meet payroll and other obligations, and still found time to be his loving, caring mate.

"Japanese women of Mom's era accepted the fact that their men didn't express feelings, particularly when anyone else was around," George explains, "but I've never doubted for a minute that Mom knew how Pop felt about her. When we were kids, he'd say and do little things, things only he and Mom understood, things that would make her smile or even break out laughing. Yeah, they had their little secrets, their own happy memories that they treasured and kept to themselves. And us kids, well, we didn't have to be told that our parents had a strong, loving marriage. We simply knew. We caught the signs. It was easy for us to feel good about our Mom and Pop's relationship. Sometimes it was harder to tell how Pop felt about any of us."

"Oh, don't misunderstand, as a kid I had great respect for my father, an admiration that only grew as I matured. In fact, in my adult years Pop and I had plenty of warm conversations, mostly about my own farming and business ventures, it's true, but by then Pop's feelings for me were far easier to read, and our father-son relationship couldn't have been better. Looking back, though, I see that despite the endearing nickname one of the older kids must have tagged him with, Pop was pretty reserved during our growing-up years, mainly because he was such a hard-driving man. First and foremost he was determined to be successful.

"Time for his family had to take a very distant second place. Crops, market prices, trying to buy or lease another piece of ground or build a new pen so he could raise a few more hogs, these were always uppermost in his mind. If any of us kids had a serious problem, we took it to Mom. She was a whole lot more talkative, much more patient and understanding, and far more capable of showing us love. No, in those early years Pop made sure we worked and took responsibility, but otherwise he never seemed to have much time for us."

Carefully sorting through his childhood memories, George finally added, "Well, to be fair, Pop did take the time to teach his sons about one Japanese tradition. He taught us all to fence with Kendos, those big two-handed swords. He'd ordered the swords, steel face guards, chest protectors and shoulder pads from the old country, which had to be expensive, but he took this tradition seriously.

"Pop was good with those heavy swords. He'd had expert training back in Japan, and he made the sport into a real art form. As soon as he put on all the garb and picked up his Kendo, he became a different man, a real warrior, ready to do battle. You could see it in his eyes, in the way he stood, the way he moved. Kendo was all about leverage, striking at the right moment and hitting the exact spot. When Pop let loose, he could knock a grown man right off his feet.

"Sometimes one of our Japanese workers who'd had a little experience in the old country would issue a challenge, then take Pop on in an actual match. Unfortunately, none of these guys were anywhere close to being in his league, so their bouts were pretty short, with Pop making a couple of quick moves, then standing tall above his flattened adversary. I've always wished we could have seen him go at it with someone on his skill level, to see what he could really do. Mostly, though, Pop used Kendo just to teach his sons and his young workers about the tradition and how to improve their own fencing techniques, and he was careful not to hurt us."

Still it was Kazuye who was always there for her children. George now understands that he had to grow up and take on his own family responsibilities before he would fully realize what a remarkable woman his mother was. Besides almost single-handedly raising four kids, making daily meals for seven or eight hungry people, handling the books and helping her husband with the endless field work, Kazuye spent several evenings a week teaching Japanese-language classes in Pasco.

"Our book work alone would have been a major job for one person to handle," George states, "because It wasn't only the normal farm bills that had to be paid regularly. With our labor-intensive crops and our packing shed, Mom had a detailed payroll to figure out. In the leaner years I remember her searching through those ledgers over and over, almost desperate to meet an upcoming payroll and to make sure she'd have enough dollars left over to pay a little something to every one of our creditors.

"Plus, she and Pop had big plans to send all four of us to universities for at least four years, but they thought this meant paying weekly insurance premiums, just to make sure we'd all have a college fund. There were times when Mom actually hid from the insurance collector when he came to our door because she didn't have enough money right then.

"It wasn't until 1952, long after my own and my brother Vic's dreams of college were gone, that Mom received four $1000 checks, a nice little windfall for her at that time, but those checks were sure hard earned, particularly when she'd had to pay so many of the premiums with depression-era dollars."

Four

A MOTHER'S DEVOTION,
A BROTHER'S LOVE,
A FATHER'S INTEGRITY

George, born in 1928, clearly remembers his earliest years as a time of definite financial swings. During the family's best years they lived in a comfortable home, he had decent school clothes, his father traded in his trucks and the family car every two years. At one point finances were so good that the new family sedan was a beautiful LaSalle, the luxurious forerunner of the Cadillac.

"But in 1933 something happened that came within inches of ending my personal story, and it must have been a real financial setback for our family," George now recalls. "Two days before my fifth birthday I'd gone across the highway that ran right in front of our house, just to pick up our mail. On my way back, I guess I got a little careless and didn't look both ways, or maybe I dawdled a bit on that road. Anyway, a speeding car clipped me with its left front fender and knocked me clear up to our house, cracking my scull and breaking my leg right by the hip. A slightly more direct hit, and I'd have been finished.

"As it was, I ended up in the Pasco Hospital for an agonizing three summer months, with no way to escape the intense daily heat. My leg break was so high up that the bone would separate every time I turned over a little too fast or made any other wrong move. Three times during that miserable summer I had to endure a doctor coming in and re-breaking and resetting that leg. Then the whole healing process had to start all over. I was a skinny little kid and that horrible cast rubbed right up against my meatless bones. I swear I could smell the stench of my own deteriorating flesh in that sweltering ward.

"Yeah, that was one miserable summer for me, but it sure brought out the best in my family and left me with memories I've always treasured. Mom must have been terrified that she was about to lose another child because she stayed with me the whole time, despite the heat and everything she had to be neglecting at home. I couldn't have asked for a better nurse. She had no way of keeping me cool or taking away all my pain and discomfort, but she did everything she could, bathing me with wet towels, reading to me to pass the hours, even watching over me while I slept, fretting every time my fever went up half a degree. "

Frank and Louise visited the young patient every single day, bringing food and clean clothes for Kazuye, sometimes small gifts for George. Elmer was also a regular and enjoyed cheering up his younger brother up with bits of teenager humor, but unfortunately one of his jokes terrified the little invalid.

"Getting bounced across the pavement like that, I'd ended up with a couple of egg sized knobs on my head," George now laughs. "I remember gingerly touching them each day, wondering if they'd always be there. Even at that age I knew I didn't want to go through life with a lumpy head. Maybe I let Elmer know about my fears because one morning he told me he'd talked to my doctor and the doctor explained that the biggest lump was the start of a new head. Right away I argued with him, crying that that was a lie. But he kept saying he'd talked to my doctor, and I'd soon be a two-headed kid.

"Now remember, I was barely five and this was one time when my vivid imagination was anything but wonderful. In fact, I was scared to death! I'd lie there in that hot room at night, seeing myself as a real freak. I'm sure Elmer was totally clue-less about what this little charade was doing to me, but that didn't help me much for a month or so, until those knobs started shrinking."

If Elmer's little joke gave the bedridden tyke long days of terror, his brother Vic's thoughtfulness was destined to leave a warm impression, an impression about the very nature of this older sibling.

"Vic wasn't even eight that summer, but he'd already developed that kind, giving nature that became his trademark," George fondly recalls. "Every day he'd bring me a Dixie Cup, one of those little half-pint containers of vanilla ice cream that every kid back then craved. No matter how hot the day was, and many of them had to top a hundred, Vic would first ride his bike better than a mile to the grocery store to pick up my ice cream. Then he'd have to double time it all the way to the hospital before it melted. Half a pint of ice cream isn't much, but those daily Dixie Cups became the joy of my life, the one little treat I could look forward to in that stifling heat."

George has no idea what his long hospital stay and his doctor bills cost his parents, but he does know that right after he was finally sent home, the family moved onto a lower grade farm. They went from living in a very nice modern home to a place that he now describes as little more than a shack, with tiny little rooms and no running water. Later Frank was able to purchase this particular farm, but at the time George feels his entire family was forced to take a real step backwards.

"I can't say for sure," he says, "but there's better than an even chance that this was a step Mom and Pop had to take because of the costs of my hospital stay. If that's true, it must have been a real hardship on Mom, going from that dandy little home with running water and everything to that borderline house across the road. Neither Mom nor Pop ever told me this, maybe because they worried I'd feel guilty. They just quietly adapted to their new home, like they did to everything else.

"I do know that our economic times must have been a lot tougher around 1936. By then the depression had gone on long enough to really hurt the vegetable markets, and hog prices were terrible. Suddenly Pop wasn't trading cars and trucks every two years. When he did upgrade, it was never to a brand new model."

In George's earliest years the Yoshinos always celebrated Christmas with a big feast and a few presents, but when the tough financial times hit, these festivities were suddenly eliminated.

Christmas became just another day, with no presents and a simple meal. However, New Year's Day, a much stronger Japanese tradition and one Frank and Kazuye had always made into a family and friend's affair, was another matter.

"No, our family finances never bottomed out to the point where Mom or Pop were forced to quit celebrating New Year's," George happily reflects. "That day was far too important. For a kid like me, it revolved around wonderful food. Mom would prepare weeks, maybe months in advance, sending all the way to the old country for mail-order mushrooms and different herbs, as well as getting all kinds of traditional foods we couldn't buy locally from a Japanese specialty shop in Seattle. Once they had all their ingredients, Mom and Louise would be busy in our little kitchen for three or four days before the big event. We started the morning with a traditional New Years soup called Ozoni, a dish served with mochi, a homemade rice cake. Making mochi ahead of time was a big part of our celebration. It took a full day and involved our whole family, as well as a couple other families who lived close enough to join us.

"Years before Pop had cut two big chunks off the base of a downed tree, about a foot and a half in diameter and at least a couple of feet tall. Then he'd chiseled a big bowl shaped depression in the top of each one. We'd set these up in our yard, and Mom, Louise or a neighbor woman would bring out a batch of hot steamed rice in a muslin cloth and set it in that bowl. Then Uncle Takejiro, Elmer, Vic and I would get to take turns manning that big wooden mallet. It's head was cylindrical, about six inches in diameter and at least fifteen inches deep, flat on both ends. It had a long handle that we'd grasp with both hands, swing the head high, then drive it down into the rice. During most of those years I was too small to be very effective, but I sure fought hard for my turn.

"The problem was that the mallet swinger had to get a real rhythm going because between each stroke someone else, in our family it was always Pop, had to constantly turn the rice over and over with his bare hands. Get slightly out of sync and you'd smash his fingers. This never happened when Uncle wielded the mallet, but at least once a year one of us kids nailed Pop, leaving the perpetrator face to face with a very angry father, caught between rubbing his aching hand and delivering his best tongue lashing. But smashed fingers aside, we'd soon have that hot rice beaten into a smooth paste. Then ours went back into the kitchen, where Mom or Louise shaped the whole works into little cakes. The neighbor women took their rice paste to their own homes to finish the job.

"Our mochi was always made into squares, in the Tokyo tradition that Mom's family practiced, but other Japanese women made theirs into little round cakes because they or their parents had come from a different part of Japan. Families that still make mochi today do it with motorized machines, eliminating much of the labor but also the fun. With our traditional tools, we made mochi-making into a family and neighborhood event."

Ozoni soup and mochi cakes were a fine mid-morning repast, but the real New Years feast came in the afternoon, with a variety of delicious Japanese dishes, made so much better because most were a once-a-year treat. Later in the afternoon the Yoshinos would welcome friends into their home, mostly Japanese families who came to exchange New Years greetings, another important Old Country tradition.

"No, even in our down years we were never really destitute," George quietly remembers. "Despite the economic downturn of '36, that was the year when Pop purchased that sixty acre farm and the little house where we'd live until the war. I guess the guy who sold it to him was feeling that same economic crunch because he gave us pretty favorable terms. Not being a citizen, Pop couldn't legally own real estate, and none of his kids had reached legal age yet, so he made a hand shake deal with his attorney, a man named Charles Powell, to put the deed in his name until Elmer came of age. It was a risky way of doing business, based entirely on two men talking over the terms, coming to an agreement, then shaking hands. But it turned out that Powell was a good man, a man we could rely on to keep his word, a man who eventually became a federal judge.

"Yeah, Depression or not, Pop was pretty clever at figuring out new ways to get a little cash flowing into our coffers, even when his newest idea involved more hard work. For instance, he'd scout the outlying sheep ranches, looking for well-used winter feeding pens that were truck accessible. Whenever he located a good one, he'd make a deal with the rancher who owned it to haul away all the dried-up sheep manure.

"Then he'd load it in his high-sided truck and haul it all the way over to Seattle, where he could sell it to a fertilizer company, which in turn sold it to that area's small farmers and gardeners. I guess for those times Pop made a decent profit doing this. The ranchers were glad to get their pens cleaned out and didn't charge him anything for the manure, so his only real cost was truck fuel. As a little kid I thoroughly enjoyed riding along on Pop's scouting trips, always imagining I was heading off to far-away places, going on a real adventure into new country, though I doubt if we ever got more than thirty miles from home, and about the most exciting thing I ever saw was a jackrabbit or maybe a mangy old coyote running across the road. Later, when Vic and I had to do most of the loading, all with a shovel, then go over to Seattle and unload, that fertilizer business wasn't nearly as much fun.

"Pop did fine with his farming, but when it came to making business deals, his poor grasp of the English language was a real detriment. Without that I have no doubt he'd have been far more successful. Language hampered his ability to thoroughly investigate a deal before he made it, and in the produce business there were always plenty of vultures just waiting to take advantage.

"I don't mean to imply that this was because we were Japanese and therefore considered fair game. No, if given half a chance, these same bloodsuckers would have cheated their own grandmothers out of their butter and egg money. They were as likely to cheat a brother-in-law as they were a total stranger. With Pop, though, it was just a bit easier because he couldn't quickly grasp the details of a deal.

"Two local produce dealers, Big Y and Pasco Growers, really took advantage of him, refusing to pay up after he'd delivered the goods. After that he absolutely refused to sell to either one of those outfits, even when their buyers came to him and offered cash. Pop was so adamant about being a man of his word and expecting every other man to meet his standard that he simply wouldn't abide or deal with cheaters. It was a wonderful trait, but years later when I had to move in a world of much higher finances, I was sure glad that my father never had to deal with the real gangsters out there."

After a reflective pause George added, "But you know, there was something equally wonderful about my father back then. As driven as he was in so many ways, he couldn't always make hard-headed business decisions, even when he understood the economics. For a long time he employed fifteen to twenty German farmers and their wives, a group that had been driven out of western Nebraska during the dust bowl. Every winter Pop kept them all on our payroll, paying every worker, man or woman, twenty-five cents an hour as laborers or twenty-seven cents if they drove a tractor or a team of horses.

"I know we didn't need that many employees in winter, but those farmers were good people, honest and industrious, and I guess Pop just figured they'd suffered enough. Those were the days before welfare or unemployment insurance, so any family without a steady bread-winner was in for a tough time. Eventually a few of these families drifted off to other jobs, but most of them, including a fine gentleman named George Brummer, who was kind of their natural leader, stayed with us until the war disrupted everything."

Five

GEORGE'S WARM AND MOSTLY WONDERFUL EARLY YEARS

His early Kennewick years gave George more than warm memories of his father's integrity and kindness. Despite the occasional glitches in his family's finances, he recalls an era of solid friendships, quality play time, and growing responsibility. From early on his bicycle meant freedom. Long before he turned ten, he'd ride to the city golf course to scour the roughs for lost balls, then carry them to the clubhouse and sell them back to the men in knickers and high socks. Each week his mother entrusted him with a dollar to make a two-mile ride over a rough gravel road to a neighbor's farm, where he had to purchase five dozen eggs, then transport them home safely.

"That egg run was usually pretty uneventful," George now laughs, "but I sure took it seriously, as if the family meals for the next seven days depended on my success. But one time I was coming back with all those eggs in a big grocery bag and hit this long downhill grade that truck traffic had turned into a real washboard. Just before the road bottomed out, I lost control and headed for the ditch. Suddenly my front tire hooked a rut, twisted sideways, and flipped me right over my handlebars. I was okay, but that crash broke every last egg in my sack! Man, I was terrified, sure my folks would skin me for wasting a whole dollar. But that was just my over-active imagination running rampant. When I finally picked myself up and struggled home, Mom was far more concerned about my cuts and scrapes than she was about a bunch of busted eggs or her lost dollar."

"By the time I was ten or eleven, a much bigger thrill was going to the movies on Saturday with my friend, Bill Green. Kids' tickets cost a nickel back then, and that's all our folks would give us, but this particular theater had a couple of vending machines, where for the same nickel you could get a candy bar and if you were lucky, there'd be a ticket tucked into its wrapper. Normally neither Bill nor I would have risked our nickels, but for one whole year his older sister Mary worked at that theater. Part of her job was loading those vending machines, so she'd let us know which were about to pay off. Maybe she even stacked one when she saw us coming. At any rate she made our purchases foolproof. A movie and a candy bar, all for the same nickel. That's a big treat when you're ten!

"Then in the fall, right after the first freeze-up when watermelons had lost their commercial value, Pop let us invite all the kids over to walk the patch and kick the left-overs. A good kick and the ripe ones would bust wide open and let us absolutely gorge ourselves on the sweet centers. All the guys really looked forward to watermelon-kicking day. This paid off for Pop, too, because the word went out and summertime melon raids never hit our crop."

But life in the Yoshino household definitely wasn't all about movies, candy bars and watermelons. In so many ways theirs was the typical Japanese-American family of that era, where education was constantly stressed, where elders were respected, and children were expected to help make a go of the family enterprise. Discipline was a given, yet neither Frank nor Kazuye ever felt the need to strike a child. If a son or daughter needed correcting, either parent could mete it out with a few sharp words. Repeat offenses were indeed rare.

Frank and Kazuye had a simple but very effective system.

"What was expected of us was always made pretty clear," George recalls. "We might argue or fuss about something for a time with either Mom or Pop, but we knew our limits. When they'd had enough, they'd let us know it was time to shut up and do what we were told. Our folks didn't overly stress religion, but what I'd call basic religious tenets of right and wrong, these were pretty strongly ingrained in all of us. I can't remember Mom or Pop ever telling me not to use profanity, and like most boys back then my speech could turn pretty blue when I was around my bud-dies, but I sure knew which words to drop when my folks were within earshot.

"Actually, in our family we had a fascinating mix when it came to religion. Mom and Pop were both practicing Buddhists when they came to this country. Then in Kennewick they became very close friends with the Episcopal pastor and his wife, a fine couple by the name of Pennell, and started attending their church. Eventually they both converted to Christianity, at least partly I think because of their warm friendship with the Pennells and the examples those two set. But my parents couldn't simply abandon their childhood and young adult religious training either. Yes, they became Christians, mostly attending a Christian church, but they never entirely gave up being Buddhists. We always kept a shrine at home, and they still worshipped before it on special days. Mom went to the Buddhist church in Wapato occasionally, and years later she and Pop befriended a Buddhist priest from a Seattle church, a man who'd come over for long visits.

"I think Mom and Pop felt strong spiritual ties to both reli-gions, though towards the end Christianity may have held a stronger sway. When they died, we had Episcopalian funerals for both of them. They'd made it clear a few years earlier that that's what they wanted. I still have their Buddhist shrine in my home, though for me it's now an important part of my family's long spir-itual tradition, going all the way back to my Japanese ancestors, and no longer a religious icon."

In many parts of the American West anti-Japanese sentiment ran strong long before the bombing of Pearl Harbor brought it to a fever pitch. Particularly in parts of California, where 110,000 of the West Coast's 125,000 Japanese resided, resentments ran very deep. Instead of being admired for their industry as Frank was in Kennewick, in parts of that state Japanese truck garden farmers were loathed and feared as talented and unrelenting competitors. Their lands, many of poor quality before hard-working families converted them into productive vegetable farms, were coveted by their Caucasian neighbors. It was pressure from California that led to the despicable 1924 immigration law.

In their little corner of the Northwest the Yoshinos had been spared almost all of this. As a grade schooler George was a quick student, big for his age, a natural athlete who became much better because he often competed with older boys. Race mattered very little. His was a childhood of strong friendships and acceptance. He knew a few Japanese lads through his mother's language classes in Pasco, but his schoolmates and neighborhood friends were Caucasian, young lads and a few girls who unconditionally accepted him. He recalls only isolated incidents of racism, fleeting moments he could easily disregard.

"When I was in first grade, we had a kid move in from somewhere in the South," he recalls. "One day at recess this kid was suddenly in my face, yelling 'dirty Jap.' I was pretty tough for a little kid, and for a minute I considered pounding him into the schoolyard, but fortunately I didn't. Instead I just went off with my friends and ignored his ignorance. I knew this kid was a little slow, sort of at the bottom of our class, someone my friends and I regarded as kind of a low life. Yeah, I'm afraid we had our own little system of judging classmates, but it sure wasn't based on race. No, I really wasn't bothered by anything that lad said to me. This happened one other time, I think in fourth or fifth grade, but again it was a kid I didn't take too seriously. If those two boys wanted to play redneck and display their ignorance, I figured it was their problem, not mine.

"It definitely helped to be at the top of my class, both academically and on the playground. It put me in with a good group of kids and gave me plenty of confidence to more than hold my own in any situation. In my own little circle, I was a leader, always making plans for our next adventure, organizing football and baseball games. Whenever anyone in our group had a birthday party or planned a picnic down by the river, I was included. As far as I ever knew, none of my pals nor their parents were concerned about my race. I was accepted into their homes, and all the kids came and went freely in ours."

After a reflective pause George added, "Guys like Bill Green, Jim Boldt, Gene Graves and Charley Quast, even some of the girls like Boots Wiggins and Norma Monico, these were the friends of my youth. A few have remained my friends for life. And I wasn't the only one to gain full acceptance. Elmer, Louise, Vic, they had their own circles, again all Caucasians because those were our neighborhood kids, the kids we knew.

"The only time I ever cried in school was the day my fourth grade teacher, Miss Mueller, wouldn't let me participate in a spelling bee. But this had nothing to do with race. For me, spelling was a gift. I'd won those bees too many times in a row, so that day Miss Mueller decided it was someone else's turn. Oh, I knew my teacher really liked me, in fact I was kind of her bright-eyed pet, but I cried anyway, only because I was so competitive. I never tired of winning."

George doesn't remember a single teacher he disliked, but like most kids he can single out one who was special. His was a young woman named Gerry Dam, only nineteen when she became a sixth grade teacher. Miss Dam loved sports as much as the athletic youngsters in her class, and better yet, she knew how to coach. That winter she organized a dozen lads into a basketball team, taught them a few rudimentary plays and then worked out a schedule of home and away games, something that school had never seen before. George was in ecstasy. Now basketball wasn't simply a pickup playground game, but a real sport with referees, actual opponents, bus rides, everything the big boys enjoyed.

"It's hard to describe how excited I'd get over those games," he now grins, "especially our out-of-towners. Then as the weather warmed, Miss Dam would gather a bunch of us kids together on a Saturday and go on long bike rides, just to look at the countryside or maybe have a picnic. When summer came on and the water heated up, she'd take us to an irrigation ditch and give us swimming lessons. Now I drive by that scummy old ditch and wonder how she ever dared let us even wade in it, but Miss Dam was an athlete herself, a champion swimmer, a real outdoors woman, and she took genuine pleasure in seeing her boys learn new skills.

"Best of all, she had a way of making a simple bike ride along a dusty gravel road into something special. She was born and raised in Richland, a town just north of our little community, and she had a real love for that arid landscape. She'd point out all the different flora and fauna. She'd tell us how snakes shed their skin in the spring and explain why we shouldn't kill them because they helped control rodents. When we saw a band of young ducklings swimming in tight formation behind their mother, she said that as soon as they came out of their egg shells, the babies saw their mother, imprinting their tiny brains so they'd always follow her. One day we watched a little bird called a Killdeer run ahead of us in short spurts, dragging one wing like it was broken. Miss Dam explained that we must be too near the bird's nest, and this was her way of drawing a predator off, acting as if she'd been crippled and couldn't fly."

Ironically it was also these bike rides that gave young George his first chance to negotiate a deal, a skill that would become one of his most valuable assets just a few years later. When Kennewick was about to have a big parade, Miss Dam quickly signed up her young riders, giving them special instructions to decorate their bikes so they could all ride proudly as a group.

"She really stressed that she wanted our bikes to have class," George recalls, "but unfortunately my bike was a real old beater, handed down from Elmer to Vic, then to me. I knew I could string that pile of rust and dents with ten yards of bright crepe paper, and it was still going to come out looking like the old junker it was. For this showcase parade I needed a shiny new bike with a real horn and plenty of chrome. It was time to try my hand at horse trading!

"First I went to the Kennewick Hardware Store where I knew the owner, a man named Gravenslund who dealt with my folks all the time. Gravenslund was a nice man and he was plenty willing to sell me a bike, but he insisted on having my dad's signature before he'd take my old bike in on trade and let me make payments on a new one, which in retrospect seems pretty reasonable. But for some reason I was determined to make this deal entirely on my own. So I hopped on my old beater bike and headed across the bridge to the Pasco Hardware Store.

"Maybe the owner of that store had traded with Pop from time to time, but he sure didn't know me. Yet he sold me the most expensive Schwinn on his little show floor, a beautiful bike with all the bright chrome a kid could ask for, plus all the latest bells and whistles. That fellow even gave me a generous eight dollars in trade for my old beater bike, then let me make payments, three dollars a month, no interest, and all this just on my signature. Pretty heady stuff for a sixth grader. I made sure I never missed a payment, earning the money by working for Uncle Takejiro and delivering flyers around town.

Grinning a little sheepishly, George added, "That story makes it sound as if I was always a model citizen back in those days, but that's a bit of a stretch. My buddies and I pulled plenty of stuff we had to keep hidden from our parents. For instance, one day I was delivering those flyers with a young renegade named Lester Miller. It was three or four hours after lunch and naturally we were pretty hungry, so we slipped into a local vineyard and started eating Concord grapes. Concords are a juice and jelly grape and not all that great for straight eating, but I guess our young appetites and the lure of that forbidden fruit improved their taste.

"Anyway, after we'd each gobbled down half a dozen big clusters, Lester pulled out a pack of cigarettes and offered me one. Well, I couldn't let Lester think I was a sissy, so I grabbed a smoke and lit it up. Whether I ever inhaled or not, I don't know, but I'm sure I started turning green with my second or third puff. Before it was half gone, I was bent over, retching, chucking up all those awful grapes and everything else I had in me. Then suddenly the heaves stopped, and my head started spinning, aching like someone had cracked me with a baseball bat. My eyes even hurt. I sprawled out spread-eagle on the ground, praying this would all go away.

"Old Lester thought all this was pretty funny and ended up rolling on the ground he laughed so hard. But I was in too much misery to cuss him out for giving me that smoke or for his lack of compassion. I hurt so badly for the next hour that ten years would pass before I'd light up another cigarette. Too bad I didn't make it through two of Lester's smokes before that nausea hit. Maybe then I'd have ended up sick for a full day and come away smart enough to swear off tobacco for life!"

If a smoke with Lester was pure misery and a bike ride with friends and his favorite teacher a pleasant childhood interlude, it was sports that gave George his real confidence, an 'I can do it' feeling that would last forever. Two of his best buddies, Bill Green and Jim Boldt, were top athletes, both destined for stellar high school and college careers. As kids Jim and George challenged one another, each lad always trying to be number one, whether on the baseball diamond, the football field or the basketball court.

"Jim was a big kid and a very good athlete, fast and well coordinated," George readily concedes, "but I had a couple aces in the hole too. First, Bill liked to compete himself, but in those early years he always pushed me to be number one. Second, I had my brother Vic. I bet I wasn't eight when Vic taught me how to throw a football and a baseball and was always getting me into games with the bigger boys, the kids his age. Then he'd be right there, encouraging me, telling me 'you can do it, George. You can tackle that guy. You can hit that pitcher.' Vic was a fine athlete himself, but whenever I was on his team, he'd get more caught up in my success than his own. For a competitive little kid like me, he was the best possible big brother."

Six

A GIANT STEP INTO THE MACHINE AGE

I f school was relatively easy and sports a fine confidence builder
for the youngest Yoshino, at times work on the family farm
seemed unending. All through their grade school and junior
high years, George and Vic faced before and after school chores.
In the spring there were twice-a-day asparagus cuttings, stoop
labor that had to be done in the chill of early morning and under
the hot afternoon sun. Summer vacation didn't simply mean bike
rides and swimming. It also meant long hours of weeding, chopping, picking, and packing, and it gave Vic and George the
chance to drive the family trucks.

"Now it's even hard for me to believe, but I was only six
when I started driving a Model A Ford panel truck from our fields
to our packing sheds and storage cellars," George marvels. "It all
started when Pop, Vic and I were working outside one of our cellars. Suddenly Pop realized we needed that old panel. It was sitting
out in a field, maybe a quarter of a mile away. I'm sure he was
about to order my brother to get it, but I never gave him that
chance.

"Instead I sprinted out there, jumped in the panel and started it up, doing everything I'd seen Vic do dozens of times. Before Pop knew what was happening, I had his old truck right in front of him. He didn't say a thing, but I guess that convinced him I could handle on-the-farm driving, and he quickly realized this could be a real plus. I was too young to do as much manual labor as Vic, so by driving I became much more useful.

"But I'm amazed Mom didn't put a stop to this. She was absolutely terrified of our gentle work horses, always warning us kids to stay away from them. She was sure we'd get kicked in the head or at least stepped on if we ever set foot inside their corral, and she did a pretty good job of instilling this fear in Vic and me. I like horses, to look at, but I've never felt comfortable around the big beasts. Yet with all her protective maternal instincts, Mom didn't strenuously object to her six-year-old son driving a vehicle. If she had, I know Pop would have had to side with her. Sure, I was a bit big for my age, but even so driving that panel was dangerous. I was still so short that when I got down low enough to step on the brake, I couldn't see over that truck's dashboard. Luckily, Model A's had an extra gas lever mounted on the steering column or I couldn't have made it go and watched where it was heading at the same time."

George is convinced that he drove well for his age and size, but he recalls one bad incident that could have ended more than his precocious driving career. To haul a load of produce back to one of his father's packing sheds, he'd have to back that panel down a long narrow driveway, right between his Uncle Takejiro's stately chrysanthemum gardens. All of Takejiro's flowers were beautiful, but his real pride and joy were his giant mums, the biggest and most spectacular flowers George would ever see, with huge deep-colored blossoms. Takejiro spent part of every summer day tending his prize mums.

"Well, because I was so short," George can now laugh, "whenever I backed up, I'd have to set the gas lever at a slow speed, then open the driver's-side door and lean way out to see where I was going. This meant I'd be steering with one hand, which wasn't all that easy even for a normal-sized driver because that old panel's steering was so sloppy you had to crank hard on the wheel to make the slightest correction.

"One day as I was trying to veer a little to my right, I lost my grip and just that fast was flat on the ground. I can still see that left front tire glide past my head, inches away. A bit more torque on the wheel before I slipped, and I'd have had tire treads across my face. With its gas lever set, that old panel wasn't about to stop. It just kept rolling back, mowing down those beautiful chrysanthemums, coming to a halt only when a rear wheel spun out in soft mud, right in the middle of that bed.

"Unfortunately this had to be a time when Uncle Takejiro was out there weeding. He looked up just in time to jump clear of my runaway panel. Had it smacked him, I'd have been better off with tire tracks across my scalp. As it was, he was on me in a flash, right in my face, screaming at me, yelling that I'd ruined his best plants. My poor uncle was so excited about those crushed mums that he didn't even think to see if I was okay."

Despite this near miss and having to endure his uncle's wrath, young George still considered himself an accomplished driver, and he thoroughly enjoyed the prestige and responsibilities that accompanied his new role.

"Yeah, I liked driving that old panel," he reflects, "and as soon as I could, I moved up to our bigger trucks. Part of this was because I'd quickly figured out that driving was a whole lot better than picking and packing, and partly because climbing behind a wheel made me feel all grown up. I'm not sure why, but even at that young age I craved responsibility. Most of the time I demanded it. Whenever Mom, Pop or anyone else tried to hold me back, to treat me like the little kid I was, I'd argue loud and long, demanding what I thought were my rights. My parents, well, I'm sure they quickly concluded that giving in had two advantages. First, it shut me up. Second, it gave them a far more valuable farm hand.

"I knew, though, that I couldn't hold onto these big boy responsibilities unless I consistently performed beyond my years. If Pop or Mom had known about that crushed chrysanthemum bed and how close that front tire came to crushing their little boy's precious skull, I'd have been stuck out there with a hoe in my hand until I was at least ten. Uncle Takejiro must have known how much all this driving meant to me because mad as he'd been when it happened, he never told my folks or anyone else about my little accident until years later, when it became one of his favorite stories.

"But that one slip reinforced my desire to quickly develop just the right touch, to concentrate hard whenever I was behind a wheel. When we harvested watermelons, I'd drive while Vic and the rest of our crew loaded the fruit, sort of like they were stacking cord wood, one high row at a time. Everything I did had to be smooth, like letting the clutch out or levering on the gas. Until the truck bed was almost full, any sudden lurch would send those stacked-up watermelons tumbling, breaking their shells."

His rapidly developing skills and a little luck allowed George's driving to continue. Before he turned ten, he was delivering produce to his father's outlets in Kennewick. When he was eleven and Vic fourteen, they started having actual contests backing a truck and trailer into a narrow shed, just to see who could do it faster. Machines and speed. For George, it started way back then.

Seven

TAKEJIRO'S VALUES AND INSIGHTS

D riving a truck may have given the youngster periodic breaks from his daily field work, but it certainly didn't eliminate it. George was still expected to take his turn with the weeding hoe, the asparagus knife and the picking baskets. Despite the long hours and the tedium of laboring on a vegetable farm, he now looks back on those long hard days with few regrets, particularly when the labor involved Uncle Takejiro.

"Working for Pop was just expected, and of course we didn't get paid," he recalls. "But most years Uncle Takejiro would lease a small plot of ground near our farm and raise onions, potatoes and sweet corn, all labor-intensive crops. So he'd hire me, paying me a whole nickel a row for weeding his onions. In a long hard day I could get through ten rows. Better yet, because we'd work side by side, it gave us a chance to have long serious talks. My uncle always treated me as if I was much older, almost like an adult. He'd definitely had his problems and made his share of serious mistakes back in Japan, but he was a smart man who taught me a lot. Long before I'd hit my teen years, we'd developed a real bond. At least part of this was because he'd had such bad times with his own kids.

"Right before I was born, his son Maurice immigrated to America and moved in with the folks too, finishing high school in Kennewick. Maurice was intelligent, but otherwise he was nothing like his father. Even as a high schooler he'd already become all talk and no work, a trait he'd never outgrow. Once he was out on his own, he drifted from one job to another all across the country, mainly being a waiter or a bartender, always irresponsible, always running up debt and then skipping out, just the kind of person my uncle couldn't abide. During the fifties he came to work for me, but by then the fellow was so lazy and irresponsible I finally had to fire him, relative or not.

"A worthless son in America, a couple of others that he wasn't getting to know back in his homeland, no wonder my uncle ended up bonding with me and treating me like the son he wished he'd had. Years later, he'd give me one of his most prized possessions, a medal he'd earned in combat. And I was more than happy to become my uncle's substitute son because he was a fascinating man.

"Besides his natural military demeanor, he'd brought intriguing little customs from the old country. For instance, he didn't raise those giant chrysanthemums just for their beauty. When they matured, he'd actually pickle dozens of the blossoms. He'd eat these during the cold winter months, claiming that a regular dose of pickled mum blossoms kept him healthy, prevented colds, flus, and even strengthened his teeth.

"Far more fascinating for us kids, though, was watching how Uncle Takejiro dealt with a cut or a sore muscle, using a potent incense he imported from Japan. First he'd rub this stuff all over the damaged spot. Then he'd take a match and light it on fire. That incense made quite a flame on his bare flesh, but if Uncle felt any pain, he sure didn't show it, never flinching or changing his facial expression. He'd just stare at that little flame as it burned itself right down against his skin. This must have been a carryover from my uncle's army days because it sure wasn't typical among other Issei I knew, and it wasn't a health remedy anyone else in our family was willing to try, not even Pop. But it seemed to work. Uncle would put that flame to an infected sore and have it totally healed in less than a week.

"According to him, regular treatments with those incense fueled flames strengthened his entire body. Maybe he was right. In all the years he lived with us, I don't remember a single time when Uncle ever went to either a doctor or a dentist. In his late eighties he was still a robust man who'd work for hours out doors, and he lived 'til he was ninety-three.

"It was our serious talks, though, that brought me closest to my uncle, partly because these talks made me feel grown up, but they also showed me a deeper, more human side of this old man. One morning when we were working together, he vividly described a terrible thing he'd had to do during that awful Japanese-Russian War of 1904. Russian logistics and the primitive methods of transportation they had made holding onto prisoners impractical for both sides. Captives were quickly turned into casualties.

"As his unit's commanding officer, Uncle Takejiro had the grim task of performing all of its prisoner executions. As he described it, he'd make a captive kneel, put a foot on the fellow's shoulder, then with one swift motion behead the man and kick his body backwards, to avoid getting splashed by all the spurting blood. This wasn't a technique he'd devised. It was standard procedure, something he had to do because of his rank, but I'm sure that didn't make it any less ghastly to perform or easier to live with afterwards.

"No, this was a grim tale, this beheading story, and definitely not something my uncle told with any gusto or pride. In fact, whenever Takejiro told me about the war, and he only did this when it was just the two of us, the stories unfolded slowly and made him reflective and kind of sad. I sometimes think he told me all this because he needed to get his awful memories out in the open, to share them with someone he hoped would someday understand a little of what he'd gone through. Or maybe he felt a real need to let me know just how tough the world beyond our family farm could be.

"Yeah, I was just a kid when we had our best talks, but even then I could tell that what Uncle Takejiro saw on the Russian front, both with the death of so many of his own troops and his role in slaughtering those helpless prisoners, had taken a major toll on him. He'd come out of that war with such deep emotional scars that telling me a story only gave him a little relief, if it helped at all. I do know that he walked away from his military career with memories that haunted him for the rest of his life.

"In fact, I'm almost certain he came out of that Russian campaign at least partly traumatized, and that's what ended his military career and drove him out of Japan. As an officer he'd been a leader of men, a role that must have fit his essential character and his earlier demeanor perfectly. To this day every time I pull out our old photos and look at my uncle in his colonel's uniform, I know that I'm looking at a man who was a natural commander, a man who must have appeared destined to rise to the very top of his country's military command. Yet during most of the years he'd spend in this country, he was content to quietly tend his beautiful flower gardens and raise a few vegetables, as if he dreaded having to take on greater responsibility ever again.

"But try as he might Uncle Takejiro couldn't always help being the powerful man he was, with his booming voice and his natural presence. When he'd get mad, his eyes literally flashed, his voice boomed, and you just wanted to get out of his way. When he turned on the power, even Pop backed down and let his older brother have the last word. The established Japanese people in our area immediately recognized what kind of man my uncle was, and they were always trying to get him to accept a leadership role. But he adamantly refused.

"Back then many of the Issei still held on to that Old World custom of bowing their heads when they met a man they considered their superior, and they'd keep them bowed until he'd passed by. Uncle Takejiro and Pop both got this treatment. In later years I'd take them over to Seattle where the older Japanese did the same thing for them, bowing deeply, showing them real respect, almost reverence. It was a custom that always seemed so strange to us kids because our parents hadn't passed it on, never once suggested that we should use it, no matter who we met. That's probably because they knew it was a tradition that wouldn't fit in America, and maybe they didn't want it to. This wasn't a land with a caste system, and I think Mom and Pop both welcomed this change from their earlier lives."

Despite his commanding presence, Takejiro was never above listening to what his nephew had to say, and he did his best to pass on what he saw as life's rules and what it meant to be a man. These began with inner strength and the fortitude to endure all hardships in silence. George clearly remembers the day his uncle gave him his most valuable lesson.

"I couldn't have been over ten or eleven. We were hoeing weeds in an onion field, and the afternoon sun was blazing hot. I wanted to call it a day, to go for a dip in a nearby irrigation pond, but Uncle wouldn't hear of it. 'You never quit on a job,' he sternly told me. 'You don't even complain or ask for a break. If it's a hard task, you make a greater effort and put in more time. And you don't let people know how you feel, whether your tired, sore, stressed out.'

'Gambatte,' that's the Japanese word my uncle used. Now I understand that it's a word that has multiple meanings, revolving around trying your hardest and doing your best. When my uncle applied it to me, I knew it also meant I was to endure, to keep a stiff upper lip, to keep my feelings to myself. To him, this was the only way you could truly be a man. He expected nothing less of his favorite nephew. I guess coming from Uncle Takejiro that word had a real impact, first because I always knew he cared about me and wanted to see me turn out right. And second, by then I knew just a little about his war years, the horrors he'd endured in silence. If he'd gone through that long ugly war as an adherent of Gambatte, I could get through a hot afternoon in an onion patch.

"So I did quit complaining, particularly when my uncle was around. But gradually this became almost second nature. All that work and the long hours, maybe I was just a kid, but they were already becoming my way of life, a big part of who I'd always be. It makes little sense to complain about who you are.

"And gradually I learned to hold my feelings in, partly because of my uncle's teachings, but mainly because of the examples both he and Pop set throughout their lives. In later years maybe I carried this a step too far. In too many ways I became a very private person, not opening up like I should have, first to my parents, later to my own family and friends. When I entered the business world, this holding everything in became much worse because by then I believed that any show of weakness, even to my closest associates, was a sure way of tipping my hand and botching a deal. As both a farmer and a businessman I was a real worrier, but no one ever understood this. I'd become too good at hiding my emotions, always displaying an outward confidence, confiding in no one."

Eight

A FAMILY FLAW

George hesitated, then added, "There was one thing I did vent my feelings about when I was a kid. Vic and I both had to work practically every day, but Elmer, who was the oldest and should have been the most capable and dependable, was given plenty of time off and enough spending money to enjoy it. Oh, I don't mean to imply that he was given a complete free ride, but way too often Vic and I would be out in the fields cutting asparagus, picking strawberries or hoeing onions on a sweltering summer day, and we'd see Elmer driving off in his car, going to pick up a couple of his friends, heading for a swimming hole or the movie theater.

"I know that most of this was because of Mom. For some reason she always took Elmer's side, maybe because he was her first child to live. After losing two babies she had to be devastated, so it could be that when she finally had a son who survived infancy, she'd always believe he was special. Or maybe it was just that Elmer was her oldest son. I know that's pretty important in the old country, but if Mom was caught up in this, she had a real different version than most of the Issei I knew. Their eldest sons were expected to work at least as hard as the rest of the family, and they had to take on more responsibility, not less. The eldest had to grow up the fastest so they could eventually take over as the new heads of their families.

"Instead Elmer became our family's expert at whining, always begging for time off from his chores or asking for a new toy, even when he was in high school. He'd get a new pair of roller skates, a tennis racket, all the things Vic and I were told the family couldn't afford. During our lean years, when as a family we weren't really celebrating Christmas, Elmer always got something, mainly because he'd badger Mom until she finally gave in.

"Though Vic and I were younger, we'd have been ashamed to ask for presents when we knew our family's money was tight. Even in our financially better times we understood that we shouldn't be asking for gifts, especially for things we didn't really need. We each had a rubber football that we'd picked up free at a local promotion and made due with these for all sorts of contests. These little footballs were okay for a rough game of tackle, but as substitute basketballs, they sure had limitations. They'd never bounced the same way twice, so dribbling was out, but if you put the right arc on one, it did sail through the net with real grace. Vic became a master at the half-court shot.

"In the long run, though, this came down to a whole lot more than which kids had which toys. Our folks did irreparable harm to Elmer because he'd never become the kind of man who could stand squarely on his own two feet. He ended up getting way more education than any of us, but he was never satisfied, always looking for something new and expecting someone else to help him out, to make his important decisions. After he was an adult, he'd still run back to Mom, complaining about how tough he had it. Then she'd come after me, asking me to help my poor brother, to ease his work load. She knew Vic and I could work and simply expected that. Why she refused to set the same standard for her oldest son, I'll never understand.

"It's about the only thing I ever had big blowups with Mom and Pop over, but nothing changed. Elmer was the privileged son, the one given a car, sent off to Whitman College, an expensive private school, while Vic dropped out of high school after his freshman year so he could help Pop with the field work and drive one of our trucks to Seattle and Portland.

"I'll never forget the day Vic told me he wasn't going back to school that fall. I felt so bad for him. I begged him not to do it. He was a real athlete, a good student, and I knew what he was giving up. Our high school coach, Mr. Normile, even came by the house to try to talk Vic out of quitting because he wanted him on his basketball team.

"Oh, I understood why Vic was quitting, but that didn't make me like it. We were always faced with so much farm work, and by late that summer Vic knew how important it was going to be for Pop to have him out there on a daily basis right through fall. Vic was always so quiet, so unwilling to have confrontations or fight for his rights that to him dropping out of school seemed like the best thing to do. As it turned out, Vic did go back the following year, but that whole thing never should have happened. He should have been in that sophomore class with his buddies, packing a football or dribbling a basketball on Friday nights and going to the sock hop afterwards. Instead he was running a produce truck cross-country. I resented this when I was a kid, and I resent it now."

Nine

SINGLED OUT
BY A DISTANT WAR

D espite this one flaw in the family structure, George's life was running smoothly in the spring of '42. He was getting bigger and more athletic every day, had accepted farm labor as his early lot in life, and was busy reveling in his many friendships. He even worked up the courage to give pretty Boots Wiggins a small box of chocolates on Valentine's Day.

Events unfolding in Europe and the Far East had no more effect on him than on his Caucasian classmates. President Roosevelt's decision to blockade Japan, cutting off its oil supply and forcing its hand, may have been designed to provoke an attack and bring the American people and their congressional leaders out of their isolationist mentality, allowing him to declare war. But all this meant nothing to an active thirteen-year-old, secure in the knowledge that he was being raised in a nation where his and his family's civil rights were said to be inviolable. Even when Pearl Harbor was bombed, George's first reaction bordered on a child's indifference.

"We heard about it that Sunday, as soon as it was blared out over the radio," he recalls. "My only thoughts were 'Well, we're at war. My country's at war. Japan's our enemy.' It would never have dawned on me to think anything else. My parents were totally dedicated to life in this country, and I was a Nisei, born into U.S. citizenship and taught to cherish that. I was an American.

"Only the next day at school, when they broadcast Roosevelt's now famous 'Day of Infamy' speech over our loud-speakers, did I start feeling singled out. I really can't say why. Nobody said anything to me. None of my pals were mean about it or snubbed me. But as I listened to that speech and thought about those Japanese pilots bombing Pearl Harbor, for the first time I felt conscious of my race. Here I was, the lone Japanese among all those white kids. It had never seemed important before. Now suddenly it was. A story got back to Mom and Pop that I broke down crying during Roosevelt's speech, but that simply wasn't true. Maybe it was Uncle Takejiro' s Gambatte kicking in because as bad as I felt, I kept a stiff upper lip. Oh, I shed a few tears, all right, but they were all on the inside."

If radio announcements and feeling singled out during an emotional speech had been the end of it, thirteen-year-old George might have slid through those war years virtually unscathed because he still had his friends and the good will and respect of his teachers. Unfortunately, the Yoshino family's nightmare was just beginning. A few weeks after war was declared, both Frank and Takejiro were picked up by F.B.I. agents and taken all the way to Yakima for questioning. Though neither man had any affiliation with Japanese organizations, they were singled out because they were Issei men of prominence, men government bureaucrats had concluded posed a threat to the nation's war effort.

Ironically, men like Frank Yoshino were detained only because they had so competently fulfilled the American dream, while less successful Issei were left alone. Through insight and industry Frank had created a thriving farming and packing operation. While most of his Caucasian and Japanese neighbors still eked out livings on ten acre parcels, often raising a single crop such as asparagus, his enterprise had become much larger. By the time the war broke out, Frank owned big modern trucks, possibly seen as a fifth column threat, and he was well known and respected. Like numerous Issei men all across the western United

States, his only crimes were financial success and recognition as a community leader. His patriotism, his success at working closely with his white neighbors to bring in an irrigation district that had transformed the entire region, all this was ignored.

"As a kid I was mostly bewildered by what was happening," George now recounts. "but when F.B.I. agents hauled off Pop and Uncle Takejiro, Mom was absolutely terrified, and for good reason. We had no way of knowing when we'd ever see them again. Were they being permanently imprisoned? Would they have to stand trial? Could they be sent back to Japan simply because they weren't citizens? Now when I talk about this, it all seems so absurd, but this was an absurd time for all of us. Government actions that would have seemed impossible a month earlier became our cruel reality. A war was on, irrational fears ran rampant, rumors abounded. Even in our comparatively isolated Northwest community, everyone you talked to had a different story about what was happening."

Frank and Takejiro were released almost right away and allowed to catch the next train home. Neither man ever talked about the interrogation they had faced, at least not in front of the younger Yoshinos.

"Yes, they got out of that fiasco pretty easily, mainly because there wasn't a gram of evidence to link them to any kind of pro-Japanese movement or even to Japanese cultural organizations. However, if those F.B.I agents had known all about my uncle's war record, it might have really gone hard for him, especially if they'd known that during that Russian war one of the junior officers under his command was Tojo, now Japan's Prime Minister, a man being touted as one of this nation's most dangerous enemies. Fortunately once Uncle came to this country, he'd cut himself off from all that he'd left behind in the old country, his military comrades, its veteran's organizations, even his own family.

"Pop's arrest was even more ridiculous. For him, America was a land of opportunity, the land where years earlier he'd cast his entire lot, and the only place where he wanted to live and establish his family's future. For my uncle this country was more of an escape, a place to get away from whatever had gone wrong in his homeland. Whenever Japan was mentioned, he'd always shake his head and tell us, 'There's nothing for me back there.'

"Once in America, neither he nor Pop had shown the slightest interest in politics, not even on a local level. All either man
ever wanted was to be part of this new world and to quietly get
along with his neighbors. In Pop's case he'd done a remarkable job
of this, with close Caucasian and Japanese friends throughout our
region. With a war going on, Pop would have gladly doubled his
efforts to make his farm more productive than it already was.

"Back then it was terrifying. In retrospect it all seems so stupid. It was a time when the army, no, the whole nation, was going
to be in desperate need of food, asking people to plant victory gardens and begging them not to horde, and yet the government was
set to start interning men like my father, men with the skills to
turn out fantastic crops, men whose whole lives had been devoted
to getting better production from their land. We'd been fattening
and marketing close to 500 hogs a year. If government officials
had come to Pop and asked him to step up his meat production, I
know he would have figured out a way to double or maybe even
triple this number."

But no government agents were coming around to Japanese-
Americans with contracts. Instead, suddenly all people of
Japanese descent, whether they were citizens of the U.S. or not,
were placed under strict travel restrictions. They had to remain
within a five mile radius of their home and were given a curfew,
confining them to these homes from eight in the evening until six
the next morning. Then, for a five-day period all their bank
accounts were frozen. When this restriction was lifted, with-
drawals were limited to $100 a month. In the Kennewick-Pasco
area all men of Japanese descent had to attend meetings in
Yakima. There was plenty of talk of internment at these meetings,
with the bolder men asking pointed questions, but government
officials assured them that they and their families were in no danger. If internment did become a reality, and the feds admitted this
possibility, it would only be along the coastline.

"Yeah, those meetings definitely misled my folks and every
other family in that region," George now says, "giving us all a false
sense of security. Japanese families who lived in Seattle and
Portland, or anywhere closer to the Pacific, saw internment coming, so many of them moved inland, some only as far as the eastern

parts of their states. Others went further inland, mainly just as far as Idaho and Utah, but a few departed for points east, wherever they could find work or had contacts. If we'd have known what was coming, at least some families in our area would have followed suit, but this wouldn't have worked for us because Pop would never have left our farm.

"Tending his land, harvesting his crops, these were paramount with him. Even the threat of incarceration wasn't going to change that. The fact is, though, he didn't know. He'd been given official assurances that he'd be able to stay on his farm, so he did nothing to prepare for internment. He didn't contact his white neighbors and set up a preliminary deal for one of them to harvest his crops and lease his land in a worst-case scenario.

"He and the rest of us simply went on with our lives, plenty worried, sure, hoping like everyone else for a quick end to the war, but essentially going about our business. Elmer was in college, Louise had graduated from high school as her class Valedictorian in '41 and was planning her own university career. Vic kept right on making his weekly produce runs to the big cities. I did my chores, went to school, played sports, was under a bit of a cloud because of my race, but with no real clue that something bad was about to happen."

The 'something bad' slipped in rather quietly. It was late May, just another school day for young George. That morning this young teenager had once again donned his work clothes and gone out to cut asparagus an hour before it was time to spruce up and head for the classroom. Suddenly a neighbor drove up with the news. Notices had been posted on light poles all over Kennewick. Persons of Japanese descent, whether U.S. citizens or not, had one week to get their affairs in order, to liquidate or make arrangements for any property they owned, say their goodbyes and report to the railroad station for transfer to a detainment camp, a benign designation for what turned out to be a ramshackle prison in Portland, a converted livestock facility, now complete with high perimeter walls, lookout towers and rifle-toting guards.

"Those notices said absolutely nothing about where we were heading," George relates, his voice reflecting that long ago horror. "It was all so hush-hush, a big government secret, as if we were a worse threat if we knew anything. What did they think we were capable of, contacting the Japanese military to sabotage their plans? They treated us like a bunch of cattle, herding us onto trains without a clue to our destination. Of course rumors abounded. At least one said we were all getting shipped to Colorado, another to California, a third had us crossing the border into Canada."

A painful irony in all this was that the Yoshinos were only a long stone's throw away from retaining their freedom throughout the war. Somehow the Columbia River had become an east-west line of demarcation. People of Japanese descent who resided west of the river, in Kennewick, Richland and on the surrounding farms, would be imprisoned. Those residing east of it, in and around Pasco, would remain free.

Internment would be a horror for the whole family, but nothing could have prepared a proud man like Frank Yoshino for what was about to happen to him. For years he'd lived in harmony and cooperation with his Caucasian neighbors, not only helping to bring Columbia River water to all of their fields, but employing their sons and daughters to work in his fields, pack vegetables in his sheds or drive his trucks. His own sons and daughter had integrated their schools without incident, in every way part of the mainstream.

Frank had gone to the same church as his white neighbors, sold his crops to the same buyers, shared the ups and downs of a farm economy. Now, without any kind of rational explanation, everything he'd worked so long and hard for was about to be destroyed. He was about to live through humiliations he'd long believed were impossible in his adopted homeland. Despite those dire telephone pole announcements, his first reactions indicate that Frank still believed there was some way out of this nightmare, or that this new insanity was only temporary.

"Yeah, even after the notices were posted, Pop's biggest concern was for the crops in our fields," George remembers. "Maybe he thought internment would be over in a couple of months, or that once we were checked out in this detention facility and they discovered that we really were good Americans, we'd be sent right back to our farm and could pick up the pieces. Pop desperately wanted to stay on the farm at least until we could get everything harvested. But whoever he asked about this said there was no way. No exceptions would be made, no leniency granted. Right away Pop went to Churches Grape Juice, a big company that would later get bought out by Welches. He'd known the owners for years, had done business with them, and thought they were his friends. Maybe he planned to ask them to take on a long term lease, to work our farm until after this internment madness was over. At the very least he was sure they'd be willing to harvest his crop or to contact someone who would.

"But suddenly all those greedy owners could see was dollar signs. They knew the bind we were in, so they tried to buy Pop out with a one-time cash offer. Then they really insulted him, offering a paltry $2500 for everything we owned, our land, our home, our trucks, tractors, the crops in our fields. Our equipment alone was worth four times that amount. Pop came home furious. Here were men he'd always believed were honorable and trustworthy. But now that he had his back against the wall, they were trying to rob him. They were ready to legally steal over thirty years of his life's work, as well as his future.

"Pop was still seething when a fellow named John Davies, a California mint buyer, pulled into our yard, apparently unaware of what was happening and simply looking for new mint growers. I guess because he was so angry over Churches' offer and because he didn't know what else to do, Pop took Davies aside and offered to sell out to him for that same $2500. It turned out that Davies was a real decent fellow and right away he protested. He didn't want to take advantage of us, he said, but Pop stuck to his first offer and finally convinced the man that we had no other choice. It was either sell to him or let that glutinous Churches outfit make an obscene profit.

"As soon as the deal was made and the check signed, Davies got hold of his grown son who came up from California, spent a couple days learning what he could from Pop, and then took over our farm. The truly amazing thing about that whole deal is that nothing was ever signed, no papers drawn up or transferred until years later. When the war was finally over and we were allowed back in the Kennewick area, we could have legally taken our farm and all the equipment back, but of course that was never Pop's way. As I said before, he hated cheaters and wasn't about to turn into one, no matter how badly he'd been treated. His word and his handshake were always going to be honored as if they were a court-tested legal agreement.

Ten

A Young Lad's First Real Taste of Humiliation and Fear

For thirteen-year-old George his parents' misery was hard to take, and he hated leaving their farm, his pals and his school. Yet not until the evening when he and his family stood on the station platform, awaiting the train that would take them to Portland, did this harsh new reality sink in.

"Looking back, that whole evening seems so strange, so different from the childhood I'd known," he painfully recalls. "We had no way of knowing where we were going, and not a single person was at the station to see us off, not my pals, none of my parents' friends, not even our minister. George Brummer, the German farmer who'd been working for Pop since the dust bowl days, drove us to the station and helped us with our little bit of luggage. He was a good man, but what could he say in that situation?

"After Brummer drove away, it was eerily quiet on that station platform, the six of us sitting there with our luggage, waiting for a train to somewhere. A little ways away were four more Kennewick families, all waiting for that same train. No one said a word, not to the other families, not even to their own kin. This was all too new, too unreal. Maybe Mom and Pop had asked their friends not to come, or maybe everyone just felt it would be too awkward and cause us greater embarrassment if they showed up. I'm sure it was something like this because later on so many of those same Kennewick people stepped forward and showed us over and over again what fine people they were.

"But for me that day was terrible, not having a single friend there to say goodbye, to shake my hand and give me the old 'See ya' later' phrase. I had to wonder why. When you're a kid, you can take a lot, roll with life's punches and all, but you're also pretty quick to imagine all kinds of bad things. As I sat there staring down at my one battered suitcase, I became convinced that life as I'd known it was over, that I'd never see my buddies or Kennewick again, that I was heading off into an unknown and irreversible fate."

The long slow train ride to Portland would do nothing to dispel George's dark clouds. Instead, it became his family's next humiliation. A single soldier was assigned to guard them. Even as they boarded the train, they could see that he was reeling drunk.

"Right away this lout started cussing us," George bitterly recounts. "He was screaming out one racial slur after another, waving his .45 pistol around, threatening to shoot anyone who dared challenge him. Once we'd all found seats, he was no better, stomping up and down the aisle, still waving that pistol, threatening us. Then this slob singled out my sister Louise, a very pretty girl back then, and flopped down beside her. I was right across the aisle and at first I thought he was going to grab her, but instead he started talking filth. Man, I was mad! Never before and seldom since have I ever had so much desire to attack a man. I know Pop, Uncle and my brothers had to be just as angry. If that drunk had ever touched Louise, we'd have had to act. Maybe the coward knew this. Maybe that's why all the dirty low-life did was talk. His words were bad enough.

"Right then all I could do is direct my rage at this one lousy soldier, but in later years I'd wonder how this could have happened. Why would only one man be assigned to us? How could his higher ups have allowed a drunk with a gun to get into that situation? I can think of a half dozen scenarios that might have resulted from this madness, all of them bad.

What if he'd shot one of us? What if he'd attacked Louise and my father, still a powerful man, had knocked him senseless? What if we'd ganged up on him in our rage and beaten him so badly he died or was permanently injured? Anything with terrible consequences that could have happened on that train ride would have been blamed on us, the Japanese, considered so dangerous that we had to be herded off to prison. If we had touched a hair on that low-life's head, we'd have ended up in far worse straits than we already faced.

"Unfortunately, now when I ask the question why this happened, I immediately see the simple but ugly answer. The war had created a terrible panic in this country, and fueled by that, plus a whole lot of people's greed as well as their latent prejudices, we had been turned into scapegoats. Nothing we'd been, nothing we'd accomplished, none of our real convictions or values mattered. Only our race mattered and officially that race was now America's enemy. We'd been dehumanized."

No more drunken soldiers met the Yoshinos in North Portland, but their temporary quarters were a greater horror. A nation gearing up for war on several fronts wasn't about to put significant resources into its long-term internment camps, and the Portland stockyards was just a holding pen until the more permanent prisons were ready to be occupied. Cattle pens, still reeking with the pungent odors of their former tenants, had been partitioned off with sheets of plywood to create individual family quarters. Armed guards marched the families from the train depot into this hastily-erected prison, where the Yoshinos would be housed in a ten-by-twelve-foot cell with a narrow, doorless entry and not a stick of furniture. A single light bulb dangled precariously from a wire. Their only roof was the big wooden stockyard structure high overhead.

At least Uncle Takejiro wasn't forced into this cramped little room. He was placed in the compound's bachelor's quarters, a separate section. Elmer immediately joined the internee fire brigade, made up of young Nisei males, and boarded with them. Still, three energetic teenagers, as well as their parents, had to share a space no bigger than a small bedroom.

The family's first task was to join hundreds of other Japanese Americans who were sorting through a mountain of suitcases, searching for their last meager possessions. When evacuation orders were posted, each internee had been allowed to bring two suitcases of clothing and personal effects, supposedly enough for their entire stay. Now these had been unceremoniously dumped into one huge disorganized pile. Next the new internees were shown a big stack of loose straw that lay in the outer court and ordered to gather enough to fashion their own makeshift mattresses. Over thirty-five hundred internees were in that camp, so their meals, consisting primarily of rice and hotcakes, had to be served in two shifts in a massive mess hall.

"I quickly learned to fill my belly at every meal so I could make it to the next dinner bell," George says. "The food was pretty tasteless and monotonous, but that was the least of my problems. Because I was still a kid, sleeping on that hard concrete with some loose straw tucked under me wasn't all that painful either, but it must have been terrible for the old folks. Pop was over sixty, but at mealtime I'd see him sitting with a bunch of other men, and he always looked like one of the younger Issei.

"Some of those old fellows, and the women too, must have been well into their seventies or even eighties, many in poor health to boot. I remember seeing aged Issei just shuffling about, all bent over, a few of them shaking with palsy. What was it like for an arthritic grandmother to lie down on a bed of straw with concrete backing each night and then try to rise in the morning? Maybe these old folks didn't have much life ahead of them anyway, but I'll guarantee those camps took away more than a few good years."

"And the older people must have hated the lack of privacy. In Japanese families, privacy for bathing and all that is almost sacred, but in camp both the men's and women's latrines were nothing but row on row of toilets with no partitions. Even as a kid I was embarrassed. A modest Old World woman like my mother had to be mortified. We had big communal showers, one for the men, the other for women, that were even less private, which didn't really bother me because I'd grown accustomed to showering next to teammates after a ball game, but again, Mom must have been horrified. What I hated was that we were always running out of hot water. You'd just be soaping up, and suddenly the water was freezing. All you could do was get a fast rinse, grab your towel and do a vigorous dry off."

A tough kid like George could easily have endured this occasional frigid stream of water. But as camp life settled in, he discovered what it really meant to be incarcerated and came to hate the daily boredom. Up until then his life had been consumed almost entirely by work and play. His simple philosophy had been to get the work done so he could have time for sports or hanging out with his buddies. Now he had neither work nor play, just a dull life of sitting around with hundreds of other internees, killing the slow hours until his next meal, or lying in bed at night, waiting for the overhead lights to be turned off so he could sleep, temporarily obliterating both the boredom and his bleak prospects.

"Yeah, thirty-five hundred of us were imprisoned there, in nothing but a big holding pen until some bureaucrat could figure out where to send us," George bitterly recalls. "For the first month we kids had nothing to do but sit around and wait for our next meal. Nothing to read, no games to play, not even a daily job to keep our minds off our boredom. Man, I missed my Kennewick chums.

"For a while Bill Green wrote me letters, about one a week, and right away I'd write back. But suddenly his letters stopped. I wrote a couple more to him, then finally gave up. I couldn't understand what had happened, and it really hurt because I felt I'd broken one of my last contacts with the outside, with my home. Another good buddy, Charles Quast, still wrote and that helped, but I sure wanted to hear from old Bill.

"Years later, at a Kennewick class reunion, Bill told me how his dad had found out about our letters and ordered him to quit writing. I never understood why his dad would do that, and I don't think his son knew either. It was just an order, something kids back then took pretty seriously. Given the paranoia of those times, his dad may have honestly believed his son could get in trouble simply by having a Japanese friend. Anyway, at that reunion Bill not only explained why he stopped writing, but he told me how sorry he was. After what I'd gone through, that apology definitely meant something. It showed me what a fine man Bill had become, and it eased an old painful memory.

"As a kid, though, I couldn't mope around and long for my old buddies forever, especially in a place that had hundreds of kids close to my age. It's strange, but that assembly center would be the first place where I made close Japanese friends, both with kids from the Yakima Valley and from Portland. We were all so bored we had to do something besides hang around our parents, and it didn't take too long before we knew all the places where we could hang out, like the compound's big laundry room. It didn't have any games or even chairs, but sitting cross-legged and talking to kids our own age sure beat sitting hour after hour in a tiny room with Mom and Pop.

"After about six weeks the camp officials finally put up a couple of backboards and hoops and issued us basketballs. From then on we'd have long pickup games whenever it wasn't raining too hard. Even an all-day drizzle didn't stop us. Only a real downpour forced us back to the laundry room, where we started devising simple games, anything to break those long hours of pure boredom.

"Finally the authorities issued us bats, baseballs and even gloves and let us set up a makeshift diamond and outfield in the big courtyard. This was great, but one time I was running after a fly ball and got right up against the fence. Suddenly a guard in the closest tower raised his rifle and fired a round in my direction. Maybe that Neanderthal just wanted to give me a good scare and had no intention of hitting me, or maybe he was simply breaking his own monotony. Either way it was a stupid thing to do. He had to know I was simply trying to make a tough play and had no intention of trying to escape. And he didn't even do a good job of scaring me much. I was too young, too much of a daredevil back then. I'd already learned more than I needed to know about humiliation and boredom, but I was a few years away from comprehending that kind of danger.

"Back then I was a self-absorbed teenager, and only years later would I understand how much worse the camps had to be on our parents, seeing all us kids pulling away from them and their cherished family structure. Traditionally a big part of Japanese life revolves around the family always eating meals together, but those huge camp cafeterias immediately destroyed that. Hundreds of people, all mixed up, first forming long lines, trays in hand, then grabbing whatever rough table was available and chowing down on that bland grub. I'm sure Mom and Pop would have liked us to eat together, but right away they could see it wasn't practical. Pretty soon, breakfast, lunch and dinner were just three more hours for all us kids to hang out with our new friends.

"Mom and Pop hated everything about camp life, but throughout that ordeal they never talked about it or complained, at least not in front of us kids. I'm sure they both felt that they had to stay strong to keep us from breaking down. Again, it was our old 'Gambatte.' That word and all it stood for was so much a part of who Mom and Pop were and how they conducted themselves. During camp and in the tough years that followed, they were both determined to keep that stiff upper lip, to get through this horror none of us could understand and come out of it with their family still intact. Not once during internment did I see my mother break down and cry, though what she might have done in the middle of the night in the privacy of her own bed, when she could huddle down behind Pop's broad back, I never knew."

After reflecting for a long thoughtful minute, George added, "You know, when something like internment happens, when suddenly life as you've known it is destroyed and your new world is incomprehensible, you have to quickly get to the point where all you do is go through the motions, minute by minute, hour by hour, living through each day any way you can. Looking back I see Mom and Pop moving through their daily lives like a pair of robots, eating their communal meals, trudging off to those communal latrines and showers, rising slowly from their straw beds each morning, only to face another ugly meaningless day.

"But that doesn't mean my folks ever gave up. Mom and Pop held stubbornly to the belief that better days had to lie ahead for us, that the war would soon end, and somehow this whole internment mess would get straightened out. And the first chance he'd get, Pop would make a decisive move to improve our lives."

As the Portland summer wore on, George and his siblings continued to make adjustments. Their friendships grew, their little gangs solidified, their time together became a major solace. Only darkness and the need to sleep drove these teenagers back to the cramped cubicle they shared with their parents.

"It was a good thing that the camps had definite curfews," George now admits. "Without them there's no telling when we'd have turned in. As it was we had to be off the courtyard by dark because that's when the guards came in and locked up the compound. Then right at nine o'clock it was lights out for the whole place, which made that camp inky black, darker than the cloudiest night. If you got caught outside your own cubicle when they flipped that big switch, you had to feel your way back to your room. More than one kid caused a real row by stumbling into the wrong family's quarters. Yeah, that blackness was about the only thing that took us away from our new pals and drove us back to our parents' little hovels."

George now realizes that although his father was dismayed by every aspect of their new prison, he was particularly alarmed by what he saw happening to his youngest two sons and his daughter. Every day he could only watch while all three became more and more in tune with their peer groups and pulled further away from him and Kazuye. But even an Old World disciplinarian such as Frank Yoshino knew he couldn't keep three teenagers penned up in that one tiny room all day. How could he possibly hold them in check or influence their character when he so rarely saw them?

"For Pop it was all bad," his son acknowledges, 'but I know now that he saw our idle time without a single meaningful chore as the worst evil. Sure, maybe Pop knew that hours of basketball or baseball were better than hanging around a laundry room, but that still wasn't what he wanted. He wanted us in a good school, preparing for higher education, to have regular chores, the kind of life that would let us move on to the next level. In essence, Pop wanted his family back."

Though young George couldn't have known it at the time, the internment camps were having a far more insidious effect on men like his father, the strong Issei heads of households. In keeping with centuries of Japanese tradition, these men had not only been the respected bread-winners and patriarchs of their own families, but as the elders in their widespread communities, they had expected and been shown deference, and had naturally stepped into leadership roles. The new prisons not only took away their status as family bread winners, but immediately turned the Issei into men who had to follow rather than give orders, badly batter-ing their strong self images.

When a man is faced with a world he's never known, a world that in many ways appears to have gone insane, the questions become endless, and this is the kind of world that Frank Yoshino and his fellow Issei now looked out upon. After decades in America these men couldn't seriously contemplate returning to Japan and starting over, but their future in this new country was so clouded. They had to wonder, would a government that had seen fit to imprison them without benefit of a trial and then labeled them 'enemy aliens' also consider deportation? And if this did happen, what would be the future of their U.S. citizen chil-dren, especially the younger ones? Certainly they couldn't be deported, but without parental guidance and support, where would they go, what would they do?

Then, whether because of some diabolical design to destroy Issei influence or through a crass cultural indifference, govern-ment officials effectively pushed these elders further out of their traditional roles as community leaders. The younger Nisei were given all of the important positions in the camps. Right from the outset the War Relocation Authority had ruled that only citizens, the Nisei, could serve on the Community Councils, the official contact between the internees and camp officials. The older Issei could be block managers, though in most cases these positions, as well as the best camp jobs, were also assigned to their sons and even grandsons. If an Issei wanted to work, he was forced to accept the most menial tasks, scrubbing floors, cleaning pots and pans.

Perhaps all this was only because internment bureaucrats found it much easier to deal with the second generation, whose English language skills were for the most part excellent and whose Westernization was more complete. But for the proud Issei elders, having to watch the younger and less experienced Nisei assume posi-tions above them, it was another major blow to their self-esteem. Their lands and homes were gone, their family lives shattered, their leadership roles usurped, their futures unknown.

And the Issei soon realized that many of their children no longer viewed them as unchallengable authority figures. Of course these same children, particularly the older teenagers, were going through their own traumas of displacement and shattered dreams. For some, high school graduation with longtime classmates had already been destroyed. A college career seemed a long way off. Even marriage or the possibility of a decent job was no longer a given. Without their traditionally strong family structure, many of these kids, particularly the boys, broke away, finding a new and too often a destructive identity with their peer groups.

"Yeah, I knew lots of boys and even young men who totally drifted away from their families during internment," George sadly reflects. "Later too many of these guys turned into real drifters, moving around the country, living hand to mouth, doing whatever it took to survive, maybe farm labor, part-time gardening or simply bumming off friends. They'd lost any real sense of direction. A few recovered and ended up doing something productive, but far too many never could pick up the pieces. They'd end up living almost purposeless lives, never having a real family or building anything for their future. The camps were hardest on the older generations, but they took a toll on my generation too."

Eleven

TRADING PORTLAND'S RAIN FOR WYOMING'S SNOW

arly in September word came to the Yoshinos and everyone
else in the Portland facility that the more permanent
internment camps were now ready and that they would all
be shipped out. Everything about this second relocation was again
hush-hush, and again the rumors flew. The only certainty was that
the internees wouldn't all be sent to the same camp. In fact, the
Yakima Valley families, as well as the Yoshinos and their
Kennewick neighbors, were scheduled to be relocated to Heart
Mountain, a huge, sprawling facility in the higher elevations of
North Central Wyoming. Their fellow internees, mostly from
Portland, would be sent to the Minidoka camp in Southeast
Idaho.

Despite the uglinesses of their stockyard internment, the
long trying weeks had led to strong friendships and not only
among the children. Now a new government order was about to
rip these friendships apart. George vividly remembers joining a
host of others in shedding a few tears when their day of departure
arrived.

"Kids and grownups alike were crying their eyes out," he recalls. "It wasn't that any of us had fallen in love with life in a converted stockyard or had learned to enjoy the gray skies over Portland, but we'd made good friends and now we'd be leaving many of them behind. Oh, they wouldn't stay much longer in Portland either, but we were pretty sure they wouldn't be sent wherever we were going. Then there's always the fear of the unknown, especially when you have no control over where you're heading. At least in Portland we had established our daily routines and more or less knew what to expect each day. For the older people maybe that was a matter of putting one foot in front of the other and trying to survive, but even that beat boarding another train and heading off to another lockup. Who knew what we were getting into?"

What the Yoshinos and their neighbors were getting into was a second hastily devised and poorly built prison. Heart Mountain was one of the largest internment camps, a facility that housed 11,000 internees.

"If it had been just me, as a thirteen year old kid, maybe I could have seen it as some big adventure," George now says, "but imagine what it was like for Mom and Pop and every other parent and grandparent who climbed on that train, spent a couple days heading through wide-open country, and then ordered off with no idea where they were. It was dark when we first filed off, and for a few minutes we stood around in little huddled groups. Everyone was asking the same questions, 'Where are we? What is this place called? When we heard the words 'Heart Mountain', they meant nothing. What was Heart Mountain? Earlier rumors had us heading for either Arizona or Colorado. On that wide-open high plateau, it could have been either. "

Again armed soldiers marched the arriving internees into the compound where they were assigned to their latest dwellings. After a short night's sleep they would awake to the reality of a new camp. This one was no converted stockyard, but the harsh winter weather of the Wyoming high country would be far more tortuous than Portland's rains. Neither the military's propaganda machine nor the ludicrous attempts by this nation's press corps to put a noble spin on a facility such as Heart Mountain, calling it a

'Resettlement Camp' or even a 'Haven of Refuge,' would soften the blow for its new arrivals. High fences, topped with rows of barbed wire, marked the camp's perimeter. Soldiers, many armed with machine guns, glared down from strategically placed guard towers. The new internees weren't naive enough to believe that the barbed wire and guard towers had been put in place to protect them from the smattering of local cattle ranchers that dotted those hills or from the few hundred inhabitants of tiny Worland, the only town for miles in any direction.

Overnight the Heart Mountain Relocation Center had become Wyoming's third largest city. Rows of strikingly ugly barracks had been slapped together, each one comprised of six rooms, each room housing an entire family. Room sizes were allotted according to occupancy numbers. The five Yoshinos were crammed into a sixteen by fourteen foot box, with a big pot-bellied stove in one corner. Again Takejiro was assigned to the camp's bachelors' quarters, and Elmer rejoined his friends in the fire brigade.

"At least at this camp the government furnished sturdy army cots with straw mattresses," George states. "But when the folks wanted something else to sit on, they had to purchase two flimsy canvas chairs for ten dollars apiece. We weren't allowed to have another stick of furniture, which was irrelevant because between our beds, the stove, and a couple of small chairs, there wasn't enough floor space left for a night stand.

"The worst thing about our new home was that those barracks had absolutely no insulation. The builders had simply tacked tar-paper over the rough boards to keep the wind out. Our room was freezing cold as soon as the temperature dropped, and believe me, during a Wyoming winter it drops a long way. After the worst weather settled in, we'd spend most of the day first hauling in coal from a big pile that was dumped out in the open yard and then huddled around our stove, trying to stay warm. We had days that winter when it dropped to forty below, with a wind chill that must have been staggering. It ripped right through those flimsy walls. I remember one time when Mom had brought a tin cup of water back to our room after breakfast and set it by the head of her bed. Our stove was blazing so hot you couldn't get too close, but right across that tiny room that bit of water turned to solid ice."

When the Yoshinos first arrived in Heart Mountain, the camp cooks had almost nothing to work with. For over a week bowls of boiled rice made up the entire menu. Like most teenaged boys, George, Victor, and their buddies had tremendous appetites. By the time a meal was served, they would be so ravenous that they would add plenty of salt to a big bowl of that rice and gobble it down.

"I guess some bureaucrat had reasoned that because of our race, we'd all be rice eaters, which was true, but this stuff was nothing like the dishes our mothers made," George says. "In fact, it was pretty tasteless. That's why we dumped on all that salt. Tasty or not, though. we'd force ourselves to eat as much rice as our bellies could hold, washing it down with big gulps of water. If we didn't eat plenty, our hunger pangs were going to be pure torture long before that next dinner bell rang, and we had no chance for any between-meal snacks. Later we started getting a little more variety, but about the only meat we'd get was mutton, I guess because the local ranchers were raising so many sheep. Maybe those government contracts were a boon, a good way to get a price for their oldest sheep. We sure weren't fed any choice lambs, just old mutton. The cooks boiled big chunks of this mutton, tallow and all, into a huge rice stew. Mutton tallow has a strong, pungent smell that's pretty unpleasant if you're not used to it, and I'd never eaten any kind of sheep meat at home. I'd walk into our mess hall when those oversized pots were steaming and almost gag.

"But again, odor or no odor I knew I had to eat what I could, so when I went through the chow line, I'd heap my plate, then eat all the rice and throw that smelly mutton away. Almost everyone in camp did the same thing, but this was sure going against what I'd been taught at home. My parents would have never tolerated us coming to the dinner table and then wasting food we'd put on our plates. With that mutton, though, I had no choice. Trying to gag a piece down would have made me sick. To this day I can't eat any meat that I know once wore a woolly coat, not even high-priced lamb chops."

Twelve

HONEST LABOR AND BLATANT RACISM

Several months before that harsh winter, the Yoshino males were confronted with an actual chance to make a decision, this one involving a new government program. The internees had no way of knowing this, but a major reason that states such as Wyoming, Idaho and Utah had been willing to accept the sprawling internment camps was that local politicians saw them not only as a boon to a smattering of local economies, but also as a chance to solve a looming farm crisis. Thousands of young farm workers were now serving in the military, thousands more had left their rural environs for the big cities and their lucrative defense industry jobs, leaving labor-intensive crops in real danger of rotting in the fields, particularly in the sparsely populated farming belts of the West. In Idaho the threat was to potatoes, in Wyoming and Montana, it was sugar beets.

"Again, it was all so strange," George now reflects when recalling this new program. "One day we're designated as 'enemy aliens' and considered so untrustworthy and such a threat to our own nation's security that we had to be locked up and guarded by machine gun toting soldiers. The next, just because we're willing to sign a paper, we can walk out of that camp, board a local bus and head off to some distant beet farm. No guards, nothing to prevent us from hopping off at any stop along the way and slipping off into the night. We were desperately needed to get those crops out of the field before winter set in, so now we were okay, free to be out on our own.

"That paper we signed was a contract to top beets on this big farm outside of Sheridan. As soon as he'd heard about this program, Pop was all for it. He knew there was nothing for us at Heart Mountain, and I'm sure he saw this as our chance to make a little honest money, to do something useful and, most importantly, to get Vic and me away from that camp and all our idle hours, at least for a couple of months. I don't remember if Pop ever tried to get Elmer to go with us, but he joined his buddies on a beet topping contract up in Eastern Montana.

"Uncle Takejiro wasn't about to go. He was getting a little too old for that kind of stoop labor on a daily basis, and by then he was already settling into the routine of camp life and discovering that for him it wasn't all bad. For the first time in years my uncle had the daily camaraderie of Japanese men close to his age, men he understood, who shared his old traditions and his beliefs, who played the old games he'd learned in his home land. Funny, as much as the rest of us hated internment, my uncle more than accepted it. He enjoyed it.

"But Pop quickly convinced two other men that this beet contract program was a good idea. It was around the middle of September when the five of us set out, with modestly high hopes I guess, but we were about to embark on two and a half months of what turned out to be pure misery. We arrived at that beet farm late at night only to discover that we'd be living in a run-down shack. I hadn't had as much as a sandwich on the long bus ride over from the camp. I was so hungry I could have eaten mutton stew, sheep meat and all. But that shack didn't hold a crust of bread, and our new employer sure wasn't offering us anything out of his larder. The next day he told Pop and the other men that he'd go to town to buy us food, as long as we provided the money.

"In those days you could get big buckets of peanut butter and jam for very little, and loaves of bread were always cheap, so that's what they ordered and that's what we ate. You can bet on that first day I wolfed down plenty of those sandwiches with real gusto. But peanut butter and jam sandwiches shouldn't be a three-meals-a-day diet. Once we were into our field work, we'd all come back way too tired to do any cooking in the evening. The next morning we'd be in too much of a hurry to get back out there to fix a decent breakfast, so day after day, for the entire length of that contract, we lived on those sandwiches. Since then I've rated peanut butter and jam sandwiches almost on a par with boiled mutton."

Their food may not have been gourmet, but the worst early problem the new beet toppers faced was that their shack was literally crawling with bedbugs. These little insects were so numerous and hungry that they made the short nights pure misery.

"When you're a kid and exhausted from hours and hours of hard work, even bedbugs can't keep you awake forever," George relates, "so finally I'd get a couple hours of sleep, but then I'd wake up in the morning covered with bites. Finally Pop and the other men protested until the farmer agreed to fumigate our shack, though this meant we had to be out of it for at least twenty-four hours. He fumigated on a Saturday, so after work we walked the ten miles back to Sheridan and rented a room in an old motel. The next day we hiked back.

"Then for at least a week the fumigant in that shack was still so strong that we'd all fall asleep at night with tears streaming down our faces. Whatever that farmer used killed every last bedbug in the place. I'm sure it didn't do any of us a whole lot of good either."

Still, every morning, seven days a week, the five-man crew was out topping beets before dawn, and they would never quit until it was too dark to see. A beet-topping knife had a wooden handle, then a long arced blade with a hook at the point. In the Northwest the Yoshinos had always jabbed that hook into a beet, pulled it out of the ground, grabbed it, whacked off its top, then dropped it back into the row, all in one continuous motion. But in Eastern Wyoming's gumbo they quickly discovered they had to yank out a couple of beets by their tops, bang them together a few times just to get rid of the clinging dirt, then stack them in piles and come back later to do the topping.

"With good-sized beets this would have been slower," George explains, "but these were skinny little runts, mostly top foliage, with tiny bodies. Before we'd left Heart Mountain, we'd signed a piecework contract, so much money for every ton of beets we topped until the fields were all harvested. The kicker was that our contract had clearly stated that we'd be working on fifteen ton to the acre beets, which back then would have been a good crop for that part of the country. Right away every one of us knew, though, that this figure was a lie. Those Wyoming beets were about the size of stunted carrots. I doubt if they'd have made five tons to the acre.

"But the worst part of that whole fiasco was the way that farmer and his entire family treated us. They'd all look at us and talk to us like we were vermin. Every day at least a couple of them would come out to the field where we were trying to get as much tonnage as possible and start talking about the 'lazy Japs,' well within our range of hearing.

"I don't really remember how the other two men reacted, but Pop, Vic and I were shocked. In the camps we'd been aware that the guards thoroughly disliked us, but for the most part we could steer clear of them, and even when we did cross paths, they'd usually hit us with no more than an ugly sneer. Here this family was going out of its way to belittle us, and they desperately needed our labor. For me, this kind of racism was brand new, by far the ugliest side of humanity I'd ever witnessed."

By law internees were to be paid the prevailing farm labor wages, but of course it was easy for an unscrupulous landowner to get around this regulation. Given the anti-Japanese political climate of those early war years, very few public officials were inclined to take up the cause of these newly disenfranchised internees. Plus, figures that somehow appeared on a contract, as well as conditions in the field and the amount of actual labor accomplished, were hard to prove or disprove. What government official was going to go to the trouble of checking out the word of an established white farmer when it was only Japanese internees who were questioning it?

"Had that farmer lived up to our contract, we wouldn't have made much, given the gumbo and those stunted beets," George bitterly laments, "But then he had to go and cheat us besides. The contract said we were to be paid when the job was finished. When it was time for us to catch a bus back to Heart Mountain, he wouldn't give us a dime, said he'd send us our checks. Well, we had to go back to camp, so all we could do was hope he was a man of his word. Yes, he finally did send us our checks, but not until the following April, and then only for seventeen dollars each. All that work, all those terrible conditions we'd lived under, all the racial slurs we'd endured, and all for a lousy seventeen dollars. We didn't make enough to pay for our food and other expenses, much less get to put a few bucks aside, as Pop had hoped.

"The other two men were so mad that right away they wanted to lodge a protest, to take our cases to the camp authorities and get them to force that farmer to ante up. But Pop said no. To him this was just one more thing we had to accept, to put behind us and go on. I'm sure he had little doubt that the authorities weren't about to take our side against that farmer, and he probably figured that bringing charges would just stir things up and might make things even worse for our families. Years later I'd understand that Pop was right, but right then I sure hated to see him simply capitulate."

Thirteen

THE TEDIUM
OF CAMP LIFE

ife back at Heart Mountain didn't include any more stoop
labor or racist farm families, but it had other drawbacks.
Less than a month after their return, Wyoming's winter set
in with a vengeance, making even a trip to the communal latrine
a real ordeal. At times these outings meant bucking a biting wind
and busting through a foot or more of fresh snow with totally inadequate footwear. The more fortunate adult internees at Heart
Mountain could at least get jobs around the camp. A monthly
wage for common labor was $8.00. Professionals, mainly doctors
and teachers, earned $16.00. The pay wasn't much, but young
George would have gladly taken on the most menial tasks if officials had been willing to hire him. Instead he was stuck in an
undersized and overheated barracks with sixty other kids and a
single teacher.

"Unless you got there early and grabbed a seat in the first
three rows, you couldn't possibly hear," he recalls. "They gave us
pencils and paper but no books. Instead the teacher would read to
us and put our math problems on the chalkboard. I'd sit right up

front and try to stay interested, but that room would get so stuffy and that overworked teacher so hard to hear that pretty soon I'd be drifting off. It seems hard to believe, but as cold as our living quarters were, between the potbellied stoves and sixty kids' body heat by mid-morning that classroom would get hot and stuffy. Somehow my teacher or maybe some clerk figured out that I earned six credits that winter, which helped me later on, but if they'd measured what I'd actually learned, they'd have taken at least five of those credits back.

Faintly smiling, George added, "I had another problem in that classroom, and I have to admit that this one was partly my fault. At Heart Mountain it was our small group of Yakima Valley internees and then a whole lot of Californians. Most of the California kids were okay, a couple even became good friends, but a few saw themselves as big city toughs, sporting Pachuko haircuts and hanging out in tight gangs, getting surly whenever we came in contact. Right away my Yakima gang and I decided these guys looked weird and treated them to some pretty graphic descriptions.

"Unfortunately, we were just a bunch of naive farm boys, maybe tough enough for a little one on one scrap, but completely unprepared for real violence, and we sure didn't know anything about sending half a dozen or more guys against one or two. A couple of our kids ended up getting cornered one morning and severely beaten, for no real reason. Sure, there might have been an earlier word or two flipped out, but we'd never dreamed you'd get punched and kicked into unconsciousness for that.

"Looking for protection from the camp guards was plain ridiculous. Those guys didn't care what went on in that center, just as long as we stayed clear of the fences and didn't give them any lip. You didn't have to see those guards in action very long to know they were the dregs of our military, unfit for combat duty, so they'd been stuck with us.

"At school my problem was that most of my close friends were older, more my brother Vic's age. Then suddenly I'd been thrust into that classroom with close to a dozen of these California lads. These younger guys weren't all that tough, but they were plenty bold when they had their own little rat pack and my pals weren't around. Those boys made it pretty rough on me, tossing out their daily insults and throwing a few pretty harmless punches when the teacher wasn't looking. I was pretty lippy as a kid, but that was one time when I knew enough to hold my tongue and just duck away from that occasional flying fist. Back then I enjoyed a good fair fight as much as the next kid, but when you're outnumbered ten or twelve to one and the other side isn't about to stop just because you cry uncle, well, there's no use being stupid.

"For a while I was sick that winter with a bad ear infection. In the camp infirmary an internee doctor named Kinoshita was treating me. One day he had to clean out my ear before putting some drops in and ended up breaking that eardrum. Dr. Kinoshita was a good guy, and I really think he was an okay doc, but he and his staff were terribly overworked, seeing steady lines of patients every single day. My ear problems had to be a rush job because the old folks in that line had far more serious problems.

"Before camp Dr. Kinoshita had been a respected Boy Scout leader and wanted to see those values instilled in us. Late that fall he formed all the boys who were willing to join into an Explorer Scout group, and before the really bad weather set in he took us on a couple of long hikes up Heart Mountain, explaining all about the plants and the animal tracks we'd see along the trail. I guess the irony of being interned and still saying the Boy Scout pledge was lost on us, which now I see as a good thing. Our lives were going to need plenty of rebuilding anyway. Coming out as a bunch of little cynics would have been deadly.

"Plus, those day hikes were sure a welcome break from the tedium of camp. Their only drawback was that we'd never get to pack any food along, and we'd always return so late the dining hall was closed. We could usually buy something at the canteen, though about the only thing they ever stocked was dried prunes. You could get a big bag full for a nickel. Prunes don't make much of a dinner, but when you're a kid and hungry, food is food."

Fourteen

HARD DECISIONS AND
A GLIMMER OF HOPE

W hile the Yoshinos were living through the miseries and
uncertainties of their detention, this country's bureaucrats and politicians kept struggling with what became
known as the 'Japanese Problem.' Panic, politics, ignorance and
greed had combined to hastily intern 110,000 people, many of
them born into U.S. citizenship, many others rapidly aging, and
virtually none of them any kind of threat to the war effort.

The bombing of Pearl Harbor had triggered a wave of rumors
about Fifth Column activities, ranging from radio signals sent to
enemy ships lying off our western shores, to harboring Japanese
paratroopers in secluded root cellars. However, F.B.I. and Army
Intelligence investigations had failed to turn up a single case of
enemy collaboration.

More and more fair thinking Americans of all races were seeing the injustices and stupidities of the War Relocations Act.
Besides disregarding the civil rights of all those thousands of people, it had created another drain on the nation's resources, and it
had locked away a highly productive segment of its population, as

well as thousands of potential soldiers who now were badly needed. Politicos could point with pride to their farm labor program, and one, Senator Mansfield of Montana, would heap glowing accolades on the internees for having saved the West's sugar beet and potato crops. But now those harvests were over. Justice seekers were making demands. Still unsympathetic but practical bureaucrats knew it was time to figure out new ways to make these people useful and to ease the government's burden of maintaining its far-flung system of internment camps. Those with higher ideals were searching for politically acceptable ways of repatriating the internees back into society.

From the outset an organization called the Japanese-American Citizens League (JACL) had pushed hard for the right of Nisei men to serve in the military, seeing this as a way to demonstrate loyalty. Instead the Selective Service had classified these young men 4C, branding them as enemy aliens. Almost all of the 5,000 Nisei who were in the military when the war broke out had been stripped of their right to bear arms, and no matter what their rank or their previous military duties, they were assigned to full-time K.P. duty.

But now that the war was raging on several fronts, a ceaseless cry for more recruits had to be heeded. Plus, the Pentagon was coming under increasing pressure to separate the 'loyal from the disloyal Japanese,' a concept that had been totally ignored in the early chaos following Pearl Harbor. This combination led to the hastily devised and poorly thought out loyalty oath, a simplistic document that was supposed to allow the bureaucrats to clearly see which Japanese deserved their freedom and which needed a lengthier and perhaps harsher incarceration.

Late in the winter of 1943 military officials arrived at Heart Mountain, paperwork in hand. The loyalty oath was a fairly lengthy document that contained two key questions. The first, 'Are you willing to serve in the armed forces of the United States on combat duty, wherever ordered?' had to be answered by all Nisei over the age of seventeen, regardless of sex. Nisei girls found the question confusing, even alarming. By U.S. law females of any race were forbidden to serve in combat. The girls had to wonder, was this a trick question? If they answered no, they could be branded as disloyal and punished accordingly. But what did a yes answer really mean? Would these young women then be forced into some form of military duty, or would they be charged with attempting to break the law?

Nisei young men were faced with even greater dilemmas because they knew yes answers meant they would soon be in the military. If there had been no internment, these lads would have served as willingly as their Caucasian counterparts, but now they had several things to consider. Do I put aside my bitternesses and serve the country that has unjustly incarcerated me and my family? And if I do, some had to wonder, what will happen to the aging parents I'll leave behind? If freed, most of these elders would now be jobless and many would either be homeless or faced with 'Jap bashing' if they dared to return to their former communities.

The second question, 'Will you swear unqualified allegiance to the United States of America and faithfully defend the United States from any or all attack by foreign or domestic forces, and forswear any form of allegiance or obedience to the Japanese emperor, or any other foreign government, power or organization?' had to be answered by every adult internee and posed a real dilemma for the older Issei.

Not only had they been incarcerated by the United States, but this country had long denied them the opportunity to become citizens, no matter what oaths they were willing to take. Now it was asking them to forswear allegiance to the only country where they could still claim citizenship. What if they answered yes, rejecting their homeland, and then were deported? Would they end up as citizens of neither nation? Given the hysteria and uncertainty of those times, this question couldn't be disregarded as irrelevant. Eventually this second question would be rewritten to the more benign and sensible 'Will you swear to abide by the laws of the United States and take no action which would in any way interfere with the war effort of the United States?' but not before the original wording had added to the general turmoil and fears of the older internees.

Camps such as Heart Mountain quickly split into two factions, the Yes-Yes group, individuals and families who were willing to answer both questions with affirmatives, and the No-Nos, largely made up of those internees who were so bitter over their unjust imprisonment and the losses of their lands, homes and jobs that they weren't about to serve in this country's military or seriously consider denying allegiance to their former or ancestral homeland, no matter how they had felt when the war broke out.

Besides the moral and ethical issues, young Nisei men knew that their answers could have immediate practical consequences. Despite the uncertainties, Yes-Yes responses probably meant quick military service for them and the likelihood of far better treatment for their families, perhaps even an immediate release. No-No answers could just as quickly get one branded as a dissident and very possibly whisked off to a real military prison with all the lifelong stigmas that would entail. In fact, although the Heart Mountain internees who answered No-No had no way of knowing this, the Tule Lake Stockade in California would be their next destination.

And of course once again the rumors abounded, many based on nothing but misinformation and fear. After all the hatreds and the violations of their civil rights that the young men had experienced, they had to wonder, what was their government's real intent? Did Yes-Yes simply mean being drafted and a quick return to civil rights for them and their families or was it something far more sinister, such as a military ploy to gather thousands of Nisei men into segregated units that would be shoved into the front lines on suicide missions? If nothing but their race had brought on imprisonment, was genocide out of the question?

"In our circle it mainly became a matter of how you dealt with your bitterness," George clearly remembers. "I'd never know how much Pop resented the indignities we'd all suffered up to that point, but I do know he was as determined as ever to put those and everything else the camps represented behind us, to move ahead, to rebuild our lives.

"Just as soon as he understood the essence of that loyalty oath, Pop was adamant that the only way to do this was for him and everyone else in his family who was old enough to give Yes-Yes answers, so that's what they all did. My parents, Elmer, I guess even Louise had to take the loyalty oath.

"Whether Pop agreed with the whole thing or not, I never knew. I doubt if he talked it over much with anyone, and he wasn't about to trouble a son my age with his problems. But by then he and Mom were both desperate to get us kids far away from Heart Mountain and into a real home again. For them, that was reason enough to sign almost anything."

All across the West these loyalty oaths were causing deep rifts among the thousands of internees. Bitter men who answered No-No quickly turned on those in the Yes-Yes crowd, accusing former friends of pandering to a government that had disregarded their civil rights as well as their years of unblemished patriotism to this country. Internees who answered in the affirmative often retaliated, calling these No-Nos fools, traitors, or worse. In-fighting at all the camps, including Heart Mountain, was always ugly, at times violent.

"Yeah, it was pretty painful," George now says quietly. "In our camp I never heard of anyone coming to blows, but a good friend of mine, Satoshi Koyama from Wapato, Washington, and his parents were so bitter over their internment and everything they'd lost that they weren't about to give 'yes' answers. When Satoshi found out how my family had answered, suddenly he hated me. It didn't matter that I was too young to take the oath myself. I was a Yoshino, part of a family he now detested.

"In our last hour together Satoshi called me every rotten name he could think of. Less than a week later I woke up one morning and discovered that he and his folks were gone, shipped off to the Tule Lake Stockade, just as we'd feared. I really liked Satoshi, so I wrote him a long letter, trying to repair the damage, but the one I got back was another long tirade against me and my folks."

"Pop was definitely right about one thing. Positive answers quickly opened the camp gates for our whole family and everyone else in our crowd. Within a few weeks Elmer was released to attend the University of Utah. Later he'd enlist and end up serving in Japan as an interpreter during the occupation. Then Louise went off to the University of Chicago. When Mom, Pop, Vic and I got our release papers. we headed for farm labor jobs back in the Northwest, near a little settlement in southeastern Oregon called Milton, later renamed Milton-Freewater."

Only Takejiro stayed behind. Like a sprinkling of older Issei bachelors throughout the camps, he had come to see his incarceration as less threatening than whatever awaited him on the outside.

"Uncle sure didn't have to stay," George affirms. "My folks had always given him a home and they were more than ready to then, but he was past seventy and not at all anxious to be uprooted again, to go outside and make another new start, even if it was as part of our family. And for him camp life wasn't all that bad. Oh, he was missing out on Mom's home cooking, but he had other things going for him on the inside. The bachelor's quarters weren't exactly luxury apartments, but with single occupancy his little room sure beat the cramped quarters the five of us lived in. Sometimes I'd stay the night with him, rolling up on his floor with my blanket and pillow, just because it gave my folks more room.

"Besides the strong camaraderie of the other bachelors, something he still cherished from his military days, Uncle was getting to see many of the old Japanese plays, and he could listen to the old music, the songs he'd grown up hearing. He'd even joined one of the camp's musical groups and from time to time had the chance to sing a solo, using that powerful voice of his to belt out a traditional song. There were some brilliant and talented internees at Heart Mountain, and as soon as they had the chance, they banded together and did their best to make camp life more endurable, especially for the old people. Whenever I'd go over to bunk with Uncle, he was always heading off somewhere, to see a play, listen to a recital, get in on singing practice.

"That first full summer at Heart Mountain the Issei organized work crews, planting flowers and vegetable gardens. They even made stone walkways all around that camp, anything to give the place where they were forced to live a little more dignity and a hint of beauty.

"No, for an old man like my uncle, with nothing left on the outside except living with his relatives who were also starting over, camp life looked a whole lot more appealing than its alternatives. Uncle refused to leave until the place was shut down in '46. After that he came to live with us, but I heard stories about elderly bachelors who kept trying to return to camp, simply because they didn't know where else to go."

Fifteen

FOUR TEENAGERS'
INCREDIBLE GIFT

The Yoshinos had a small house waiting for them on a farm near Milton. It turned out that the owner, a man named Heidenreich, only needed one hired hand, and for some reason fourteen-year-old George was picked for this job. Frank and Vic would work for a neighbor.

"I had no objections when that decision was made, but it turned out that Pop and Vic were definitely the lucky ones," George grimly remembers. "They went to work for a man named Stiller who worked them hard, but he treated them decently. At first Mom worked over at Stiller's too, helping prune his small orchard. Then that summer Pop and Vic put up his entire hay crop. In the fall we all topped beets on several farms, once again doing piece work but this time for honest farmers. With decent beets and a reasonable per-ton price, this was the quickest way for us to make a little extra cash.

"But most of the time I was stuck working for Heidenreich, one of the nastiest men I've ever met. Here I was, still a kid, and old Heidenreich thought he had to spend a good part of every day insulting me, telling me how terrible the 'Japs' were, how they'd never accomplished anything as a civilization, were simply bums who'd tried to take over the rest of the world to make up for their own shortcomings. It was as if he held me personally responsible for Japan bombing Pearl Harbor. Man, this guy still had a strong German brogue, and I remember thinking, 'Hey, weren't we at war with your people too?' There were days when Heidenreich almost pushed me into saying something nasty about his ancestry, to call him a Nazi, but I needed that job, and my family needed the little house he provided.

"The man paid me sixty cents an hour, which was an okay farm wage back then, but he'd turn all my working hours into pure torture. If pruning his orchard was bad, putting up hay in the hottest weeks of summer was sheer misery. Loading was hard enough, walking alongside that wagon and pitchforking the loose hay on. The real killer was unloading it. Heidenreich would stay on the wagon and toss the hay up, while I was in the loft, doing all the final stacking. I'd done plenty of farm work, but I'd never stacked hay before, and Heidenreich wasn't about to teach me how to do it right when he could get so much satisfaction out of seeing me struggle. He seemed old to me, but he was still a big strong man, able to pitch that hay up so fast he'd bury me with it.

"Anyone who's done summer field work in that country knows what intense heat is, even when you're away from buildings and picking up a slight breeze. By late afternoon the heat trapped in that loft was almost unbearable, and of course with that boss, I'd never get to take a water break. Old Heidenreich would push and push, screaming at me the whole time. His favorite line was 'I'll kill you or make a man out of you!' He didn't do either. If becoming a man means knowing how to work, I'd learned that lesson long before I met that racist. All he did was give me another lesson in bigotry. Maybe I was only fourteen, but I came away knowing that it's the Heidenreichs that make this world a whole lot worse than it has to be.

"Every day when I'd be out there working, I'd see his two teenage sons go off in their car. I don't know how their father figured they were going to turn the corner into manhood because neither one ever touched the farm work. I guess only the 'Jap' kid needed that lesson. Somehow those two boys discovered I was a pretty good athlete because early that fall they came over and asked me to enroll in Milton High and play on their football team. I flatly refused.

"By then I had almost as much contempt for those boys as I had for their dad, and I had no desire to spend any more time than I had to in Milton. The few times I did go into that little town, I felt unwelcome. No, the shop owners didn't call me names like old Heidenreich did, but their looks, their brusque actions, the whole air of the place made me feel unwanted.

"Again Mom and Pop didn't talk about it, but I know they felt the same way. Just to avoid the place Mom would go all the way to the bigger town of Walla Walla, about thirty miles away, to do her shopping."

If his daily life in Milton was no great improvement over internment camp, at least George recalls two good things that came out of it. The first was the day four of his Kennewick pals made the long trip to Milton and sought him out. Recalling that early summer afternoon still brings on a smile.

"I was out in the orchard pruning when suddenly this car pulls up. Out jumps Jim Boldt, Gene Graves, Glen Mowrey and Charles Quast, all old buddies from back home. Somehow they'd found out where I was, and they'd taken the time to look me up. It turned out that they could only stay for a couple of hours, but, man, after what I'd gone through since I'd seen those four guys last, they were going to be two very special hours.

"There I was, fourteen years old, living near a town where I knew I wasn't accepted, without a single friend. Sure, I still had my brother Vic, but it always seemed like when I did get an hour or two off, he was working. I'd been so lonely that I'd found enough scrap lumber to build a set of parallel bars and with the little free time I had, I was teaching myself new acrobatic moves, building on a few tricks I'd learned back in camp. It was about the only entertainment I had my entire time in Milton, from May all the way into January. When those boys showed up, I bet I didn't know how to act, having real buddies around again.

"Later I'd realize that they'd helped me with much more than my loneliness. I'd just gone through about a year and a half when a few really mean-spirited people and a couple of huge events seemed to be conspiring to break me down, to destroy my self-confidence, to turn me into the kind of person I knew I didn't want to be. Then here came these four, just being my friends, just being the decent kids they all were.

"Maybe they were only a couple of years into their teens that summer, but somehow every one of them had escaped the hatreds and prejudices that entrapped so many adults during those terrible times. But I guess that shouldn't have come as a real surprise. After the way we'd been in school, out on the playing fields, in each other's homes, these four guys and a bunch of the other Kennewick kids simply were never going to see me as some kind of potential enemy or even as any different.

"And now these four had cared enough to come see me, maybe because they missed me, maybe just to let me know how they felt. Either way, they'd end up giving me much more than part of an afternoon of pure enjoyment. That little visit, a meager two hours, was an incredible gift, one that would partially erase those months of pain and go a long ways toward restoring my battered self-image."

Sixteen

THE FAMILY'S SEARCH
FOR A FRESH START

The second good thing was that George's sojourn on the Heidenreich farm was destined to be blessedly short. At first the Yoshinos thought they were going to have an opportunity to start farming in Moses Lake, Washington, at that time a tiny town in the arid central part of the state, where they knew several Japanese families. Frank sent his two young sons on an exploratory trip.

"Vic and I headed for Moses Lake in the '37 Studebaker Pop had put in storage just before we left for camp," George recalls. "We'd made it all the way from Milton to Connell, Washington, about forty miles from our destination, when we blew the left front tire. Our spare was almost paper thin, and you couldn't simply go out and buy another tire during those rubber-rationing war years. You had to find someone who had one and who was willing to part with it. Connell had nothing, and we had our doubts about what we'd find in Moses Lake, so we had no choice. We had to double back to Pasco where at least we still knew a few people who might help us out.

"In Pasco it turned out that a family named Ogata, some of the nicest people we knew, had a panel truck that before the war they'd used to deliver laundry. Gas rationing had put a quick halt to that service, so they'd put their panel up on blocks, waiting for the war to get over. The tires were about the same size as the ones on our Studebaker, so we offered to buy one, but they insisted on making it a gift. Well, we argued because tires were pretty precious right then, but finally, just to make us feel better, they said it would be a loan. How do you loan a tire?"

To make this trip, it had taken Vic and George a month to save just enough gas ration coupons, issued for three gallons per week per vehicle, but now the miles of backtracking and driving around Pasco were going to leave them way short. They either had to purchase more fuel in Pasco or abandon their quest, pointing their Studebaker back toward Milton. Finally they found a Pasco filling station where the attendant said sure, he'd sell them fuel, as long as they had ration coupons

"No coupons, well, he'd gladly sell us those too," George laughs, "five bucks each for three gallon black market chits. This guy had a bundle of them. Once again we had no choice. There wasn't another station around the corner that was going to give us a better deal. We forked over ten dollars for two of his coupons, paid him his regular price for the gas, and once again headed north, praying hard we wouldn't blow another tire."

They had no further road problems, but when the brothers finally made it to Moses Lake, they found a dismal little village with just a handful of buildings, a couple of dusty unpaved streets and almost no services. Pulling into town around noon, they discovered that the town's lone cafe had a line of men strung out along its sidewalk, waiting to get a seat. Moses Lake's only grocery was a place called Hochstatter's General Store, where everything from food to hardware was sold. Vic bought a loaf of bread and cold cuts, the boys' lunch, dinner and breakfast during their day-and-a-half sojourn. The town did have a small hotel, but renting a room wasn't in their budget. They slept in the Studebaker.

"As young kids the things we'd hoped to see in a town where we might locate, like maybe a roller rink or at least a movie theater, just didn't exist," George recalls. "In a vacant lot we saw rows of wooden benches, all facing a big concrete block wall. I guess after it turned dark enough, they'd haul out a projector and show films. Vic and I weren't exactly big city boys looking for all the amenities, but we had to admit, this place looked pretty bleak."

Still, the brothers knew that getting an acreage was way more important than a roller rink or malt shop. The reclamation project that would turn this whole area into a mecca of irrigated farms was better than a half dozen years away, so except for a few wells all the irrigation water had to come out of the lake. That afternoon they talked to two farmers who did have the right ground, but lease costs were way too high. Vic and George left Moses Lake convinced that this was one town they didn't want in their future. Little did they know.

"The only good thing that came out of our first little trip was that while I sat in the Studebaker eating a sandwich, Vic went back into Hochstatter's and bought me a brand new shirt. None of us had much in the way of clothes back then, but maybe Vic thought that my shirts were getting a little too threadbare. Or else he just wanted me to get something nice for a change. That might have been the first brand-new piece of clothing I'd had since before internment. Vic could sure be thoughtful."

Moses Lake had proven to be a temporary bust, but that winter the Yoshinos were contacted by an old Kennewick friend, a man named Naegel. Naegel's sister and brother-in-law, an older couple by the name of Stringer, were ready to retire and wanted to lease out their eighty acres near Weiser, Idaho, a small community right on the Oregon border. The Stringers would still live in the main farm house, but the Yoshinos could immediately move into a second house they had on their property, their former employee's quarters.

Naegel was certain that this would be the perfect place for the hardworking Yoshinos, a place where they could again become vegetable farmers. That spring the family moved into the small but comfortable house and started seeding their crops.

"The Stringers were fine down-to-earth people, just like their brother-in-law," George remembers, "and they had a nice farm, almost the ideal setup for us to get started again. With all four of us working for wages in Milton, we'd been able to put bread on the table and somehow Mom had managed to send enough money to Elmer and Louise to keep them both in college and to even save a few bucks. But having our own place again was always Pop's goal. By then I guess a farm was my goal too. I'd already missed a whole year of school in Milton, and my earlier dreams of going on to college and maybe into a profession were fading fast. In fact, when we hit Weiser, I wasn't sure I'd make it through high school.

Seventeen

GEORGE STEPS INTO THE BREACH

A s much as Pop wanted us on our own, I knew he wasn't ever again going to be able to run a real farming opera-tion without a lot of help. For one thing, now we'd have to move into a totally different kind of farming than the truck garden type Pop understood. We'd have bigger fields, different markets, more of a commercial operation. If he'd been able to stay in Kennewick and farmed every year, he'd have changed with the times and been a real success, but that didn't happen. And by then I also knew that Pop was never going to regain his old confidence.

"Mom wasn't the same strong woman she'd been either. Before camp she'd handled all our finances and helped Pop with the major decisions. Now she wasn't nearly as sure of herself. She'd never say much about our internment, but Portland and Heart Mountain had changed her. She could still be warm and gregarious with her host of old friends, and she could be plenty assertive with her own family. But now the outside world scared her, particularly when it came to business deals."

Perhaps eighteen-year-old Vic should have been the decision maker, but with his usual unassertiveness, he seemed more than willing to let his aggressive younger brother take control, a role George stepped into quite naturally. Before he turned sixteen, he was deciding what, where and when to plant. He sought out new markets and determined how much to spend on equipment. He now understands that part of his willingness to take charge was also the aftermath of Heart Mountain.

"For years I denied it even to myself, but, yeah, those two camps had a profound effect on me too," he quietly reflects. "Before internment I'd worked so hard and taken so much responsibility that from about the age of six on, I wasn't really what you'd call a normal child. Oh, as I've said, I had plenty of friends and fun times, sure. I did all that kid stuff that most lads did back then, but I spent far more hours out in our fields than I did skipping rocks in a nearby reservoir or harassing wildlife with a homemade sling shot. All that work, it changes you. It gives you a different self-image.

"And the more Pop saw what I could do, the more leeway and responsibility he gave me, like driving our trucks and just a few years later letting me hop on a tractor and do some pretty tricky cultivating. Deep down all that responsibility was satisfying, maybe because I was the youngest kid and needed to prove myself. I bet I wasn't yet five when I first learned to resent phrases like, 'You're too young yet,' and 'Let Vic do that!' The worst one was 'Wait 'til you're older!" I hated it when Mom or Pop treated me like the baby of our family, so I was constantly out to prove myself.

"Then came the camps and I was forced to be just a child again, a thirteen-year-old without a single meaningful responsibility. I ate my meals when the dinner bell rang. I went to bed at lights out. I spent all those free hours hanging out with my little gang, playing games, getting into minor trouble, just like every other kid in camp. Pop saw all this and he didn't like it a bit. He'd seen what I could do, and I'm sure before internment he had nothing but high hopes for me. Now he was seeing me as just another irresponsible little kid, and no, he sure didn't like it. But neither did I. I'd been battling that image since I could remember. At the grand old age of thirteen, I no longer wanted to be seen as a kid in anybody's eyes, especially not my father's.

"So when we moved to Weiser, I know I over-compensated, working doubly hard at everything, stepping forward to make the important decisions, going way out of my way to make bigger deals. From day one I took on every responsibility that came my way. Given all the voids in our family right then, maybe I had to be the responsible one, but the truth is I thoroughly enjoyed this new role. Oh, like any other teenager, at times I complained about all the work I had to do, but I don't think I did this too often and never with much conviction. My folks saw me taking charge, and they both knew that I wouldn't have had it any other way."

Apparently neither his parents nor that area's businessmen were inclined to think of this youngest Yoshino as a kid because soon fifteen-year-old George was making deals with produce houses and purchasing on credit from local seed and equipment dealers.

"Reflecting back, I wonder why these people trusted me so much," he now muses, shaking his head. "I was so young when I took charge of our Weiser farm. Why would someone sell me a piece of equipment on time or rely on me to hold up my end of a vegetable contract? I was barely fifteen when I made a deal for our lettuce crop with a fellow named Dave Haraguchi, a field agent for the big Simplot corporation. We'd do all the planting, irrigating, weeding, whatever it took to raise a good stand, and Simplot would come in with their men and machinery to do the harvesting. They paid us a thousand dollars an acre, which was a pretty good deal because not counting our labor, I'm sure we didn't have much over a hundred and a half per acre into that crop.

"Two years in a row Simplot didn't harvest our lettuce. By the time it was ready, we were having so much rain that our fields had turned into pure mud. They couldn't run their machinery, so the entire crop rotted. But that was Simplot's loss. We'd lived up to our agreement and had our money. Harvesting was their problem, their risk. Of course ours wasn't a huge acreage either year, around ten acres, and a big company like Simplot had lettuce contracts throughout the Northwest. They knew they were going to lose some. That's the volatile nature of the lettuce business, a high-risk crop with enormous profits when conditions are right.

"No, it wasn't any big deal for Simplot to lose a small plot here and there, but what still throws me is that they'd sign any kind of contract with a kid. Later, when I was in business, if some fifteen-year-old came to me with a $10,000 lettuce deal, I'm pretty sure I'd have told him to get back to school, then work for somebody else for a couple of years before he started trying to make grown-up bargains. But for some reason these people all seemed to have faith in me. They'd take me at my word, contract for my crop, extend me credit, write me out big checks even before I had anything to sell them. To this day I don't really understand it. I'm just glad I didn't let any of them down."

It was fortunate for the Yoshinos that George could make profitable deals because although the costs of starting a small farming operation weren't enormous, they quickly strained the family's small budget. While still residing in Milton, Vic and George had purchased a 1940 Ford truck for $2000, only $500 less than their father had been paid for his entire Kennewick farm and all his machinery, including two trucks that were far superior to this one. This latest truck blew a piston before it was five miles off the lot and would go through four more motors in the next couple of years.

"The whole civilian machinery industry was still suffering because so much production had to be diverted to the war effort, building military trucks, tanks, jeeps," George recalls, "So when you needed a farm truck or anything else, you had to really shop around. Even then, you didn't want to be too particular. Maybe you suspected that a truck or tractor might have problems down the line, but if you thought you could make do, you bought it, simply because you didn't have many options."

Finally the Milton truck was proving too unreliable, so George negotiated a deal in Weiser, this time purchasing a slightly newer ton-and-a-half Ford, almost entirely on credit. Then to give his family an immediate cash flow, he rigged this vehicle to pull a semitrailer and started hauling other farmers' lettuce crops from Weiser to a produce house in Ontario, Oregon. At the time fourteen-year-olds could get an Idaho driver's license. At a grown-up fifteen, George attained a legitimate chauffeur's license, allowing him to legally drive this tandem rig. For this ambitious youngster, speed meant money.

"Yeah, I definitely developed my lead foot way back then," he now laughs, "always floor-boarding that '42 Ford, running it faster than it was meant to go. Other guys who were making that Weiser-Ontario route would get so mad because even when they'd take off while I was still loading, I'd catch and pass them somewhere on that road. Was this safe? No, of course not. Sure, I was a good driver and we didn't face much traffic, but I was always pushing my limits, driving as hard as that old Ford could go. Like a typical kid, I had no idea that I was mortal, and getting things done in a hurry was already second nature. Everything I did had to be fast, as fast as a machine or my physical limitations allowed. Whether it was loading or unloading lettuce, racing over an open stretch of highway and not slowing up when I hit a curve, extra speed meant an extra load or two per day, which translated into a fatter paycheck at the end of the week."

High-speed lettuce runs weren't going to be the only time when young George would get the chance to test his driving skills. Somehow John Davies, the man who bought Frank out, heard where the Yoshinos were and came down to Weiser to see if they could do business. Before he left, he had convinced the family to put in a small acreage of mint, the first ever raised in the state of Idaho. A mint crop is started by planting root stock, and for this George had to make runs all the way to Kennewick.

"Well, actually I'd have to stop right before I hit the bridge because the war was still on, and Japanese-Americans couldn't cross the Columbia River. I guess the army thought I was a threat to come there with a truckload of dynamite and blow up their link between towns. The mint farmer Davies had tied us in with would meet me in Pasco, drive my truck across that bridge and load it, then bring it back, while I sat by the side of the road twiddling my thumbs. Maybe because the camps had inured me to that kind of stupidity and this guy was seeing it for the first time, that farmer hated the inconvenience far more than I did.

"As far as my driving, those mint root runs to Kennewick and back were more of the same, the old 'pedal to the medal' the whole way. After getting a couple of speeding tickets early on, I didn't learn much of a lesson. I simply developed a knack for spotting the patrol cars before they had me clocked. The Oregon trooper academy was located in LaGrande, and their young recruits found out who I was in a hurry. As soon as they knew my truck, they were always on the lookout for it coming down the road.

"But they couldn't write a ticket until they'd tail me long enough to get an accurate speedometer reading. Fortunately for me, that old highway twisted like a snake, making it easy to pick them up in my rear view mirrors the second they left their little off-the-road concealment spots and tried to slip in behind me. Ah, those were the days, before all this law enforcement technology. If highway cops had had radar way back then, I'd have had to change my ways.

"Yeah, all my life I was in too much of a hurry, especially when it came to driving the highways, whether I was in a car or truck. It didn't always pay either, especially early on. Sure, I made extra money with speed, but those old Ford motors could blow up even when you drove them right, and they sure didn't stand the kind of abuse I put them through. Before I traded that '42 off, I'd burned up four engines."

Eighteen

REBUILDING FAMILY IN THE WEISER VALLEY

A s the Yoshinos had hoped, this relatively arid region that by the early forties was already made up of small irrigated vegetable farms proved an excellent fit for their displaced family. They had the lettuce contract, their first venture into raising mint quickly proved profitable, and they were able to turn out small but impressive acreages of potatoes and onions. Better yet, this valley was the home of dozens of other Japanese-Americans, well established farm families who had gained the respect and trust of their Caucasian neighbors and the local businesses. Their school-aged children had blended into the local schools, many proving to be top students. In the entire valley, as well as in the small town of Weiser itself, Caucasians and Asians alike accepted the newcomers and treated them fairly.

Yes, once again the planting, irrigating and weeding involved in raising vegetables seemed never ending, but at least here the Yoshinos were a family again, eating most of their meals together, at times working side by side, always helping one another in a dozen little ways, enjoying their traditional camaraderie, even having a bit of privacy when they needed it. For the sons and the father, growing and harvesting crops of vegetables was simply more of the steady grind they'd known before internment, but in later years George had to wonder how his mother coped with everything her disrupted life had thrown at her. Before they were forced out of Kennewick, Kazuye's duties had certainly been demanding, but at least then she had possessed a few modern conveniences, including a small refrigerator and an electric ringer washing machine.

"Along with almost everything else, these appliances were lost when we had to leave the farm," George recalls, still stung by his memories, "and with the war on, we couldn't buy Mom replacements, even when we had the credit. In Weiser she had to get by with a flimsy Montgomery Ward's ice box that was so tinny and poorly insulated you had to replace the heavy ice block about every other day. We were constantly having to stop at Weiser's one ice house, where they cut big blocks of ice in the winter, stored them in a huge warehouse with lots of sawdust for insulation, and then sold them all through the year. Even with fresh ice it was hard to keep anything cold in that hunk of metal. Milk and cream would turn rancid in no time, and the butter was so runny you could pour it on your toast easier than spreading it.

"The worst part was that without her washing machine Mom had to get all our laundry cleaned in a big old tub, sudsing everything up, then grating it back and forth over a rough scrub board. Despite this, on my school days she'd never let me out of the house without a clean and pressed shirt on my back. To this day it's hard for me to think of my mother for very long without picturing her standing over an ironing board late at night, a big stack of pressed clothes piled up on one side, on the other a couple of basketfuls still waiting their turn. And this was always after she'd put in a long hard day of cleaning, cooking, maybe helping outside by hoeing weeds or picking potatoes, whatever the time of year demanded.

"I remember those ironing scenes so vividly, but what I can't remember is Mom ever complaining. As she saw it, she had a good husband, two kids off at college, a couple of hard-working sons. She had her little home and her family around her again. Best of all, the uglinesses of camp life were behind her. She readily accepted those endless days of labor as her lot, the price she'd gladly pay for family unity. When Louise came home from college during the summer, Mom turned the cooking and house cleaning over to her and spent even longer days helping us with our field work.

"Yes, as a family we'd taken a giant step backwards from our Kennewick days, but at least we all felt good about working together, as well as doing many of the little things that our former life had revolved around. Simply having a sit-down meal together, sharing that single hour of camaraderie, that was vital. Sometimes those meals were a time to air our concerns or to share our hopes and dreams. More often we used these moments to relax, to get into light banter and laugh at each other's stories, even the ones we'd heard dozens of times. With all the over-the-road running I was doing and the farming demands we all faced, a family meal wasn't always an option. Lunch-time was especially tough. Many days it was eat when you could, no matter what the rest of the family was doing.

"Back then I had a tremendous appetite, always coming off a produce run or out of the fields ravenous. I remember a lunch when Louise started making me toasted cheese sandwiches, using one of those little presses. I wolfed down those sandwiches faster than she could make 'em. She went through a whole loaf of bread before I'd had enough.

"But my sister could make a lot more than toasted cheese sandwiches. Louise was already developing the cooking skills that became such a major part of her life. She could whip a few simple ingredients into a wonderful dinner. Later, when she'd have better resources and could get what she needed, she'd turn out traditional Japanese dishes that were pure art, both to look at and to savor."

A major figure in the Yoshino's Kennewick household was still missing, but that was also going to change in the fall of 1946. That was when the federal government finally closed the last internment camps, forcing Takejiro to finally leave Heart Mountain. Perhaps because he felt that he had no other options, he again joined his brother's family. Leaving camp may have been yet another unwelcome disruption in a life that had been too riddled with disruptions, but he quickly blended into the family's new world.

From that point on, though, Takejiro totally gave up trying to lease small plots of ground and raising crops. He seemed content to stay in his new home, to plant and then tend his flower and vegetable gardens in the spring, summer and early fall. Once the cold Idaho winter set in, he mainly stayed indoors.

George still admired the only uncle he had ever known and was pleased that he was back in their home, but his own demanding work schedule and his budding friendships with his new schoolmates left him little time to spend with the aging Takejiro. Besides running the farm and making road trips, the younger man was again trying to finish his education.

Nineteen

CLASSMATES, IN THE FINEST SENSE OF THAT WORD

"Amazingly I'd somehow make it through high school in Weiser," he now says, grimacing slightly, "though this almost came to an end shortly after it started. In late 1944 our local draft board rejected my brother Vic's Four-C, a farming classification, and made him 1-A. We were all so sure he'd be drafted before spring planting that I went to my principal and explained that as soon as this happened, I'd have to quit school. It was tough enough anyway, with everything we had to do on the farm. Without Vic, I knew I'd have to be out there full time. The draft board kept threatening, especially when the Battle of the Bulge was raging, but for some reason they never pulled Vic in.

"By the time I started classes in Weiser, though, I'm afraid I wasn't much of a student, not that the school's academics were all that challenging for me, but between my duties on the farm and running produce several times a week, I could only attend classes for half a day, and I'd still end up with more absences on my record than days spent in class. I vaguely wanted my high school diploma, and I definitely wanted to stay eligible for sports, so each semester I'd carefully scrutinize the schedule, then sign up for the three easiest classes I could get. Even then I'd get in trouble.

"At the end of one term Principal Riggs called me in and showed me my attendance record. It was pretty dismal all right, but there was nothing else I could do. Finally he said 'Look, if you can't do better than this, why come at all?' I had to agree. I was at a point where dropping out so I could concentrate on everything else in my life made a lot of sense, even if it meant giving up sports and the fine friendships I was developing.

"But Mr. Riggs was a good man, a fellow who paid more than lip service when it came to caring about his students. And Weiser was a small town where people tended to know what everyone else was doing. Yeah, I'm sure that principal had a pretty good idea about my situation, and I guess he figured that if he let me stay in school, I'd get something out of it, at least the camaraderie of sports and a little more time with kids my own age.

"I know now that I agreed to stick it out only for those two reasons. If it hadn't been for my football coach, Mr. Gill, I'd have flunked several classes, particularly typing, where you were graded partly on your attendance. Coach Gill would go to my teachers and talk them into passing me, just so I'd be eligible for the big games."

If sports were going to be his high school mainstay, at least George used his limited free time to make the most of them. He did okay in basketball and track, but football became his show-case. If he'd had time to practice with the team, he might have been their star quarterback, throwing touchdown passes to his fleet-footed pals. Instead he became a pulling guard on offense and a defensive mainstay.

"Nowadays I think they call it having a nose for the ball," he says about his defensive prowess. "Coach Gill told me to call the defensive signals and once the other team lined up to quickly switch positions as I saw fit. Teams back then had more set patterns and were easier to read than they are now, so I could look at a formation and guess where a play was going. One play I'd be up on the line, ready to cut off an end run, the next I'd drop back into pass coverage."

Despite his demanding work schedule George did find time to socialize. Going to movies, roller rinks, the high school dances, and sports led to close friendships with lads like Bill Maxwell, who to this day keeps in touch, Dave Chadwick and Nick Speropolous. Bill and Dave were Weiser's two multi-sport stars, fleet halfbacks in football and dominant figures on the track. Between them they'd get out of high school owning all of that state's sprint records. But though most of his life in this little town was free of racial incidents, not every Caucasian in Weiser was willing to accept George as a total equal.

"Just once I dated a white girl," he recalls. "My high school buddies had no problem with this. In fact, I think one of them set us up. But a small group of guys in Weiser got pretty upset when they heard about it and started making nasty noises, threats that you wouldn't exactly describe as veiled. These guys were just the local pool room hangers-on, fellows who'd grown up in that valley and whose own lives were going nowhere, so I guess a little crude bigotry gave them a much needed ego boost. They never came after me or said anything when I was around, but the word was out.

"Had I never experienced anything except life the way it was during my years in Kennewick, I'm sure I'd have reacted differently, maybe fought for my right to date any girl who was willing to go out with me. But after all I'd been through in the camps and while working for a couple of racist farmers, I was a little gun shy. I sure wasn't in love with this girl or anything, so it was just easier to back away, to let it slide. I had enough going on in my life. I didn't need the hassle of dealing with the local rednecks."

If Weiser's few petty racists could make George feel uncomfortable, his teammates knew just how to make him feel accepted. It was after an out-of-town basketball game during his junior year when he had the chance to see these young men at their best.

"We'd stopped in the little town of Payette, just down the road from Weiser, for a post game meal," he recalls, his voice reflecting the significance of that particular evening. "I'd just sat down and was reading the menu when suddenly a gruff voice bellowed 'We don't serve Japs!' I glanced up and was staring at a glaring restaurant owner, standing right in front of me, looking as if he was ready to personally toss me through his front door.

"Before I had time to react, Nick Speropolous, who was sitting right next to me, jumped to his feet, tossed down his own menu and said 'Let's get out of here.' Not one person hesitated. My team, my coach, even our school superintendent, we all walked out together, leaving that owner staring at his empty restaurant.

"He was only a sophomore and couldn't have been more than sixteen that year, but Nick sure knew the right thing to say and the right thing to do. Five forceful unhesitating words, then he led us out. That's all it took to turn what could have been a very ugly scene into one of the best memories of my young life. Yeah, Nick set the tone. He led the way, but the really great thing was watching all those other guys immediately walk out too. I don't remember worrying about being accepted and respected by my teammates even before that night in Payette, but having them display their feelings so openly and decisively sure made me feel good."

Before going on George hesitated, reflecting on his youth. "You know," he finally added, "many times in later years I'd be asked how I kept from getting bitter over the injustices of internment and the bigotry I had to sometimes face when I got out of Heart Mountain. Well, the incident in that little Payette restaurant might help explain it. I don't doubt that other Japanese-Americans had it many times worse after internment and weren't around the right people, but in my case there was always a Nick to counter a small-minded cafe owner. For every Heidenreich who tried his best to belittle me, there were guys like Nick, Bill, Dave, Jim and many many others who stood by me. Most of the time this was just a matter of being my friend, standing with me in the face of bigotry, but at other times it meant helping me when I was down, giving me the chance to rise again and rebuild my self-esteem.

"If it hadn't been for all those friends, well, I just don't know. From the time we were toddlers, Mom and Pop had done their best to instill a sense of integrity in all us kids, mainly by example. Then the camps and a couple of twisted farmers came along and taught us far too much about injustice. As a teenaged kid I was headstrong and feisty enough that I know I could have gone either way. I could have embraced that injustice, then spent the rest of my life seeking some kind of petty vengeance or simply turning bitter.

"My other choice was to fight injustice, to make sure it never dominated my life. Thanks to my folks and my friends, I was able to take that second option. Why let a Heidenreich pull you down to his level when the Nick Speropolus's and Bill Maxwells of this world can pull you up to theirs? In fact, I discovered along the way that if you play it right, the bigots out there can actually improve your life. I know they did mine. When I was able to finally walk away from those two racist farmers, I knew two things for sure. First, they didn't represent all white people, and second, I wasn't going to spend my life at the mercy of people like that. What those two guys put me through in a few short months, when I had no choice but to put up with their garbage, drove me to better myself, to make sure I didn't ever feel forced to work for their ilk again. Even before we ever left Milton, I was determined to some-day become one of the bosses rather than the bossed.

"And reflecting back, I now realize those two racists gave me something else. When I did become an employer, I had a whole lot more compassion for my employees. Oh, I doubt if many people who worked for me are now going around describing me as a soft touch, but I hope they're willing to say that I treated them fairly and with respect, the two things I always felt I owed any worker, at least until he or she proved me wrong.

"Unfortunately, over the years I've met too many former internees who let the injustices of the camps eat at them, destroying a big part of their lives. Sure, I can understand their feelings and see why this would happen, but in the end what good does all that bitterness do? It doesn't make past wrongs a bit better, and it only hurts the person who's bitter and those closest to him. The good thing is, I've met a whole lot more guys who came out of the camps and did just what I did. No, none of us will ever entirely get over what happened, but at least we've been smart enough to put the wrongs behind us and go ahead with our lives.

"When I happened to land in Weiser as a teenager, I was doubly lucky. Not only were most of the Caucasians I dealt with decent people, but I had a fine role model in a fellow former internee named Tom Hayashi. Tom was two years ahead of me in school, had been interned with his family at Tule Lake, and now was doing his best to pick up the pieces. Because of internment the Hayashi family had lost a farm that was destined to become downtown Bellevue, one of Washington's premier cities. A few years after the war it would have been worth millions, just as raw real estate. But Tom had already left all that in his past. As a senior in high school, he was involved in sports, studying hard, getting straight A's, making sure he was prepared for college. Even back then all his classmates knew Tom had a real future, that he'd make something of himself. He was a natural student, bright and disciplined."

Tom Hayashi's college career was about to be put on hold. A military that was still anxious for replacements was snatching most of the recently released Nisei men up as fast as they were eligible. Tom's local draft board had him on a bus and heading for basic training before he could go through his high school graduation ceremony. After a two year stint in the military, he was able to use his G.I. Bill, enrolling in the University of Washington, earning an engineering degree and going to work in California's burgeoning aerospace agency. While he was in the military, he and George would exchange a few letters, just enough to keep in touch, to retain what would become a lifelong friendship.

Tom wasn't the only Japanese-American at Weiser who was destined to have a major impact on George's life. The summer before he started school there, another Japanese-American family had moved to town. Their daughter Frances was just his age, pretty and very intelligent. Within a couple of months she was helping him with his schoolwork. That winter they started dating.

"Actually, as time moved along, Frances did more and more of my schoolwork," George now admits, "and without her help, maybe even my coach couldn't have saved me. I'm sure the teachers knew. Our school was too small to hide much, but they never said a thing, just let me slide by and stay eligible for sports. Frances was smart and from a family that definitely stressed education. Her brothers all went on to college, becoming medical doctors or getting other advanced degrees. She should have gone on to college too, but back in the forties few girls were encouraged to do that, and most of those who did go on used it as a stop gap before marriage."

If his parents' security hadn't come first, George definitely could have entertained his own thoughts of a college career. After watching him on the football field, several college recruiters were more than willing to overlook his poor academic record and open their school's doors for him. As a senior he made Idaho's All-State team. But it was a game against perennial power Boise that gave him the most notoriety.

"Boise had a winning streak that dated back several years," George relates. "We went down there, played 'em pretty tough all game, but when the final gun went off, they still had that streak intact. I must have had a good game, though, because the next spring Boise's coach, Bob Gibb, contacted me. He'd been hired to take over as the University of Idaho's head coach for the next season and said he wanted me on his team. Coach Gibb talked me into coming up to Moscow, to look over the university campus, to talk about my possible role on his team, and listen to his offer. It turned out that he was willing to give me a real scholarship, tuition, books, a part time job that would have covered my room and board. For a small town kid walking around that campus, looking over their big stadium, and thinking that I might have the chance to be a star, well, that was all pretty heady stuff.

"A little later I made another trip to the Lewiston Normal School, where they also offered me a football scholarship. Deep down I must have been harboring a slim hope that something was about to break, that somehow I'd get my shot at college, even if I had to delay it a year. But mostly those trips were a formality and maybe a chance to bask in the moment. When you're young, it's good for the ego to hear a college coach tell you what you could do for his program. Coming back to reality, I knew I couldn't leave the farm and my folks."

That fall a near-fatal accident turned a college football career into a moot question. To make extra money George had rented a beet-loading machine, hired an operator, and was busy doing custom work for his neighbors.

"I'd quickly figured out that the beet loader could go only so fast no matter who ran it, so that's where I put the fellow I hired. If I was behind the wheel of my truck, I could make top speed runs back and forth to the beet dump and get in two extra loads a day. To save a couple of minutes, whenever I'd get back to the field and pull up next to that machine, I'd hop out of my truck cab, grab a lever and raise the front end of the loader, then jump in my truck again and back under it so we could transfer the beets.

"Just once I got too careless when I grabbed that lever. Trying to get better leverage, I stepped back, right into the loader's power take-off. In a flash it hooked my pocket and sucked me in, completely ripping off my brand new coveralls. This all happened in seconds, but before I'd pull free, that square shafted power take-off severed a major nerve in my right arm, lopped off the tip of my right ear and snapped my neck around hard, doing permanent nerve damage. Over my lifetime, that neck injury has been the worst, at times creating almost unbearable pain. I was lucky to get out alive. If my coverall material had been a little tougher, that moment of carelessness might have ended a whole lot more than my potential to make tackles on a football field."

Twenty

VIC'S REBELLION, FRANK'S INTEGRITY, A MAJOR MOVE

D espite George's injuries life in Weiser looked pretty good. He had his first real girlfriend, a few top-notch buddies to pal around with and a reputation for athletic prowess in a town he liked, a town where he'd gained the trust and admiration of the agricultural industry. Add to this the fact that he was running a productive little farm with the chance to eventually lease or perhaps purchase more land, and it's possible Weiser could have become his permanent home.

Suddenly, though, his brother Vic was becoming a major flaw in this otherwise operable machine. Both in Milton and when they'd first moved to Idaho, Vic had been every bit as willing as his younger brother to work hard, building a future for their entire family. Together the brothers had brought in their first mint crop and put together a still to extract its oil. While George did most of the over-the-road truck runs, Vic put in his own long hours, running their old tractor, hoeing weeds, harvesting vegetables, willingly taking on any chore that came his way, the same conscientious brother that George had admired so much during their

Kennewick years. Then with little warning he changed, shirking his duties, spending money foolishly, staying away from the farm for days at a time.

"From our camp days on Vic had always had four or five of his old Heart Mountain pals hanging around," George grimly remembers, "guys whose families had fallen apart during internment. After camp these fellows had turned into drifters, with no real purpose or aim in life. In Weiser a couple of them even moved in with us and wouldn't leave until Mom had to blow her stack and kick them out. As long as my brother did his work, though, neither the folks nor I saw these guys as a real problem, just sort of a nuisance at times. But then suddenly Vic started acting like them. He'd take our only car and go off for days at a time, too often just when we desperately needed his help. It didn't matter if we had irrigating and cultivating that needed his attention or a crop of vegetables that had to be harvested. It was as if Vic's life with his buddies suddenly meant more to him than his own family.

"In fact, Vic became downright devious. At that time I'd been able to buy a nice little '36 ford that I drove back and forth to school. Vic talked me into trading up, for a much roomier '42 Buick that he said we'd share. Then he and his pals started taking off with that Buick, going on long road trips, leaving me with nothing but our old truck that went through engines about as fast as oil changes.

"I'll never entirely understand just what happened to Vic back in Weiser, but I'm sure a big part of it was that he was finally rebelling against Mom and Pop. For years he'd been such a good worker, so steady, never complaining. At fourteen he'd been running our produce all the way to Seattle and Portland, most of the time making those runs in a single long day and taking care of all the paperwork. No matter what the folks asked him to do back then, he did it, always totally trustworthy. I think, though, that he had deep-seated resentments building up because he worked so hard, and Elmer got away with so much.

"Vic's nature was to be quiet, holding everything in, but a few times he was willing to talk to me about this, angrily letting me know exactly how he felt. With the folks he'd just clam up. That's just one place where he and I were different. It didn't happen very often, but when I was really fed up, I'd go to both Mom and Pop and blow off steam. A five or ten minute tirade and at least I'd walk away knowing that they knew where I stood. Better yet, those short screaming sessions let me get my worst rage out in the open and at least partly out of my system. Vic could never do that. Not once did he go to Mom or Pop and tell them exactly how he felt. No, it wouldn't have changed how they treated us or Elmer, but it might have been the emotional release Vic needed. Instead, all his rage built up inside him until it finally busted loose in that crazy, destructive rebellion that wouldn't stop until it had driven the folks and me out of Weiser.

"When that craziness all started, I was sure I was the one who could get through to Vic, to talk some sense into him. We'd always been so close and he'd been so good to me that I just knew I could go to him, say a few of the right things, listen to his side of the story and get this mess straightened out. But every time I tried, he'd just get mad, go completely irrational. He couldn't explain a thing, not even to me. Finally his anger would set me off, and we'd end up screaming at each other, making that terrible situation worse.

"Then, seeing what he was putting Mom and Pop through and destroying everything we'd all worked so hard to build up, well, I just couldn't understand it. Day by day my own anger and resentment grew. The worst part was that all this was driving a bigger and bigger wedge between Vic and me, the brother I'd always felt so close to."

The practical ramifications of this family rift were quickly becoming insurmountable. Besides crippling the entire farm operation with his prolonged absences, Vic was rapidly spending it into bankruptcy. Unfortunately, because he was the oldest son at home, Frank and Kazuye had put him in charge of the family's finances. The checking account was in his name, and when he and his pals went off on an extended foray, Vic took the only checkbook with him. Suddenly George found himself trying to operate a farm with no access to ready cash.

"Besides handling our own farming, I was hauling other people's produce from Weiser to the Ontario market every day," George says, "trying desperately to get enough dollars coming in so we could stay afloat. But it was no use. Week by week we just kept sliding deeper into debt. By the winter of '47 Pop and I both knew that Vic wasn't going to quit doing whatever he was doing any time soon, and we couldn't keep going on the way we were. We had to make a change."

A few years before his second son's rebellion brought his family's Weiser sojourn to a close, Frank Yoshino's inflexible honesty standards were given a remarkable test, one that had he failed would have given him plenty of cash to weather his family's financial storm. When he had sold out just before internment, no documents of any kind had been signed. John Davies had given him $2500 on a verbal agreement and a handshake.

Frank's former attorney, Charles Powell, had continued to hold the legal deed. Living up to the earlier promise he had made to the Yoshinos, Powell had transferred this deed to Elmer as soon as this oldest son turned twenty-one.

"Suddenly Elmer gets a call from a big land developer, offering him $70,000 for just twenty acres of our old place," George recalls. "It turned out that our farm was right in the heart of what was about to become a big Kennewick shopping center that would eventually be surrounded by other businesses. Elmer was still in the army when that call came, and as soon as he'd listened to the deal, he was hot to take the cash. But Pop wouldn't hear of it. 'That's not our land,' he firmly told Elmer. 'A deal was made, our word was given, we're going to honor that.'

"Elmer argued and sputtered, but Pop was adamant and finally brought him around. Right away Pop got hold of Powell and had the land put in Davies' name. Seventy thousand was a whole lot of money back then. It would have allowed the folks to buy plenty of farm land, get the right equipment, and still have dollars in the bank. But I'll always be proud of Pop for holding firm. A lesser man would have thought about everything he'd just gone through and used that as an excuse to grab his land back. Internment camp did real damage to my father, but it didn't destroy his convictions. He never questioned that decision or doubted it was the right thing to do."

Frank's strong sense of Old-World honor again came to the fore when he learned that Vic's girlfriend, Betty Yabuki, was going to have his son's child. Despite the young couple's commitment to one another and their pending marriage, Frank could only view this as a family disgrace.

"This would have been hard for Mom and Pop to take in any case," George maintains, "but after what they'd just gone through with Vic, it was the final straw. Pop immediately disowned him, kicking him out of our house. The fact that all of us really liked Betty and that Vic intended to marry her didn't change a thing. I guess they were married someplace in Idaho shortly after that, but I'm really not sure just when or where. Not a single person from our family attended their wedding. Our split was too severe by then for Vic to invite me. This was a terrible time. I really believed I'd lost my brother forever."

Again it would be a former friend from their Kennewick years who would help decide the Yoshino's next move. A man named Harry Yamagami had been one of the Japanese Issei who had relocated to Moses Lake and earlier had encouraged Frank to join him. Now he stepped forward again, citing the thousands of acres of irrigated land that would soon be available through the newly formed Columbia Basin Reclamation Project. Harry did more than encourage his old friends. He found them all jobs, working for an established Moses Lake farmer named Percy Driggs, jobs that included a barracks that the family could temporarily call home.

"After that earlier excursion with Vic, I sure wasn't thrilled about heading back to Moses Lake," George recounts, "but when I listened to Harry, it did sound like the best place to make a fresh start. In the five years since I'd been there, Moses Lake had changed. Now it was much more of a town and had more irrigated land around it, and the big reclamation project was about to make far greater changes."

Financially, making any move wasn't going to be easy for the Yoshinos. They were so broke that Frank had to borrow a few hundred dollars from a friend in Payette, and George was able to get a small loan from a produce house where he had been selling their vegetables. Because the Buick was in Vic's name, they couldn't get it back.

"Yes, it was pretty grim," George admits. "Though I still owed the local garage from the last time our Ford truck blew a piston, a year and a half before we left the valley I'd finally figured out that I'd better dump that old engine eater. I'd traded it in on a ton and a half '46 Dodge, a much better rig and the only vehicle we'd have to make our journey. We'd arrive in Moses Lake with a mortgaged truck, a handful of I.O.U.'s, and very little else."

Despite his painful break with his brother Vic and his family's seemingly bleak prospects, nineteen-year-old George still had plenty of faith in himself. He left that valley with a couple of huge regrets, many wonderful memories and his determination to succeed stronger than ever.

"If life had been perfect, I'd have still been in Kennewick," he now reflects, "but Weiser had been good to me, no doubt about it, though even back then I think I knew that it was time to move on. Farms in that beautiful little valley were too small. The chances of developing the kind of big commercial operation I'd already envisioned ranged from slim to none. I only had a vague idea of what it might mean for me, but as soon as I'd heard about the big reclamation project that was about to turn Moses Lake and the surrounding countryside into a real agricultural center, I was intrigued."

Before continuing George flashed his soft smile. "I guess I did have real confidence in my future. I must have because before I left Weiser, I asked Frances to marry me. We both knew that this couldn't be right away, but we did become engaged. I even bought her a ring, again with borrowed money. That's the best part about being young. You might not have a dime to your name, but you can still have faith in your ability to create a great future. Those first two years in Moses Lake, even before we were married, Frances really helped me get started, and she sure eased the loneliness that was going to be a big part of my new existence. She and her dad would come up to Moses Lake and stay with us, both of them helping out in any way they could.

"Long hours are always part of farming, but when I started out in the Basin, I knew I had to work way beyond the norm. Our tractors back then were small, nothing like what you see out there today, so if I really wanted to get anything done, I had to be out in my fields day and night, grabbing a couple hours sleep in snatches. That's just one place where Frances really helped me out. She'd make sure I had hot food, even if that meant bringing my meals to the field so I could keep on going. Then in 1950, when I had a big potato crop over by the little town of Wilson Creek, she and her dad helped out with the harvest, picking spuds for regular piece-work wages. They were two of the best pickers I'd ever have, with real fast hands and tireless backs."

Twenty-one

EMBARKING ON A
REMARKABLE CAREER

With Frances and his parents forming a home front support team, George could concentrate on his many other
tasks. It was a good thing too because not yet twenty and
with a negative net worth when he arrived in Moses Lake, this
young man was about to embark on a farming, packing, marketing
and finally a processing plant career that in retrospect seems truly
amazing. By the spring of 1956, on the day he was celebrating his
twenty-eighth birthday, his Moses Lake accountant, Herb Quinn,
brought over his financial ledger. 'Well, George, you've hit that
first big plateau,' Herb announced. 'You're now worth a million
dollars.'

The fifties were years of tremendous expansion in
Washington's Columbia Basin, but they were anything but a
series of windfall profits for most of its farmers. 1952 brought in
the first Columbia River water, diverted from the huge reservoir
that had been created by Grand Coulee Dam and channeled into
this arid region through a series of canals. Entitled 'The Columbia
Basin Reclamation Project,' this was an undertaking that created

over a million irrigated acres and hundreds of new farms. Yes, there were other farmers who came into this project, started on the proverbial shoestring and prospered, some simply making an adequate living, a few eventually becoming wealthy landowners. But for every newcomer who stayed ahead of his creditors and eked out a living during those early years, at least four others would have to sell out or have their farms fall to an auctioneer's gavel. Why did George and a handful of others get rich while so many farmers were going broke or barely making ends meet? When this question was posed, George had a simple answer: "Desire and hard work."

"Well, what I should say," he quickly clarified, "is, for me at least, it was more desire and more hard work. Almost every farmer I've ever met had quite a bit of desire, but after what my family and I had lived through since Pearl Harbor, mine was at a fever pitch. It drove me, almost non-stop. Oh, I'd be less than truthful if I said there weren't times during those first couple of years when I wondered about this new life of mine. More than once I'd look around, think about what I was doing day in and day out, then realize that at least for the near future I'd have to keep right on doing it. It was in those moments when I'd question whether it was all worth it. Stuck on the hard seat of a tractor through scorching hot afternoons and bone-chilling nights isn't any nineteen-year-old's idea of a good time.

"Sure, I'd worked hard in Weiser too, but at least there I had my school chums. Whenever I did get an evening or a Sunday afternoon off, I had a real social life. Now weeks or even a couple of months could go by when I didn't get to spend an hour with a single pal or to even talk to a guy who was anywhere close to my age.

"Maybe what helped me most during those low times was knowing that whatever I faced was nothing compared to what my father had gone through when he started out. Whenever I'd get to feeling too sorry for myself, I'd remember Pop's early farming world and start making comparisons. Everything that I was doing from the seat of a tractor, Pop had to do walking behind a team of horses with his incredibly primitive tools. My little John Deere and two bottomed plow weren't much by today's standards, but they sure beat walking behind a plodding team all day with your hands clenched on the handles of that old single bottom.

"Then I'd get to wondering, how did Pop buy that first team, where did he find a plow or all the other equipment he needed, and how had he learned to handle it? He must have learned the basics of irrigating, seeding, cultivating and harvesting when he was working for Rudkin, but in those few short years, he couldn't have mastered everything he later knew about raising vegetables and hogs, to say nothing of his packing and marketing. Obviously Pop was picking up new ideas all along, but from whom?

"When he first moved to Kennewick, all his closest neighbors spoke English, and Pop was in no position to travel far and wide in search of new ideas. He came there as a young man raised in a big city by parents who'd sent him to the best schools and expected him to go into law. Now suddenly here he was, a hardworking dirt farmer and all alone. I just couldn't fathom how he'd kept from being overwhelmed by those long years of labor and isolation. I still can't. To this day I find it incredible that Pop stuck to his dream.

"At least by the time I started farming on my own, running machinery was second nature, and I had a pretty good handle on irrigation and crop rotation. Plus, whenever I needed information, all I had to do was hop in my pickup and make a quick call on one of my many competent and helpful neighbors. And I always had Frances bringing me hot meals and Mom keeping my clothes clean, cooking me a big breakfast, doing everything she possibly could to make sure I had a comfortable home life. Yeah, my long hours on the tractor were tough, but when I did finally climb off, I knew I had a family waiting for me.

"From 1910 when he moved up to Kennewick until 1915 when Mom joined him, Pop must have come out of his fields night after night completely exhausted, grimy with all the blowing dirt and his own sweat, only to face a cold stove in an empty shack. Before he could cook a simple meal or heat enough water for a sponge bath, he'd have to haul in wood and fire up that old stove. No one was there to wash his clothes or mend his socks.

"Apparently Pop got on fine with his Caucasian neighbors right from the start, and eventually he and Mom developed fine friendships all around Kennewick, but given the language barrier, communication had to be pretty minimal when he was just starting out. To me, that almost complete isolation would have been the worst part. An hour or two of pondering Pop's world always put mine back into perspective. He came to this new land knowing nothing about farming and not only survived but prospered, creating one of the biggest and best truck garden operations in our state. Then it would hit me! If Pop could succeed in early twentieth-century Kennewick, with everything that was against him, I had no excuse for not making it in mid-century Moses Lake.

"My real success keys were going to be the same as his, hours and hours of hard work and carefully planning ahead. And I knew that my hard work couldn't just come in spurts. Every young farmer is going to work hard for a time, maybe for three or four solid months, but then he'll figure he's earned the right to a little time off to socialize, to go bowling, night clubbing, or he might take a trip, maybe even a short summer vacation. In those first few years I quickly realized that my spring, summer and fall farming schedule precluded almost everything but work, and I'd have to spend the winter finding equipment and working out land deals. As soon as I started in the Basin, my goal became to double my acreage year after year, to use any profits I made to buy or lease more land."

"That's where desire really came into play because right from the beginning I knew that I wanted to be more than a small farmer, to drive a tractor around the same few acres all my life. To get to that point I had to be willing to put luxuries and small pleasures on hold for a while. My philosophy became 'Don't start spending money as soon as you have it. Instead, use it to expand, make it grow, let it build toward a meaningful future.'"

The expansion part of George's philosophy would not be easy. Even when he located a suitable acreage and had the necessary financing, buying land in the Columbia Basin back then was complicated. Because the whole region was now part of the federally run Bureau of Reclamation Project, the government had set appraised prices on all the farm ground, seventy-five to a hundred dollars per acre for undeveloped land, two to three hundred for developed parcels. Buying or selling for more than this appraised price was strictly against the law. More than one deal resulted in a prison sentence for the purchaser and seller alike.

"Our problem was that the government had imposed totally unrealistic land prices," George explains. "All their figures were based on what those farms had been worth when the reclamation project was just getting started way back in the late thirties. By the early fifties we'd had so much inflation that no land owner with half a brain was going to sell for those figures. If you seriously wanted a piece of ground, you had to be innovative, to figure out a way to give the seller something more than that set price, something that would satisfy him and wouldn't land you in jail. One way was to throw in a luxury car, something most guys and their wives really wanted. I'd buy a brand new Buick or maybe a Pontiac, make out a bill of sale for a fraction of the car's real value as a down payment on a piece of ground, and it was all perfectly legal.

"Bigger land deals might involve a house, something a family leaving the farm needed anyway. Say an owner wanted $15,000 above the appraised price of his land. I could buy a $20,000 home in Moses Lake, then sign it over to him for a fourth of that amount as part of my purchase price, and the government couldn't say a thing.

"Or we could set up a simple lease with an option to buy contract. If a piece of raw land had an appraised value of $150 an acre and the owner wanted $350, I could sign a two year lease-option that paid him an extra $100 an acre per year on the lease. Anyone with an ounce of common sense could see right through this, but once again it was strictly legal. As soon as I had all the paperwork signed, I'd start leveling and putting in the irrigation system, treating that land as if I owned it because for all intents and purposes I did. The law was both silly and tough, making crooks out of all of us, buyers and sellers alike."

Yet all the desire, hard work, and innovative land deals that can be packed into one person don't entirely explain George's early successes. He's now quick to acknowledge how fortunate he was to have a mother and father who were also willing to do whatever it took to rebuild their family's future, as well as a wife who quietly went along with his decisions, worked in his fields when she could, and, ultimately, raised his children.

"Those first few years were rugged for all of us," he says. "That worker's barracks the folks and I lived in our first year wasn't terrific, but it sure beat the shack we moved into our second year, just to save a precious few bucks on rent. That place was riddled with cracks and loose boards from one end to the other, and it sat right by the lake where the shoreline vegetation crawled with rodents. This shack didn't have enough bedrooms either, so I ended up sleeping out on our living room couch. Many nights I'd wake up feeling something weird and discover a mouse or rat crawling right across my face or my neck."

"I've had a real rodent phobia ever since," he admits, involuntarily shuddering. "I hate their beady little eyes, even in photographs. The folks, they just took it all in stride, the vermin, the dust that blew in and everything else that was bad about the place. After all, Mom was quick to point out, we were living there rent free!"

George also acknowledges that at times he was incredibly lucky to progress so rapidly, but it was luck made possible by the insights of a budding entrepreneur, one who was willing to do whatever it took to bring his plans to fruition. This started that first year in Moses Lake, when Percy Driggs not only gave the Yoshinos jobs and adequate housing, but also the use of a small plot of ground, fifteen irrigated acres to grow their own produce.

"Percy was a fine man," George affirms. "Besides the fifteen acres and giving us a place to stay, he paid us fair wages for that time. I don't recall what he paid Mom and Pop when they worked for him, but I made $1.25 an hour driving tractor, better than average back then. Right away, though, Percy saw what I could do, whether it was seeding, cultivating or plowing. He'd come out and watch me run his machinery and go away nodding his head, really pleased, plenty willing to pay a little extra for having someone who could do the job right. Still, our paychecks only covered our living expenses. It was those fifteen acres that gave us the jumpstart we needed.

"That spring I borrowed Harry Yamagami's tractor and seeded it all to onions. Then throughout the summer we did all the weeding and irrigating ourselves. Whenever one of us had a couple hours off from our regular jobs, we were out tending that little patch. Then a few weeks before harvest, I started nosing around for the best buyer, finally choosing Pacific Fruit Company. They were willing to buy our whole crop at $3.50 per fifty-pound bag, delivered to their cold storage sheds in Spokane and Walla Walla. An in-the-field sale wouldn't have brought half as much, but delivery meant I had to get them there."

'Getting them there' entailed a solid month of solo labor, loading the old Dodge truck with seven and half tons of sacked onions each night. Long before daylight the next morning George was on the road for a fast trip to Spokane. At the storage terminal he had to unload the sacks on a hand truck, take them by the elevator to the basement, then restack his cargo onto a pallet. As soon as he had a full pallet, he would grab the company's manual floor jack to move it into cold storage.

When the last pallet was tucked away, it was time to floorboard the Dodge back to Moses Lake for a second load. Five days a week he made these two-a-day two hundred mile round trips, hand loading and unloading fifteen tons of onions. Saturdays his two loads went to Walla Walla, approximately the same distance but a tougher round trip. When it was all over, George had a check for $12,000.

Twenty-two

REVERSE DISCRIMINATION, NEW FRIENDS, THE MACHINE AGE

"I gave Mom a third of that money for our family's upkeep and put the rest into machinery and start-up costs for the coming year. I knew, though, that eight thousand dollars wasn't going to be enough for what I wanted to do, so I went to the guys who had leasable land, dealerships, seed and fertilizer companies, guys like Carl and Marshal Burress, Mode Snead and George Shuster. Every one of them extended credit. They didn't even ask me to sign a paper. They'd just say 'Pay me back in the fall.'

Carefully selecting his words, George added, "You know, it's strange but after all the racism our family faced when we were sent to camp and everything Mom and Pop lost because of that, by the time I came up to the Columbia Basin, it actually helped to be Japanese. The people I had to deal with, from the implement dealers to the bankers, I know now that they just trusted me more. They had more confidence that I'd succeed as a farmer and pay my bills. Here I was, not yet of legal age, just starting out, brand new to this area, and right away I was making some pretty big deals, leasing and even buying valuable land.

"I know now that this was because of all the good Japanese farmers who preceded me in the Basin. Guys like Chi Omori, Yoe Nishi, Spud Yamamoto, Harry Yamagami, the Hatori brothers and many others. They'd set the tone with their honesty, their skill and their industry. All I had to do was live up to their high standards. Sure, the old hatreds of the war years were still simmering, and not every Caucasian in the Basin thought highly of our race or wanted to see us prosper. But I was only hurt by blatant racism once during those early Basin years, and I had to go all the way back to Payette, Idaho, to get hit with this.

"In late 1952 I found out about a good piece of ground that was for sale just east of Moses Lake. The owner had moved to Payette, so first I gave him a call, then on a Saturday drove over to discuss the deal. At our first meeting the guy seemed a little distant, but we agreed on a price, and everything seemed in order. Then suddenly he asked me to come back the next day. I figured he wanted to run the deal past his wife or maybe just have a night to think it over.

"So I took a motel room and the next morning showed up at the fellow's place. Immediately he went into a tirade about the Japanese, how we were immoral people who didn't go to church, and now here I was, showing up just when it was time for him to go off and worship. The whole thing was absolutely ridiculous, but I wanted that land deal enough to hold my tongue. Finally the guy settled down, we talked over the details again, and he said, 'Okay, you have the papers drawn up and send them to me.' We shook hands on the deal, and I left.

"Well, to make sure everything was done right, I hired Darrell Reis, a local attorney, to do the papers and mailed them the next week. About ten days later they came back, unsigned. When I called this fellow, all he'd say is that he'd changed his mind. He'd give me no explanation and of course wouldn't consider paying half the cost of drawing up those papers. I should have walked away from that guy the minute I heard him belittle my race. Why expect a racist to honor a verbal commitment or a hand-shake?"

Despite this single confrontation with post-war bigotry, George clearly understands how fortunate he was to have landed in a place where members of his race were not only accepted but admired, particularly in the field of agriculture.

"The older Japanese farmers helped me in many other ways too," he pleasantly recalls. "Farming around Moses Lake was different than either Kennewick or Weiser, and these guys had been there long enough to know the right techniques and more than willing to set me straight. For instance, the second year I was in the Basin, Yoe Nishi saw me out in a field in early April and came over to ask what I was doing. I told him I was planting watermelon seeds. 'Oh no,' Yoe warned. 'Around here this is too early for melons. They'll freeze out.'

"We'd always planted that early in Kennewick with good results, so I figured I could get away with it here, not yet realizing that I now faced a much shorter growing season. At least I was smart enough not to argue with Yoe. I just told him that watermelon seeds were cheap. If I had to, I could always replant, then went ahead and finished that entire field.

"In the melon trade, the earlier you get a crop to market the better. After Labor Day, forget it. When that weekend is over, people quit eating melons even if they're still plentiful. Well, in any other year Yoe's advice would have been right on target, but that April turned out to be a rare frostless one in the whole Basin, so right after the Fourth of July, many of my melons were ready to sell at premium prices, while Yoe's were still a month away and wouldn't be nearly as profitable. Despite this, Yoe came over and taught me which watermelons to pick and which needed more time to ripen. In Kennewick we'd gone by the curlicue on the stem. Around Moses Lake you had to do it by the color of the rind. It took a good man not to resent this brash youngster who'd ignored his sound advice and then through sheer luck came out with a far better cash crop than he'd end up getting.

"Another fellow who helped me was Chi Omori. Chi had been at Heart Mountain with us and liked to remind me that he'd been my camp basketball coach. I don't remember Chi being any great shakes as a coach, but he was a heck of a fine potato farmer. Without his and Spud Yamamoto's guidance I'd have made far more mistakes than I did.

"As a kid I'd always asked a lot of questions about anything that I didn't fully understand, and I sure didn't break that habit when I started farming on my own. Even before I came up to the Basin, I'd seen too many guys get burned by plunging into raising a new crop without knowing enough. I learned to do my homework, to ask for help, not only from the other Japanese farmers in our area, but from anyone who I thought could teach me something. If you go to people with questions and show them that you're sincere and willing to listen, they're almost always willing to give you honest answers. The real keys are to ask plenty of questions, but don't argue, don't second guess, and don't act as if you already know what they're trying to tell you. Any one of these is a sure turnoff for a fellow who's going out of his way to explain something.

"Farmers are particularly willing to help the guy who knows how to ask. Oh, I guess there was a time or two when I ran into a potato or onion grower who clammed up or rudely put me off, but that was rare. Way more often I'd have a fellow take hours of his valuable time to teach me things that he'd learned the hard way."

Asking questions and buying farm equipment became George's major priorities during the winter of '48 and '49. To make the most of his limited funds he spent a big part of those cold months hitting auction sales back in the Weiser Valley. He bought planters, cultivators, the tools he needed to fix them, all for a fraction of their retail price. A potato planter he picked up for $35.00 served him through that spring. That summer he sold it for $150.00 when he needed ready cash.

"In those days the Weiser Valley had many more auction sales than we had up in the Basin, mainly because it was a much older agricultural area, so a lot of farmers were hitting retirement age and selling out," George explains. "With plenty of sales to choose from I quickly learned to read a crowd. Sometimes you'd hit one only to discover that the auctioneer had already succeeded in getting half a dozen buyers whipped up, bidding everything way too high. As soon as I saw that, I'd jump in my rig and head for another sale a dozen or so miles down the road.

"Not only did I make good buys around Weiser, but then I saved a few more bucks by talking my brother-in-law, Louise's husband, into hauling all that equipment up to Moses Lake, using his own truck. When you're just starting out like I was, you definitely have to be frugal, cutting corners wherever it's possible. In fact, in those early years I had to figure out ways to economize because at times that was my only way of turning a small profit or of going too deeply into debt as I expanded.

"In 1952 I bought a couple of pieces of raw land that had to first be leveled, a costly item when you contracted it out. Right away I figured that this was another task I'd better do myself. So I purchased a well-used TD-9 International Crawler tractor and attached a six-and-a-half-yard carryall to it. This rig was much smaller than commercial outfits were using to level fields, but I could once again employ my 'everything at high speed' philosophy. I'd hit a piece of ground in fifth gear, pick up a load of soil, then dump it in a hollow spot without ever slowing down. Sure, this was more work for me, but while my neighbors were paying twenty-five dollars an hour for a guy with a D-8 Cat to level their ground, I was doing my own just as fast and at a fraction of their costs."

When he couldn't afford or locate a piece of equipment he needed, George became adept at making do with what he had. In 1949 he bought a used onion planter and figured out how to modify it to plant watermelon seeds.

"Unfortunately I was no mechanic, either then or at any other time in my career," he's quick to admit, "but both as a farmer and later as a packing shed and plant owner, I did develop a knack for looking at a machine, figuring out what it could and couldn't do, then come up with a way to make it do a job faster or at least better. Maybe this is just another thing my parents did for me. When Pop let me start driving his trucks before I was a grade school graduate, maybe he built this into me. At any rate, I know I wasn't very old when I developed a real affinity for machines, those wonderful labor-saving devices.

"At least part of this was because of my time and place. As a vegetable farmer's kid, I'd spent all those long hot hours doing stoop labor, everything from picking potatoes and strawberries to topping onions and cutting asparagus. Then as a very young man I started seeing how even our earliest machines could do these jobs so much faster and better. That's why I always wanted the latest and best. In 1949 a man named Fred Krueger started manufacturing a single-row potato harvester right there in Moses Lake. Chi Omori bought the first one and I took the second.

"This machine dug the potatoes, ran them onto a conveyer, and a man at the back end caught them in sacks as they came off. It cost $1200 and was too slow for my big fields around Wilson Creek, but it sure saved labor costs on my smaller Moses Lake acreages. Instead of hiring two dozen or more pickers, I could get by with a crew of four. I drove the tractor, Mom and Pop rode on the harvester by a turntable, tossing off all the debris that came up with the potatoes, and my old Weiser buddy, Tom Hayashi, was on the tail end sacking the spuds.

"My folks had a dirty job, but they could easily keep up. Tom was the real key because I could only push that harvester as fast as he could sack and then set the spuds on the ground. Given what he faced, Tom did an outstanding job, but that never stopped me from riding him, constantly telling him to pick up the pace. He'd try, pushing his limits.

"Years later Tom could laugh about that harvest and how worn out he'd be at the end of every day. Now he likes to tell me that I made up for the half wages I paid him by making him work double time. Half pay may be a little strong, but back then I did-n't have much so I sure didn't pay Tom what he was worth. Instead of remembering myself as cheap, though, I like to think I gave Tom something far better than wages. I gave him motivation! For three straight summers he'd be my only regular hired help, and every fall he was hot to get back to his cushy university life where he could wear clean clothes, let the blisters and sore muscles heal, and he'd again earn top grades, just to make sure he wouldn't end up working for me the rest of his life. Yeah, I deserve a little credit for his later successes.

"Besides, Tom got a little unintentional revenge for those potato harvesting days. His last summer he'd be out in the field with a pack of Lucky Strikes in his pocket, so whenever we had a few minutes together, I'd join him for a smoke. He went back to school that fall and gave up tobacco, but by then I was buying my own Lucky Strikes and had a real start on a forty year addiction."

Compare the speed and efficiency of George's first potato harvester to the human pickers who preceded it, and it was a vast improvement. Compare it to the machines we have today, and it's a real dinosaur. Historically, it was simply one more step in the movement of this country's agricultural industry towards greater and greater mechanization and efficiency. George enjoyed being on the cutting edge of this movement.

"When you think about it, getting any job done is all a matter of time and motion," he explains, "how long and how much energy it takes to accomplish a given task. Time and motion, that's a concept I've thought about my whole life. Whenever I look at any machine in action, whether it's mixing concrete, slicing vegetables or plowing a field, I start analyzing the process. Then I ask, 'how could it be made more efficient, faster? I still tend to do this even when I'm looking at machines that aren't part of my life and that I'm never going to alter.

"But back when a piece of equipment did affect my operations, I made some significant changes. Lots of my earliest ideas came to me in the long days and nights I spent on that little tractor. I'd be plowing, going round and round the same field, pretty much by rote, so I had plenty of time to think. Then I'd start asking, how can I do this job faster or make this machine more efficient.

"One night it hit me, here I am, plowing up this field, then I'll have to go over it all a second time with a packer and a third with a harrow before it's ready to seed. Why couldn't I pull the packer behind my plow and save a step? Or better yet, why couldn't I attach my harrow to the packer and combine three steps into one? My tractor was slow but it had just enough power to pull that trio. In that irrigated ground we had to use a two-way plow, so this meant I had to engineer a simple sliding mechanism to move the packer over each time I switched directions, which turned out to be pretty simple. Within a few years almost everyone in the country was turning this into a one-step operation, but back then it was brand new. When word got out about what I was doing, farmers came from all over to see how I'd set this up and started copying my sliding mechanism."

Twenty-three

STEPPING INTO THE COMPLEX WORLD OF AGRI-BUSINESS

Time and dollar-saving innovations were helping George survive, but bank financing was an absolute necessity. In the spring of 1949 he purchased the tractor that could pull his plow, packer, harrow trio, a brand new $1200 John Deere, entirely on time. He found this dandy machine at an implement dealer in Coulee City, a small community fifty miles to the north, and arranged finances through the Grant County State Bank in Ephrata, thirty miles closer to home.

"Yeah, like just about everyone else I dealt with in the Basin, the local banks were really good to me when I started out," he gratefully acknowledges. "But because I expanded so rapidly, it wasn't possible to pay off my loans or all my other creditors as fast as they and I both would have liked. So I had to come up with a workable system. Fortunately, I remembered what Mom had taught me way back in our Kennewick days.

"When Mom took care of her bills at the end of each month, she made sure every single one of our creditors received a payment, no matter how small. 'Pay everyone at least a little bit,' she'd say. 'It's only fair and that way no one gets too impatient.' This worked for Mom back then, and it sure worked for me when I was starting out. If I paid each creditor something, they all understood that my account was still open and active, and they could all see I was trying.

"Too many young farmers felt that they had to pay every dollar they could scrape up to their few biggest accounts, or maybe to the one or two creditors who squealed the loudest. Then they'd let the rest stew, maybe for months, without getting a dime. No matter what business you're in, that's a sure way to get served with repossession or even foreclosure papers. With Mom's system I never let anyone feel they were being totally ignored, I could gradually retire all my bills, and I was able to keep right on expanding. Debt never worried me as long as I knew I had the potential to raise and market the crops that would pay it off."

The expansion part of this scenario had its beginnings in 1949, a year that was far more than a doubling of the fifteen-acre plot of onions the Yoshinos had raised the year before. For starters George leased fifty acres from the Welch and Kandra partnership, land he used to raise onions, paying cash rent after his crop was sold. George Shuster, a man Frank had known in Kennewick and who now owned land and a potato shed in the Moses Lake area, offered the young farmer the chance to raise potatoes, onions and watermelons on 200 acres. The potatoes would be a partnership, with Shuster furnishing land, seed, fertilizer and water for 52% of the crop. George would do all the farming and pay the land owner $35.00 an acre cash rent for his onion and watermelon ground.

"Getting in with Shuster was a major step for me in more ways than one," he explains. Sure, it was a good farming opportunity, but more important, our potato crop that first year gave me another early lesson in what it meant to have more control of your product after it comes out of the ground. We raised a beautiful White Rose variety, but in the heat of July or early August they developed Heat Necrosis, tiny little spots at the blossom end of the potato. It's really just a tiny blemish that doesn't harm a spud at all. In fact, in states like Wisconsin, Minnesota and Colorado they freely ship and market all the Heat Necrosis spuds they want to.

"But in Washington, Idaho and Oregon, we have a more stringent quality standard that requires federal inspections before our potatoes hit the fresh market. The inspectors have labeled Heat Necrosis as one of the internals, a blemish, and if they find over five percent in a shipment, they'll kick it over, which simply means you can't sell it on the fresh spud market.

"In one sense these inspections are good because they allow us to retain our U.S. No. 1 grade status here in the Northwest, but unfortunately those harmless little brown spots have broken too many capable farmers, guys who didn't do anything wrong.

"Just starting out I'd have been in real trouble that year, but because Shuster owned his own packing shed, he could spread our potatoes out, mixing them in with the thousands of tons of unaffected potatoes he'd purchased. That way the inspector wouldn't see enough blemishes to kick any of his shipments over, and we'd get paid the full price for our crop. If I'd been strictly on my own, selling my potatoes to a packing shed that didn't try to protect me, that single harvest might have put me out of business."

Shuster's produce house may have saved his potato crop, but everything else the young farmer was doing that year was totally up to him. Now, fifty years later and with far greater financial successes behind him, George looks back on 1949 with justifiable pride, partly because it was his first year of real profits, but far more because he accomplished so much with little help.

"I had the potatoes with Shuster and another 175 acres of onions and watermelons on my own," he says, his face reflecting the pleasant memories. "Once Tom's spring quarter was over, he was right there for me, doing a lot of the manual labor like changing irrigation water, but to save dollars, I did all the tractor work myself, setting up rills, seeding, cultivating, plowing. Oh, Pop would be out in the fields every day too, doing whatever he could, like helping with the irrigating. But even that was hard for him because it was so different than the irrigation systems back in Kennewick and Weiser. Soil in that upper Columbia Basin was so sandy our irrigation channels had to be lined with heavy paper we'd get by saving fertilizer bags. Otherwise these little ditches would wash completely out, sending water every place but where we needed it."

Without a 'nose to the grindstone' attitude he may not have survived at all, but it was one of George's early innovations that paid real dividends. Typically, once onions were topped and put into gunny sacks, they were left in the field to dry for a week to ten days. After that most farmers hauled them into a commercial packing shed. To save time and money George borrowed a portable onion sorter and did his own grading in the field, separating the jumbos from the mediums and putting them all in new fifty pound mesh bags. This not only cut his sorting and packing costs by more than fifty percent and had the entire crop ready to sell without first being hauled to a shed, but it left the culls and debris behind, awaiting the plow.

"That year I sold the mediums right out of the field, making a nice little profit, but I decided to put all my jumbos into cold storage and hold out for a better price," George recalls. "That sure turned out to be the right decision. In December the jumbo onion market absolutely skyrocketed, and I sold. When all my bills and checks were in, I'd netted over $40,000 on those jumbos alone! Right about then I figured I was about the smartest man in the whole world!" Flashing a grin he quickly added, "A year later I was going to find out that wasn't true. I think that's what they call growing up."

Perhaps George didn't have this planet's top I.Q., but he was smart enough to plow his windfall profits back into expanding his operation. That spring he purchased an additional forty acres east of Moses Lake, raw land he had to clear, level, have a well drilled, then develop an irrigation system. He leased another one hundred and twenty acres of developed ground close by and took on two hundred as well as a small potato packing shed in Wilson Creek, a tiny town forty miles to the north. Again he was on the run.

"By then I was completely convinced that having my own packing facility was essential. Well, in a few years it turned out I was right, but that first little Wilson Creek shed sure tested my faith. I signed a year's lease, brought in a couple of key people I'd need to run it and spent a whole bunch of dollars fixing it up, just so I could pack my own spuds because everything else in that country was hay and cattle.

"I'd counted on picking up the laborers I'd need locally, but all the good hands around Wilson Creek already had steady jobs. The only available laborers were the hobos who came in on the railroad. From day one my new crew and I developed our own little ritual. They came to work for me with practically nothing so had to be paid as soon as they'd put in their eight or ten hours. Then they'd head straight for the tavern. Before their meager pay was gone, they'd be both drunk and disorderly, the local cops were called in, and my gang would get tossed in jail, where they'd sleep it off until I arrived the next morning to bail them out, supply them with coffee and rolls, drag them back to work, ready to start this whole scenario all over again.

"That's definitely no way to run a packing shed or anything else, but even with this crew maybe I'd have been okay. Unfortunately, I'd picked absolutely the worst year I could to get into this business. It was 1950, a terrible year for all Basin farmers and packers. Our potato market absolutely bottomed out. I'd made a deal with George Shuster to market the spuds that went through my shed, but even with his contacts he couldn't find a buyer. We had to sell every potato to a government diversion program, to be destroyed.

"This would have been bad enough, but the federal inspector couldn't make up his mind on how we were supposed to handle these throw-away spuds. First he said we had to pack them all, using brand new burlap sacks, then find a pit and dump them. His men would come behind and pour this awful looking purplish dye all over our potatoes, to make sure no one retrieved them later and put them on the market.

"A couple days of this, and the inspector decided that all we had to do was get the spuds out of the ground and haul them to the pit. Next, he told us to dig them up, he'd determine our tonnage, then have us run across them with a disc. Finally he said 'Well, just dig up two rows out of every forty, we'll figure out their tonnage, then average out the field from that.' His last solution was sure the best and saved us a fortune in labor costs. I just wish it hadn't taken him three weeks to turn practical.

"But despite my potato shed woes, what I saw in 1950 reaffirmed what I'd started to see back in '48 with that first fifteen acres of onions. None of our crops were worth much in '50, but by packing my own onions, I still made a profit on those, a profit that kept me out of bankruptcy. I knew then that just being a grower was never going to be enough.

"Sure, on a good year a grower does okay, but every time he hits a depressed market, which happens way too often in all of agriculture, but especially in perishables such as potatoes and onions, he'll slide backwards. In 1950 I watched way too many good Basin farmers go under simply because of that one terrible market. If I didn't have some way to improve my odds, I knew this could easily happen to me.

"By being both a grower and a packer, I'd at least break even on the bad years, and during the good ones I could more than double my profits. Yeah, my first venture with a potato packing shed had fizzled, but I was still convinced it was the way to go. A few years later I'd start thinking seriously about the next step and embrace an agriculture strategy called 'Vertical Integration.' It simply means that you start with farming the ground, then go to packing, next on to marketing, then into other products. My final step would be processing, but with 100% vertical integration you'd take your crops all the way from the field to the grocery shelf."

Twenty-four

THE ANDY JEAN SAGA

Surprisingly, just as his budding farming, packing and marketing careers were getting off the ground in the Columbia Basin, George became involved in another time-consuming enterprise, this one all the way down in the Arizona desert. It had its innocent beginnings in 1948, when a man named Andy Jean pulled up to a field he was cultivating and waved him off his tractor. The newcomer was full of questions, mainly about raising onions. He'd been nosing around among the local farmers and implement dealers and had been told that the Yoshino lad was a potential up-and-comer. In the next few weeks he made several more stops, always quizzing George, always testing his knowledge and his confidence levels.

"Andy owned the Jean Seed Company in Twin Falls, Idaho," George relates, "but he was never going to be satisfied with that thriving enterprise. No, he was a real wheeler-dealer, always looking for bigger and bigger projects. Every chance he had that first summer and fall, he'd look me up and talk about agricultural possibilities. The next year we went partners on a small plot of onions near Moses Lake.

"Then in the summer of '49 Andy came to me all excited. Earlier he'd put in a bid to lease 14,000 irrigated acres on the Gila Bend Indian Reservation southwest of Phoenix and had just been awarded the contract. Now he wanted me to go partners. What he was offering sounded too good to be true. I wouldn't have to put up any money or sign for any bank loans. I'd just have to come down to Arizona and be his farm operations manager and get fifty percent of the profits on his onion crop. Andy envisioned us growing tremendous crops of onions in that desert heat, and right away I saw the chance to step up to the kind of huge commercial operation I'd been dreaming of.

"If I'd been willing to move down there, Andy would have made me a full partner on everything, including the cotton and sorghum he was growing. But until I knew more about him, his huge operation and how our partnership was going to work, I sure wasn't going to give up my Moses Lake farms. By the time our Gila Bend project was rolling, I'd already planted over 300 acres. This meant that I'd have to plan my irrigating so I could be gone a few days without letting my crops go dry, then jump in the car and tear all the way down to Arizona, an eighteen-hour non-stop trip. I bought a '47 Buick Super just for these treks and shot across the wide open stretches of Washington, Oregon, Nevada and Arizona at a hundred miles an hour.

"It turned out that I'd spend parts of two years on Andy's Gila Bend project and never make a dime. But I've never regretted our partnership nor looked at all those long days of driving and working as time wasted. No, Andy didn't help my bank account, but he did give me a real education. First of all, he was a top-notch negotiator, really smooth at setting up contracts, dealing with banks and government agencies, and he could get all the equipment he needed on credit. In the very near future one of my most valuable skills was going to be as a marketer, and I'd soon be negotiating my own high-dollar deals, sometimes face to face, more often over the telephone. What I learned from watching Andy in action during those two years was going to prove invaluable.

"Unfortunately for him, Andy also reaffirmed my belief in doing your homework before plunging into a new venture. It turned out that the man knew a whole lot more about negotiating big dollar deals than he did farming, especially in that Arizona desert, and he didn't talk to a single farmer around there before plunging into that contract. Right away I was convinced that this was wrong, so every time I had a chance, I'd go talk to those local farmers, once again asking all my questions. These were good men, fellows who'd been farming down there in that heat long enough to know what worked and what didn't, and as soon as they knew me a little, they were more than willing to share their knowledge.

"What I discovered was that we were trying to grow certain crops where they simply weren't going to make it. The intense summer heat of that desert would wipe out our white and red onions. But Andy didn't want to hear that. He was a born plunger, always believing that he could get bigger and bigger. He was convinced that he could grow onions or anything else wherever he chose, as long as he had lots of sunshine, the right fertilizers and plenty of irrigation water to dump on them. His worst mistake was believing he was a whole lot smarter than that farmer down the road, even when that guy had three or four decades of practical experience.

"Another major glitch was that the reservation contract called for us to hire Indian labor whenever we could. But too many of these men simply didn't understand or take to this kind of farm work. Everything had to be carefully explained to them, and you had to be there to make sure they did it right. That whole 14,000 acres was perfectly flat, laid out in quarter-mile squares, all flood irrigated from the Gila River. It was a good set-up if you raised the right crops and watched what you were doing.

"Too often, though, I'd get down there late when our night crew was supposed to be out changing water. The first thing I'd do was drive around until I spotted their lanterns in one of our fields, but way too often when I went over to see how the men were doing, those lanterns would be all I'd find, propped up on a piece of high ground with irrigation water spilling over the dikes, running all over the place. Our whole crew, even the foreman, would be off at a local bar.

"Yeah it was a mess. Still, if Andy had done more planning before he started and then brought in half a dozen good supervisors, guys who understood irrigated farming and who'd have set the right work tone, we might have been okay. Unfortunately

Andy had too much confidence in me. He thought I could come down there and correct all his labor and crop problems and quickly turn this huge undertaking around. Before that first year was over, I knew that wasn't in the cards. Even if I'd moved down there and devoted full time to it, this was one project that was already way beyond my control.

"When I finally decided to call it quits, Andy was still expanding, still plunging ahead without enough of a farming background to know half of what he was getting into. Besides Gila Bend he'd leased another 1700 acres near Chandler, Arizona, where he was raising cotton and sorghum, all with complete government financing. Talking your way into mega deals is great, but at some point you have to start producing. Before long he lost everything, which I hated to see. Despite his shortcomings, Andy'd been good to me and taught me a couple of valuable lessons."

Twenty-four

MARRIAGE AND TWO NEW PARTNERSHIPS

Not many months after his final split with Andy Jeans, George entered into a far more significant partnership. On December 29th, 1951, he and Frances were married in Moses Lake. Like so many young farmers of his day, George had to schedule their wedding for the dead of winter, the one relatively quiet period in his otherwise hectic schedule.

"It was a great day for us and our families," he fondly recalls. "Despite the bad roads our friends and relatives came from all over, Seattle, Kennewick, Weiser. People even came up from California. We had to hold our reception in the big hall out at the county fairgrounds. the only building around with enough room. For some reason lots of our guests thought expensive goblets and dishes called Foster Ware made the perfect wedding gift, and they totally bought out the local hardware store's stock. Just starting out like we were, that stuff wasn't going to be much use to us for years to come. But that was okay. All we really cared about was getting married and sharing our special day.

"Mom and Pop fairly glowed they were so happy. I think our wedding was one more sign that life was definitely turning around for them. We had farm land again, a little prosperity, and now I was marrying a girl they really liked. I'm sure they saw this as a real step toward solidifying our family. I think our wedding was about as special for Mom and Pop as it was for Frances and me."

After a honeymoon through parts of California and Nevada, George and Frances settled into a modest two-bedroom home that he'd purchased on the north side of Moses Lake for $6,800. Until the children came along, Frances would spend long hours working in their fields, particularly during the onion harvest when she'd help supervise the large topping crews. Even after their first daughter was born, she was back out there in the field, counting sacks, tallying what each topper was owed, sometimes with her baby girl nestled comfortably in her left arm.

That spring would bring a second significant Yoshino partnership. Vic, with his parents' blessing and encouragement, would join his brother's farming operation, with no money changing hands.

"I suppose from a purely economic standpoint, it wasn't my most practical move because I made him a full partner in everything I'd already built up without getting anything in return," George now states. "But then this partnership wasn't about economics. It was about my brother Vic and healing family wounds. Despite what happened back in Weiser, I'd always wanted Vic back in my life, for him to again be part of our family. Sure, maybe I should have been more practical, but I'd spent too many painful hours cursing the rift that had pulled us apart to pass on this chance. A partnership looked like the perfect way for Vic and me to get back to what we'd once had.

"Plus, by that time Pop had at least partially forgiven Vic. No, the wounds of those last Weiser years were never going to heal, but he and Mom both understood it was time to move on, to accept Vic back into our family and to start bonding with his wife and child. Although we'd never talked about it, I'm sure my folks knew how much losing Vic had meant to me, just one more reason why the Weiser fiasco had hung over the two of them like a dark cloud. This new partnership seemed like the ideal way to rebuild our family.

"Having a wife and child to support had forced Vic to grow up in a hurry, to break away from his rudderless friends and get way beyond that crazy rebellious period. He'd already moved up to Moses Lake, had gone right to work for Percy Driggs, and was again proving to be the steady, hardworking Vic we'd always known. He was terribly ashamed of everything he'd done to all of us, so when our partnership kicked off, he worked doubly hard, trying to set things right.

"Forgive Vic? For me that was the easy part. All I cared about was that I had my brother back in my life. I remember so many days when the two of us would be out in a field, it would be getting late, and I'd tell Vic to knock off for the day, to go spend a couple hours with his family and have a good dinner. But he'd just shake his head and tell me I should go home and let him finish up. We'd both end up staying out there, getting tremendous amounts of work done.

"Unfortunately, in the coming years it meant we'd be spending too little time with our wives and kids, but as young farmers we sure made a great team. I still took care of all the financing, including land purchases and leases, and I did our marketing. But Vic definitely had a major say in what crops we planted and how we handled various other aspects of our operation. Within a couple of years we were farming over a thousand irrigated acres, with little outside help."

Rapid expansion didn't come without another price. George quickly realized that his bankers would be more than a little nervous if they knew just how much land he and Vic were farming, possibly to the point where they would pull his financial plug. He decided he'd have to be careful about how much information he gave them.

"I didn't out and out lie. I just withheld a few pretty significant details," he now laughs. "I'd take out a production loan to farm a little over five hundred acres when in fact we were farming a thousand. Then because we were doubling our acreage every year, the next season I'd take out a loan for fifteen hundred and farm two thousand. Of course this put a lot of pressure on us to turn a profit, and it meant we had very little money for outside labor. When our harvest revenues came in, those bankers either had a pretty good idea of what we were doing or they thought we had one hell of a crop!"

Their first Columbia Basin season together was tough for the Yoshino brothers, with depressed potato and onion prices. But a year later they hit a real farming and marketing bonanza. This was 1952, the first season of sugar beet production in the Columbia Basin, a crop that from that time on gave the brothers a steady and relatively secure income. That year they sold their potatoes directly to Basin Produce and made another solid profit, but once again their real killing would be in onions.

"Even the straight onion growers did well in '52, but by packing and marketing our entire crop, we quadrupled our profits," George states. "Our onions were sorted and packed out in our fields, and again I sold the mediums right away and sent the jumbos to cold storage. These weren't sold until I'd located the right markets. I ended up selling half to an Idaho shipper, then scrambled around and found equally good sales for the other half. From that one crop alone we netted over $200,000. And that was after our accountant had scrambled hard for every deduction he could possibly use to reduce our tax bill."

Add in what the Yoshinos made on beets and potatoes and 1952 definitely was one terrific farming year. It gave them the economic base they needed for major expansions in 1953, with real working capital and far more status with the local bankers. Right away George purchased another 160 acres and took on additional leased ground. Then in 1954, just as they were starting this next round of expansions, George and Vic took on a third partner, their older brother Elmer.

"That definitely wasn't my idea, and I know Vic sure didn't like it," George now states, shaking his head. "In fact, it was a real mistake. When Vic joined me, I'd continued to make almost all of our major business decisions, but he was a real asset because he was one terrific farmer, who knew what to do and when to do it even before I did. Elmer was neither a farmer nor a businessman. He'd always have to be told everything.

"When Mom and Pop first asked me to take him on, I said no way. But Mom kept after me, bringing it up every time we'd get together, breaking into tears, telling me I had to do this for my poor brother. Elmer was working for wages down in Los Angeles, and I'm sure he'd gone to the folks and whined about how tough he had it. He got to Mom and she'd finally get to me. It was just typical. When he was going to Southern Cal back in 1950, Elmer had cried so loud about not having a car that Mom and Pop pushed me into buying him a brand new Chevy. Back then I'd had to borrow the money and make payments, and I wasn't driving a new car myself. Now I was going to be stuck with him again, a man who'd never be more than a farm worker, but he'd be getting a full partner's share.

"Maybe I shouldn't have given in, but that's not how I dealt with my family, partly I guess because those were such comfortable years for Mom and Pop. They had a nice little home on a farm I'd bought east of Moses Lake. We'd put in a four or five acre apple orchard that they pruned, watered, directed the picking, and kept any profits. They both thoroughly enjoyed spending long hours working in their orchard, getting a real kick out of doing little things, like grafting cherries, apricots, and peaches onto a single apple tree. As the years went by, their flower gardens became more and more elaborate. We put in two concrete ponds with water ladders and circulating pumps so they could have those big goldfish they liked so much.

"I never thought Pop would be interested in this non-commercial stuff, but in his later years he was fascinated by it. He and Mom turned that whole farm yard into a beautiful Japanese garden, the kind they both remembered from their childhoods. Later, when I traded away that farm, I bought them a home in town where they did the same thing, even putting in their own little green house so they could get an early start on the growing season.

"Then whenever I had an hour or so to spend with Pop, I'd tell him all about our farming operation, what we were raising, what land I hoped to buy or lease next, what new piece of machinery I'd purchased or was looking into, about the seed potatoes I was bringing in from Montana or our latest variety of onions. Pop would just nod his head, taking it all in, always one hundred and fifty percent in agreement with everything I was doing. I knew he was pleased. By the early sixties, when we'd really taken on a sizable acreage, he'd just laugh heartily and say 'Too bad I'm not a few years younger. We could farm the whole Basin!'

"Even by the early fifties, I knew too well that his sons' successes had gone a long way toward repairing the damage that the camps and losing his own farm had done to Pop's world. Seeing both him and Mom so happy, well, that's about all it took to make me feel good. If keeping them that way meant taking Elmer on as another partner, then that's what I'd have to do."

Twenty-six

NEW FRIENDS, COLORFUL CHARACTERS

Despite his feelings towards his newest partner, George wasn't about to let his farming operation stagnate. Using the windfall profits of 1952 as his springboard, he was on a real quest to constantly expand his acreage. However, even by 1954 leasing or purchasing good irrigated ground close to Moses Lake was becoming difficult and often prohibitively expensive. Too many of that region's other farmers were also trying to expand, and newcomers were constantly moving into the area.

Finally George turned part of his attention to the agricultural ground forty miles to the northwest, around the little town of Quincy, where the Reclamation Project was just starting to bring in irrigation water. His initial important contact in that area was a man named Ray Young, a big jovial fellow who quickly became an important ally and a close friend.

"Ray was one of the Basin's more colorful characters back then, with a real history in the potato industry," George recounts, laughing a little over his memories. "During the war, when the government had placed a ceiling on what farmers and shippers could charge for potatoes, Ray was working for a Tacoma distribution house that would send him down to Bakersfield, California, with a whole satchel full of cash, up to half a million dollars, all of it in big bills. Farmers down there were raising tons and tons of potatoes on irrigated ground, and Ray's instructions were to use this cash for under-the-table payoffs, a thousand bucks per carload of spuds. It was the only way his bosses could get the tonnage they needed to meet their customer demand.

"Absorbing that extra thousand bucks per carload was no problem for those Tacoma guys because wholesale and retail prices were totally unregulated. Once the potatoes had cleared the shipper, they could be sold to grocery stores or directly to consumers for any price they could get. It was just one more example of a ridiculous government program. All it did was hurt honest farmers and shippers, and it didn't save the consumer or the military a dime."

"Anyway, when I came over to Quincy, Ray was working for a big outfit called Williams Brothers, managing a thousand acres of their land and farming 160 acres of his own. Right away we hit it off, first in a business deal when I leased a couple of the eighty acre units he managed, then as pals. He was a big man and an ex-prize fighter, but he must have left all his aggressions in the boxing ring because unless someone really pushed him, he was about the most good-natured fellow I've ever met. With his broad smile, his hearty laugh and a ready handshake, he couldn't be in a place for ten minutes before he'd made half a dozen new friends, which made him a great companion for me. Unless I could talk about farming or a related business, I was pretty reserved when I walked into a new situation, so Ray became my ice breaker.

"I'd been buying my seed potatoes from along the northern Washington coast, as well as out of North Dakota, but Ray convinced me to go with him to Deer Lodge, Montana, and check out their growers. He didn't have to ask twice because the coastal seed potatoes were getting costly, and their lower elevation and wet weather created too many insect infestations. Montana's quality and prices were on par with North Dakota's, and my shipping costs would be much lower.

"Yeah, financially this was an excellent move for me, but it also added a whole new dimension to my life, throwing me in with

Ray's pals, particularly Wild Bill Anderson, who owned a big seed potato shed in Deer Lodge, and Bud Balch, who grew up with Ray and by then was a mint and potato farmer out of Wapato, Washington. Bud always came along on our trips, sometimes to buy his own seed potatoes, but far more often just to get in on the party that was sure to erupt when Ray was around.

"For the first time in my life I found myself spending time in bars. In fact, after a couple of trips to that state, I started believing that Montana had an unwritten law that said business deals had to be either made or celebrated in a place where alcohol was served. That sure held true for the likes of Wild Bill and his cronies. At one time Anderson had been a professor at Montana State University, but if academic sobriety had ever been part of his life, it had faded into a very distant memory.

"But those guys were all real two-fisted whiskey drinkers. Our regular spot was the Rocky Mountain Tavern in the little town of Drummond, where Ray and Wild Bill Anderson knew everyone. As the new kid on the block, I became the target of Wild Bill's gags. The first time I was in there, he hired the barmaid to saunter over and suddenly flip a stuffed rattlesnake right at my chest. I jumped back so violently that I smashed heads with the guy next to me, bloodying his nose. Immediately I was apologizing to this fellow, a man I hardly knew. But he was part of that Montana bunch, where a little spilled blood was just one more reason to roar with laughter and order another round. I'd never been around guys like these, but their little gags didn't really bother me. Instead they were just the break I needed from the tensions of constantly trying to swing big agricultural deals. I'd get with Ray, Bud and Wild Bill, and at least for a night, sometimes for a couple of days, I was caught up in their crazy world and partially forgot about mine.

"My real problem was I simply couldn't handle that much alcohol. Two drinks and I'd start getting flushed, three or four and I'd be woozy. Canadian Club and water became my choice, and I quickly learned to nurse a drink, sipping it slowly. But I had to make Ray and the boys think I was doing some serious drinking, or else they'd really get on me. So I'd slip a few bucks to the bartender to mix my cocktails extra light, with just enough whiskey for a dash of color. At times guys from all over a bar would be ordering us rounds, and I'd end up with half a dozen drinks stacked up in front of me. When this happened, I'd wait 'til no one was looking, then saunter up to the bar and dump a full glass or two down the drain, or I'd wait until Ray and Wild Bill left the table and push a couple of mine in front of their chairs. As much booze as those two downed, I figured a few extras weren't going to matter.

"Wild Bill could definitely hold his booze, but even he was no match for Ray, and if I'd ever tried to match my buddy drink for drink, they'd have carried me out of the place before the first hour elapsed. One time Ray rode with me on about a three hundred mile jaunt and polished off two fifths of Jim Beam, his favorite whiskey, finishing the last swallow just as we hit our destination. Yet when he stepped out of my car, he was able to walk, talk, and he even sat down in a restaurant and ate a big dinner less than an hour later.

"A stranger wouldn't have known he'd been drinking. Oh, maybe all that whiskey made him a bit more jovial, but with Ray that was always a matter of degrees anyway. Drunk or sober he was quick to laugh and quicker to make everyone around him crack up. The down side of having all that capacity to hold and enjoy so much liquor was that it encouraged Ray to drink steadily. By the time I met him, he was well on his way towards being a hard-core alcoholic, a disease that shortened his life by way too many years.

"Bud Balch and Wild Bill, were a lot of fun too, and they had their own problems. Both loved to gamble, and Bud was generous to a fault. One time he won a fantastically expensive Swiss watch called a Petite Philippe in a high stakes card game and insisted on giving it to me. I protested, but Bud kept saying 'No, it looks good on you. You're the only guy I know with enough class to wear a watch like this.' It was a nice gesture but one I wasn't about to accept. Fortunately I knew a Montana dealer who was crazy about anything he considered top quality, so I talked him into making a trade, that watch for two thousand dollars worth of seed potatoes, which I then consigned to Bud. That was something he needed and couldn't very well refuse, and I didn't have to go home feeling guilty."

A year after he met Ray, George bought a three bedroom home in Quincy and moved his family over. He then rented an additional five hundred acres from his pal, including part of the land Ray owned. Farms in that district had a little better soil than those around Moses Lake, and they had the added advantage of being laid out in bigger fields. Plus, competition for good potato and onion ground wasn't nearly as keen. The move threw him in even more with Ray and all his pals. Almost fifty years later George still has a hard time explaining the close friendships he developed with Ray and Bud, two men whose temperaments and lifestyles were drastically different than his.

"Yeah, both Ray and Bud were easy going and could get pretty wild, while I was more uptight, more of a worrier, and far more conservative. Those two were always ready for a good time, whether that meant going on a Las Vegas gambling spree or heading off on a Montana big game hunt. No matter where we went, whether it started out as a business trip or simply a little vacation, sooner or later the booze flowed freely and the party began.

"Maybe I liked being with those two guys because they were so fun-loving and easy-going and could draw me out of my shell. When you're as deeply involved in an ever-expanding business as I was back then, it sure feels good to let it all go once in a while. I watched my alcohol consumption, but other than that holding back wasn't a realistic option. Ray and Bud both had too many little ways of breaking down my defenses, of getting me caught up in the moment.

"One of our craziest episodes happened in the late fifties. It started with a call from Bud. 'Chum, have I got the car for you,' were his first words. He was in Chicago on other business, and he'd come across an almost brand new Chrysler Le Baron at an estate sale that was way under-priced. We quickly agreed that I'd wire him the money, he'd make the purchase and drive that Le Baron to Las Vegas. I'd fly down there, we'd spend a couple days hitting the casinos, then drive home together.

"The real craziness started the second night when we went to the Sands. We dabbled at blackjack and the slots for a while, but when we moved to a craps table, suddenly I was into an incredible hot streak. Bud was making his own bets, losing almost as steadily as I was winning. Every time his stack of chips ran low, I'd shove him some of mine. Any real gambler would tell you I did everything wrong that night, letting huge stacks of chips ride, making totally wild bets, but this was one time when it didn't seem to matter. It was just my night. At my high point I was $50,000 to the good and felt completely invincible.

"Bud was usually the guy who could party all night, but he'd already spent a long day on the road, so around midnight he gave up and went off to bed. By then I was so wired over my hot streak that I knew I couldn't sleep, so I took my winnings and started looking around for more action. Frank Sinatra, who owned a piece of the Sands back then, had acted on one of his many quirks and had taken over dealing at a blackjack table. When I spotted him, he was flipping out cards for a whole bunch of women. I guess because it was my big night, my normal inhibitions didn't keep me away. It just seemed natural to walk right over and join them.

"Don't ask me why, but right away Sinatra seemed to like me, which was a good thing because that man definitely had a sharp tongue. When a second guy tried to get the game, Frank really leveled him. He'd only deal to those women and me. After a dozen hands or so, Frank and I started getting chummier and chummier. He started refusing to rake in my chips when I lost a hand. The women would lose and he'd scoop in theirs, but when I tried to throw in mine, he'd shove them back across the table. That game finally broke up around five in the morning, and Frank actually invited me up to his suite for an ongoing party. But by then my big night elation had worn off, and I was so exhausted I had to beg off. It's kind of too bad. How many times in your life are you going to be around someone like Old Blue Eyes, especially when he's the one doing the inviting?

"But saying goodbye to Sinatra and heading off to bed didn't end all the craziness. The next day Bud and I spent more time at the blackjack tables, and of course my hot streak didn't last. Between us we dropped over half of my earlier winnings. Finally we moved up to Reno, hit their craps tables and lost another big chunk of change. By the time I made it home, I figured that I'd paid for the Chrysler and my trip, but the rest of the fifty grand was gone. No wonder the casinos don't mind a big winner. I'd created plenty of excitement with my hot streak, and if I'd stayed another day, they'd have had all their money back.

"Yes, sometimes it was Bud, sometimes Ray, sometimes both, but between them those two brought out a whole different side of me. Of course friendship's always a two way street, and reflecting back I have to believe that Ray and Bud were even more drawn to me than I was to them. They were the ones who always kept up our contacts, giving me a call or stopping by my place at least a couple times a week. Ray would drop whatever he was doing to go along on one of my road trips.

"Both guys were definitely intrigued by how fast I was expanding and by how quickly I'd make decisions. Part of this was because although they were hard workers and knowledgeable farmers, they were also real dreamers, always coming up with new get-rich-quick schemes they weren't about to carry out. I think they saw me as a guy who was actually willing to take on something new, who was acting on a few of his ideas, not just dreaming about what could be."

As George's business enterprises rapidly expanded in the next ten years, several more men would get caught up the excitement of it all, wanting to be part of it or at least to observe from the closest vantage points. Dedication to the man at the center of all this excitement naturally followed, a dedication that in one case nearly had tragic consequences.

In the early sixties a man named Carl Doud had moved to Quincy from Idaho because he wanted to work for George. His allegiance to his new boss grew rapidly, and he stuck George with the nickname 'Big G', a moniker that rapidly caught on.

"Carl was a good man, an excellent worker, and yeah, he was dedicated to me," George acknowledges. "He was also a big powerful man, whose only real flaw was a violent streak that showed up when anger impaired his judgment. Late one fall I had about a dozen pheasant hunters coming over from Seattle, so I booked half a dozen rooms at a Quincy motel. Well, that afternoon the Cascades were being hit by a real snow storm, so I wasn't at all sure anyone was going to make it. Finally Carl and I went over to the local restaurant to have dinner and give our guests a couple more hours.

"As we sat there, the motel owner came stumbling in, already full of booze, and started asking me what I was going to do about the rooms I'd tied up. I tried to tell him not to worry. If my hunters didn't show, I'd take care of his bill. This didn't really satisfy the guy, but finally he went back to the bar, only to stagger back to our table fifteen minutes later and start that whole scenario over again. This went on for at least a couple of hours, the guy completely unwilling to listen to what I was saying and constantly coming back, a bit more soused and belligerent each time. Finally I gave up on him and my hunters and headed for home. Unfortunately, Carl ordered another drink and stayed on.

"The next time that drunken motel owner came back, he was really badmouthing me personally, telling everyone within earshot how I'd cheated him out of all that room rent. Finally Carl blew up and invited the guy outside. To this day I'm not sure what happened.

"When the cops arrived, that motel owner not only had some nasty bruises, but a couple of knife cuts as well. Carl admitted he'd roughed the fellow up, but he swore he'd never pulled a knife. I sure wanted to believe my friend, and what he said had a ring of truth. Doud was a tough man, physical enough to break that other guy in half with his bare hands, so using any kind of weapon made absolutely no sense.

"But I knew Carl could get irrational, and the guy had visible knife wounds, so I just couldn't be sure. The motel owner let the charges slide, mainly because his own drunken conduct was going to look pretty bad in a full blown trial. The local police were more than willing to drop this mess, partly because they all liked Doud and didn't think much of his drunken adversary, and partly because they'd be doing me a real favor. Still, I felt that I had to really lecture Carl and warn him against unleashing that temper of his. I knew he thought he was doing this for me, but I let him know in no uncertain terms that violence was one kind of help I was never going to need."

A man who became equally dedicated to George, a much closer friend and a far more important political and business contact was Harry Blackfield, who along with his brother owned a fair-sized Seattle bakery. Again Ray Young made the initial introductions, and after a few years George counted this new man as one of his closest friends. He and Frances named their youngest after Harry and asked him to be the boy's godfather.

"At first Harry just came over to the Basin with a group of guys Ray knew," George recalls. "They'd all show up every fall, ready to hunt pheasants on our farms. But almost as soon as we met, Harry became more intrigued with everything I was doing and started making trips over at any time of year. He enjoyed hanging around my farms, seeing how everything worked and watching our various crops come on. Then when my first big packing shed was up and rolling, Harry, who was into high volume baked goods sales, was immediately fascinated by that operation, especially by the way I handled marketing.

"Before long, whenever I had a conference to attend or a big out of state business deal to look into, Harry'd tag along, just to be with me and see what this latest venture was all about. For me this was great because I always enjoyed Harry's company, and he was a good guy to bounce ideas off. He had a quick mind and had been in sales long enough to pick up lots of business savvy. Plus, like Ray, he was a real pro at meeting people and breaking down their defenses.

"Harry definitely liked a good time, too, but he wasn't nearly as free-wheeling or wild as Ray and Bud. His business and political connections, though, were incredible. Our state's governor, Albert Rosallini, as well as his cousin, Vic Rosallini, who co-owner of the prestigious 6-10 and the 4-10 restaurants, were just two of his close friends. Yeah, Harry became my 'In' person west of the mountains, the guy who knew everyone, who could always make the right introductions.

Twenty-seven

THE EARLY WOES
OF A BASIN FARMER

L ong before any of this could happen, George had to firmly establish his own prominence as a land owner and business-man. The fifties were going to be very good years for the Yoshinos, but they were also destined to be a time of overcoming one major problem after another. In the early part of that decade, the brothers were opening up acres and acres of new land and despite George's early research, he still had a lot to learn.

Rill irrigating in the North Basin's sandier soil was a constant headache. He or Vic would spend several days on a tractor, care-fully going over a piece of ground to build up its rills, little ridges that channel the water. Then a late afternoon wind would kick up and in less than two hours wipe out three days of tedious work, flattening every rill. A more prolonged blow would dump enough fine sand into the main ditch to plug it, sending the canal water cascading through a freshly seeded field, creating huge washouts.

"Yeah, we definitely had our early problems," George recounts, "In the summer of '53 one of my neighbors east of Moses Lake pastured cattle in a field that was stripped of feed and so poorly fenced that those cows would bust out and start feeding on our crops, stomping our rills flat, breaking down the irrigation ditches. I'd have to get out there, herd them to the road on foot, then hop in my pickup and push them back onto the neighbor's land. Next I'd have to mend his fence before I worried about the mess those four-legged beasts had made on my ground.

"One day as I was herding them with my pickup, a calf hopped off into the road ditch, then bolted back. Before I could hit the brake, I clipped its head with my right bumper, killing it instantly. All I could do was drag the little fellow back into the ditch where my neighbor found it about an hour later. He never mentioned it to me though. Maybe he was just glad I hadn't turned him in for pasturing his cows in that barren field."

As if their losses on new ground onions weren't bad enough, that same year George had shipped ten carloads of his good crop, all sorted and packed into new bags, to a broker at the Ide Street Terminal in Spokane. There they went into the basement, a huge area used by many of that area's fresh pack distributors, a cool storage facility.

"This looked like the clear deal," George recalls, "but unfortunately someone else's mistake ended up costing us big time. There were several outfits down in that basement that were making salads for Spokane's restaurant trade. Apparently one of them kept dumping its refuse into the drain until it totally plugged up, backing up the water and flooding the whole level. By the time I heard about it, our onions had been sitting in water for several days and were already rotting. We had no insurance, no one to come back on for our loss. Oh, maybe if we could have proved what company created that mess we could have sued, but that wasn't possible.

"To make matters worse, we were still responsible for our onions. Vic, his wife Betty, Frances and I took a big truck up there, and the four of us spent several miserable days loading out all those rotten bags and hauling them to a local land fill. Besides our other losses, we had to pay Spokane's high dump fees. Once again, all we could do was shrug our shoulders and say, 'Well, in farming you don't make money on every deal.'

"In fact, in those early years it seemed as if I was going through one major or minor crisis after another," he now muses, "and only in retrospect can I find any humor in a few of those deals. For instance, the first non-farming deal I got involved in turned out to be more amusing and embarrassing than costly because right about then any big losses would have totally wiped me out. This little fiasco happened way back in '49 and started because of those miserable government-appraised land prices we had to work our way around. I'd purchased a small house in Moses Lake to throw in as partial payment on a farm.

"Well, this deal fell through, I got stuck with that little house, and before you know it, I'm a landlord. I did okay at a number of things in my life, but being a landlord wasn't one of them. The first mistake I made was letting this guy move in who turned out to be quicker with an alibi than a rent check. By the second month he was delinquent. Then the next thing I knew he had his girlfriend living there with him, a barmaid at one of our local taverns.

"Finally I went to see this woman, figuring that maybe she'd have the cash and might be more reasonable. But her solution was to offer me sex for the rent they owed. At first I was so shocked I thought I'd misunderstood. Next I was horrified, not only because of the way I'd been raised but because she was a much older woman. I'd never heard a woman talk like that, and I sure wasn't interested in what she was offering. I just wanted my rent.

"Looking back, this all does seem kind of funny because I don't think she was all that old, but when you're twenty-one and very naive, thirty-five is ancient. This woman was all it took to convince me of one thing: if this was what being a landlord could lead to, I was definitely the wrong man for the job. Fortunately I was able to use that little house as a bargaining chip on another deal and never did take in another tenant.

"Even little incidents could be either painful or humorous, depending on how they turned out. During the summer of 1954 I'd ordered an onion grader from a small manufacturing firm over in Sunnyside, Washington, a bit over a hundred miles from our farms. That company hit me with one delay after another until finally around the first of September they called and said it was ready. I went over with my pickup to haul it home, but again there was some production glitch, so I had to spend the night and didn't get that grader hooked up and on the road until after lunch. In those days the only highway out of that valley was a narrow, winding canyon road, with plenty of bumps. Every time I hit a slight uphill grade, I'd have to shift to low gear, grinding along at fifteen miles per hour, tops.

"This would have been bad in any case, but that happened to be the day before Labor Day, a fact that never hit me until I looked in my rear view mirror and saw the line of vacationer's autos stacking up behind me. Then when I was right down at the bottom of that canyon, all the bumping and grinding started flipping chains off my machine. Before I found a place to pull off, at least half a mile down the road, I was watching car after car swerve around my chains. It took me better than an hour to retrieve them.

"But I guess I was lucky on at least two counts. Those flying hunks of metal hadn't caused an accident, and all that road rage only resulted in drivers rolling down their windows as they went by and making highly uncomplimentary statements about my character and mental capacity. A couple dozen verbal barrages and an obscene gesture or two weren't all that much to endure, considering I'd backed up traffic for a good ten miles.

"Then there was my short stint as a bowling alley stockholder. This all started that same fall when I sold onions to a fellow named Henry Toll, who owned a Spokane produce house, and was suddenly cash strapped. But Henry had some shares in a Spokane bowling alley called the North Bowl, and after a little convincing, he got me to accept part of this stock for my onions. At first this seemed like a pretty good deal. We'd get regular quarterly dividends, a percentage of the alley's profits.

"But time kept passing, and I wasn't receiving a dime. When I confronted him, the owner tried to tell me that his business was down, that there simply weren't any profits, but I wasn't about to buy that. Every time I was in the place, it had plenty of bowlers, mainly sporting their league shirts. Every weekend the place was absolutely packed. Finally I demanded to see his books. Well, it didn't take a CPA to figure out what he was doing. He'd purchased a second establishment, Spokane's East Bowl, and because he owned this one outright, he was transferring all the North Bowl's profits as well as some of its assets to it.

"Harry Cooper, a friend of mine who owned Produce Supply in Spokane, also owned some of these shares, but when I told him what was happening, he just wanted to let the whole thing slide. He had so many ties to that area that those little dividend checks were less important to him than avoiding controversy. Of course I had no such ties and even though no huge dollar amount was involved, I wasn't about to sit back and let this crook sift off profits that were rightfully mine. I was just starting to contact the other stockholders and make a real scene when the owner offered to buy back my shares. That was one check he was willing to cut in a hurry, if only to shut me up."

George can now laugh about his little bowling alley fiasco, but his memories of a severe labor shortage that hit the whole Columbia Basin in 1954 and 1955 are anything but humorous. When his onions were ready to harvest that first year, he couldn't find nearly enough toppers. Finally he had to put high racks on his big flatbed truck, then drive thirty-five miles to Wenatchee every morning to pick up the hobos and winos who slept out around that town's railroad station.

"That sure wasn't any way to get this country's best toppers," he now freely admits, "but I had no other choice. With enough bodies out there and every man working for piece-work wages, we'd eventually get our crops harvested. Trouble was, they all needed to be paid at the end of each day, then hauled all the way back to Wenatchee. I couldn't pay cash because then I'd have no record for the tax collector, so after we'd run a sack tally, I'd be out at the edge of a field long after dark, using my truck's headlights to write dozens of small checks, running anywhere from fifteen dollars down to three.

"Most nights I wouldn't get home until after midnight, and every morning I'd have to be back at the railroad station by six. Then I'd always be faced with better than a fifty percent turnover from the day before. Too many of those guys immediately converted their tiny checks into enough cheap wine or whiskey to stay totally wiped out for at least a couple of days. Luckily, each new day brought a few new bodies into that rail yard, and I'd get the earlier guys whose booze had run out. After what I'd gone through as a kid, I always wanted to treat my own farm laborers decently, so this situation became downright distasteful. I'd keep telling myself that a few of the better workers might stick with us, get a little money ahead and then maybe move on to something better. But after a few days or at most a week, even the best ones disappeared, heading off to God knows where.

"Yeah, it was a nasty business, trying to get a crop harvested by men who'd fallen that far. I had a big fellow, a black man named Willie Jackson who worked as my harvest boss all during the '50's and into the early '60's. As soon as Willie spotted a man lying down on a pile of sacks sleeping off his last night's drunk, he'd run over, grab the fellow by the shoulders, give him a hard shake, sometimes even kick him, whatever it took to get him on his feet and back into his row, at least so he could fill a couple sacks of onions before dark.

"Willie himself was a good man who'd had his own problems with alcohol and his hair- trigger temper. During the ten or eleven years he worked for me, he pretty much stayed on the wagon and did his job, but he constantly ran up against blatant racism, all over the Basin. He'd go into one of our local taverns just to buy a pack of cigarettes only to have a bartender or tavern owner order him to get out. Right away Willie 'd get riled, then boisterous, demanding his rights, only to end up in jail. Next he'd call me, and I'd have to come down with my lawyer to straighten the whole mess out.

"As soon as the bar owners and police saw that Willie had someone with a little community standing and a lawyer to defend him, they'd back down and offer to drop the charges. But I always figured that wasn't enough and refused to drop the matter until both the cops and the bar folks apologized to Willie and promised to treat him better from that point on. Then I'd pull Willie aside and try to convince him to stay out of those places, to buy his cig-arettes in a local grocery store and avoid all that hassle. Maybe that was good advice, I don't know, but I sure understood the man's anger. And I do know that Willie wasn't the one causing the problem.

"All he was asking for was the simple right to spend a little cigarette money just like any other adult. His flaring temper didn't

help matters any, but he'd been fighting this same kind of ignorance all his life. Unfortunately, this life of confrontation had left
Willie with some pretty deep emotional scars that finally drove
him away from me. He started drinking again, then one night had
an ugly scene with his wife and disappeared."

Although he could usually get a better crew than the Wenatchee rail yard men, by its very nature seasonal labor was always a
headache for George. One year he hired half a dozen workers from
Mexico and housed them in a farm house near Moses Lake.

"This was an excellent work crew," George recalls, "but it
turned out they were all here illegally. One night they went into
town and were rounded up by I.N.S. officers. The next morning I
happened to be at the farm house when the patrol brought them
out to collect their belongings before deportation. As that big van
drove away, several of those Mexicans rolled down their windows,
waved goodbye and shouted 'We'll be back!' Maybe that was just
their way of goading their captors, but it sure backfired for me.

"After they left, I turned that house over to Willie, who
brought in a bunch of his friends to do our field work. Late one
night the place was suddenly surrounded by the feds, who quickly
burst through the doors with guns drawn. They'd seen a light and
jumped to the conclusion that my Mexican crew had returned.
Instead, they were pointing their loaded forty-fives at seven black
men, who had no idea what was going on. The I.N.S. guys would-
n't even apologize. I guess they figured farm laborers of any color
weren't all that significant and shouldn't mind having guns
shoved in their faces.

"Another time I discovered that Cedar Green, a small frozen
foods plant in our area, was bringing Philippine workers up from
California to cut asparagus. Working through their connections I
brought in about twenty of these fellows. They were definitely
better workers than the winos and transients, but immediately I
was faced with other problems. I'd purchased an old hotel in
Quincy so I'd have a place to house them, but almost as soon as
they arrived, I was hearing stories about them bringing girls into
that hotel, doing too much drinking, running the streets late at
night, getting into fights with the local toughs, all the things a
bunch of young men out on their own might do, but also the

things that were going to completely outrage a little town like ours. Although I felt responsible for these guys, I couldn't be their employer all day and their surrogate guardian at night. Our police chief knew about my labor problems and was willing to work with me, but these guys were a constant headache for him, too.

"Then, just when I really needed them to harvest a field of asparagus, that whole crew went on strike, demanding higher piece-work wages. They figured they had me because asparagus that's ready can't wait. That field needed harvesting right now, and I had no other help available. Well, I did a little quick mental arithmetic and figured out that at the wage they were demanding, I'd probably lose money on that crop anyway, and by then I was tired of these guys. If this was what it took to harvest asparagus, it was time to turn my efforts in another direction. I simply threw up my hands in disgust and said 'That's enough!' then got on my car radio and called for my tractor and disk. As soon as it arrived, I started disking under all those asparagus plants while those fellows stood at the edge of my field and watched. When I finished, I paid them all off and sent them packing."

Twenty-eight

GOOD MACHINES, BAD BUSINESS DEALS

Problems with the precarious seasonal labor market made George into an even stronger believer in moving ahead with the machine age. When a new harvester came on the market, he'd quickly check it out. If convinced that it could get his crops to market faster and with the same or less cost, he made it part of his arsenal.

"I had a pretty good eye for labor-saving machines," he says, "but one time I discovered one that I thought would solve my asparagus harvesting woes, and I ended up scrapping it, even though I still knew it worked. Yakima had a small machine shop that was turning out this handy little rig, built kind of like one of those little go-karts you see today. It was slung low to the ground, totally open in the front, and had foot controls for speed and steering. The whole idea was to keep the operator's hands free as he moved up and down the rows and cut off the stalks, then dropped them into a box behind his seat.

"This machine didn't revolutionize the harvest because you were still stuck hand-cutting the spears. But it eliminated all that bending, walking, filling and emptying your small basket, and of course traveled much faster than a stooped over person could hike. I was so impressed that I purchased eight of them. I figured I could get by with about a fifth of my regular harvest crew and start expanding my asparagus acreage. Everything worked fine, except finding competent operators. When I'd do a short demonstration, I had no trouble, but as soon as I turned a crew loose, they'd be zigzagging all over a field, flattening more asparagus than they harvested. I tried a bunch of different men and women on these machines, always with the same results.

"A neighbor had a little asparagus acreage, maybe seven to ten acres, and he had a young Mexican woman who could harvest it all in no time by using one of these machines. He paid her by the hour and must have cut his labor costs by at least two-thirds. This woman controlled that machine like she'd been born on it, but everyone I tried botched the job, and apparently I wasn't alone. Drive past an asparagus field today during harvest, and the crews are all back to the stoop and cut method."

George had far better luck with an improved sugar beet harvester. In 1953 Gemco Corporation in Boise, Idaho, had built one that handled three rows at once and brought it to Moses Lake. But they were having trouble making it work. After examining this machine carefully, George was sure that it just needed a few minor modifications, so he bought it for the bargain price of $1500.

"Even with the changes I made, that first machine was temperamental," he now admits, "but as long as I drove the tractor, kept it going at just the right speed and made sure the beets were feeding through it okay, I could get seventy or more truckloads out every single day. After that one season I sold that beet harvester to a neighbor for the same $1500 and picked up a better model for the next year. Other farmers in our area quickly came on board. Essentially we revolutionized the Basin's beet industry with those first Gemcos. Before that, beet growers just couldn't get any real tonnage out of the ground and to the sugar mill fast enough to beat the bad weather, forcing them to plant smaller acreages.

"By '54 we also had our first potato harvester that loaded directly into a truck, but it took another six years before I could find a workable onion harvester. Finally an outfit in New York came up with a dandy. Their basic concept was to have a steady blast of air lift the tops, the lightest part of an onion, have a cycle bar slice them off, and then have a conveyor dump them directly into storage bins. Right away I ordered a pair. Now for the first time we'd be able to harvest our onions without manual toppers, so we could quit worrying about the spotty seasonal labor market. We'd cut our harvest costs by as much as 90% and get our produce to market or into storage at least three times as fast."

George is quick to admit that not all of his early moves were as wise as buying those two onion harvesters. Despite the questions he asked and all of his and Vic's best efforts, many times a farming venture would go wrong. But his costliest mistakes often came when he branched out into non-farming enterprises.

Grinning, he acknowledges, "When you're young and have had fast financial success, you sometimes get the idea that you can take on almost anything, and when you suddenly have a few bucks and are capable of swinging the finances for a variety of projects, there's always somebody coming around, offering you what they swear is a red-hot money- making deal, with nothing but huge profits if you'll just go down their road. Eventually I'd realize that at least for me the two cardinal rules of the business world are don't go into anything that you don't know enough about, and don't take on any enterprise where you're not going to have control. Every time I broke either of these rules, I ended up getting hurt."

The man coming to George with the more pricey 'deals' was often his accountant, Bill Williams, a fellow who lived in Pasco. Generally after looking into what his accountant was offering, George rejected it, but when Williams came to him with the chance to buy a Pasco optical shop that turned out both glasses and contact lenses, it appeared to be a sound and very profitable investment.

"Before stepping in, I carefully went over the books myself," he recalls, "and the place had definitely been making money. It had an eye doctor, a regular Double E.E.N.T., tied in with it. I'd lease the building, give this doctor free rent and pay his secretary's salary, and he'd send all his patients to us. We had the first shop in that area that made contacts. At first everything went real well.

The doctor was busy so our optical shop was busy. Profits weren't enormous, but they were steady, and the doctor's client base seemed to be continually growing, right along with our own trade.

"Then I started hearing rumors about this doctor's gambling habits. Word was he'd suffered big losses playing poker at the local Elks Lodge. These rumors bothered me a bit, but I figured he's a doctor. Surely he's smart enough to know his own limits. It turned out that sound medical degrees and reckless gambling addictions aren't mutually exclusive. Apparently this guy's love for the cards was only outstripped by his poker ineptitude. Before long he was so far in debt that he skipped town, dumping the practice he'd built up and going to work for the Veteran's Administration down in New Mexico.

"Of course this left my optometry shop high and dry. Without a doctor in our building, our trade immediately dropped off to almost nothing. I tried hard to pull in another E.E.N.T., even contacting Frances's brother. He was definitely interested and would have done well there, but opted for a position in Hawaii where he did even better. Finally I simply had to pull all the equipment and break my lease. Then the lawyer who owned the building sued me. We finally settled out of court.

"The only good thing to come out of that mess was that I gave all the office furniture and anything else he thought he could use to Dr. Harrison, a Wenatchee orthodontist who'd opened a branch office in a little town north of us. Harrison owned a small farm over in Quincy, as well as an airplane he kept at the same little airport I used, so right away we had mutual interests. Any time he had the chance, he stopped by, mainly just to chat, sometimes to get my advice on which crops to plant.

"As soon as Dr. Harrison considered me his friend, the man adamantly refused to charge me for all the orthodontist work he'd do on my four kids. Every one of them eventually needed braces, so this went on for years. I tried hard to get him to bill me, but he wouldn't take a dime. I'm sure braces cost a whole lot more now, but even back then they weren't exactly free. At least that office furniture was a partial payment."

Two years after he closed the optometry shop, George made a bad business decision that led directly into a much costlier one.

This all started when a carpenter who had worked for him wanted to build houses in Moses Lake but couldn't finance his projects.

"The fellow was a good worker and seemed to be an honest man, so I let him talk me into a partnership. I'd take care of all the finances and he'd do everything else. Because of the demand right then, we agreed we'd only build low cost tract housing. Unfortunately, I was too tied up with my own projects to ride herd on him, and the next thing I knew he was putting up a fancy 4000 square foot home. Moses Lake had absolutely no market for a house that big and that costly, but by the time I found out what this guy was doing, I had no real options. I had to let him go ahead and finish it. Of course, that ended my financial backing. A year later the builder was long gone, and I was stuck with this beautiful home.

"Finally a guy named Harold Parker stepped forward. He'd looked at the house and said he and his wife really wanted it, but at the moment they were strapped for cash. So Parker offered me a partnership in his Buick-Nash dealership, a fifty-fifty deal in exchange for that house. I wasn't all that anxious to get into a car dealership, but I didn't like having that house on my hands either, so I called my accountant over and gave him instructions to thoroughly check this out, to go over all the dealership's ledgers, to make sure its record with G.M.A.C. was sound, that Parker had a solid credit line, the whole thing.

"A couple months later I was in San Francisco attending a produce conference when Williams called. 'Hey, I've checked everything out and this Parker deal is great,' he assured me. 'Get back here and sign the papers before it gets away!' Well, when I got back, I was still a little hesitant, but finally I did what my own accountant recommended. Less than ten days later Williams is on the phone again: 'Hey, Parker wrote a $20,000 bad check to G.M.A.C. We've got to cover it or lose our franchise!' Of course I was horrified, but by then I was starting to feel trapped. A month later Parker posted a second bogus check, again for around $20,000.

"By now I'm following my money and trying hard to find out what Parker's all about. But I could never get him to sit down and talk. When I'd call his office during the day, his secretary would tell me he was at the golf course. In the evening his wife would tell me he was out bowling. For a guy whose business was in serious trouble, this fellow had one tremendous social calendar. I started going in to see his office manager in the late afternoon, then taking him to dinner, asking him all kinds of questions. Finally, he realized that if our dealership had a future, I was going to be his boss, not Parker, so he told me everything. He showed me a drawer full of promissory notes Parker had taken as down payments on brand new cars, mainly from airmen at nearby Larson Air Force Base.

"As a business practice this is deadly, something a legitimate dealer just doesn't do. Almost anyone would be a bad risk, but these young airmen were especially dangerous because they'd soon be leaving our area. A guy about to be discharged could come in and buy a brand new Buick with zero down, move back to Texas, Alabama or some other place equally remote, and immediately start missing his payments. Even local repossessions are bad business. Every time we had to cross the country to get a vehicle back, we'd lose a thousand dollars or more.

"This practice by itself would have eventually sunk that dealership, but then I discovered that Parker was doing something far worse and totally illegal. He was taking pink slips to the county courthouse and registering new car sales under false names, then hiding the corresponding vehicles. With every phony car sale, he'd apply for and receive a G.M.A.C. financing check, money he was using to support his lavish life style.

"By the time I stepped in, things were so bad I couldn't turn that dealership around. I had to let it go under. It took me over a year and better than $50,000 to get clear of that mess, basically because my accountant hadn't done the background check he claimed he had, and I'd gone ahead on his say-so. It turned out that Pop's old Kennewick attorney, Charles Powell, was the judge who presided over our bankruptcy proceedings. One day he said, 'The wrong people are standing here in front of me. Parker should be on trial and sent to prison.' A few years later Powell's words proved prophetic. Parker ended up in the Walla Walla penitentiary for other misdeeds.

"Bill Williams apologized profusely for not doing his job. He even wrote me out a $50,000 check to cover my losses, but that was a totally meaningless gesture. He'd developed a real drinking problem, which was the real reason he hadn't checked Parker out, and didn't have a dime. He assured me that he'd soon have the funds to cover that check, but I knew better than that. I simply took my losses and got myself a new accountant.

"Taking big financial hits is never easy, but fortunately it was 1957 by the time I got involved in that dealership mess, a time when I could absorb that kind of loss. Do enough in the business world, and you're bound to lose on a few of the deals. That's okay as long as you can cover your losses and you learn a valuable lesson or two. At least I came out of that Parker fiasco knowing a whole lot more about our bankruptcy courts."

A Happy Childhood: Young George Plays Cowboy

Uncle Takijero, (L), Kazuyi and Frank Yoshino in Ceremonial Dress

Shortly After Internment the Yoshinos Gather for a Thanksgiving Feast

Strawberry Pickers on Frank Yoshino's Prosperous Kennewick Operation

Frank's Harvesting and Packing Shed Crew

Loading Sacked Onions on Farland East of Moses Lake

Frank Yoshino as a Young Man

The Heart Mountain Internment Camp

Young Japanese-American Internees at Heart Mountain

The Beginning of a Love Affair: George with His First Luxury Auto.

Quick Decisions Over the Phone. Marketing Produce Became One of George's Greatest Assets.

George Yoshino in His Later Years

Twenty-nine

EARLY FATHERHOOD, EARLY TRAGEDY, LIFE-LONG REGRETS

Despite his setbacks George's farming enterprises continued to expand, and life on the home front didn't exactly stand still. 1953 had barely begun when Frances gave birth to their first daughter, Jean Frances, born on the ninth day of the New Year. Just short of two years later, on December 13th, 1954, a second daughter, Franki Jo, named in honor of her grandfather, arrived. With the birth of her second daughter, Frances's days of helping out with the harvest were all but over. She and George both knew it was time for her to put all her energies into being a full-time mom.

"Looking back, I wish I'd spent more time with my kids, especially in their earliest years," he now sadly reflects. "All four grew up while I was working almost non-stop, way too involved with my own world. It's easy to make excuses, to say my enterprises forced me to work like I did, but once those childhood years are gone, there's no getting them back.

"When I was farming, I'd leave the house before the kids were up in the morning, and most days I wouldn't come home until they were back in bed. Later, when I got into packing sheds and finally processing, I often wouldn't get home at all, catching a few hours' sleep in my office when I absolutely couldn't go on any longer. All the parenting chores in our family fell to Frances, and I have to say that she did a terrific job."

Tragically, one part of their family life that George and Frances did have to share was the untimely death of their third daughter, Georgia Anne. She was born right before Christmas in 1956, and at first appeared to be as healthy as their other two girls. But when she was only six weeks old, she suddenly became gravely ill.

"We were living in Quincy by then and I had to rush her to Samaritan Hospital in Moses Lake, driving as fast as my car could go," George quietly recalls. "The whole hospital staff at Samaritan, the doctors, nurses, everyone, they were great. They did everything they could to save our little girl, and for three days and nights neither Frances nor I left Georgia Anne's bedside, trying desperately to keep her alive. She'd stop breathing, I'd carefully pump her tiny chest, she'd revive, start breathing on her own, then, maybe within a few minutes, maybe in an hour, she'd stop breathing again. Finally she was just too weak. Her little heart stopped, and no amount of hand pumping was going to restart it. I had to face defeat. I couldn't bring her back."

Georgia Anne had died of Sudden Infant Death Syndrome, and both George and Frances understood that a closer hospital wouldn't have saved her, but he was also convinced that childhood emergencies shouldn't require forty-mile high-speed runs by desperate parents. He started making contacts, urging community leaders to get involved, and he donated $5,000 as a start-up fund for what was to become the new Quincy hospital.

"Yes, I definitely felt we needed our own hospital," he says, "but at the same time we sure didn't want to let the Samaritan staff's efforts go unrecognized. When they had a major renovation project, we donated to that, too, and had a room dedicated to Georgia Anne."

Despite their grief George and Frances knew they had to move on. Frances still had two energetic daughters to tend to, bright, talented girls who were both taking piano lessons before they turned five. Shortly after her eighth birthday Jean Frances's music teacher recommended additional lessons at the prestigious Julliard School of Music in San Francisco. Dutifully, her mother spent a summer there with her children, then started taking her talented youngster on weekly round trips across the Cascade Mountains, even in the dead of winter, for further training.

"Yeah, all that driving and making sure the kids had real opportunities fell to Frances," George acknowledges. "I should have taken a more active role, but we did have one weekend event that lasted for a few years, though it sure didn't start out as any family affair. In fact it started in the spring of '56 in a Deer Lodge, Montana, tavern, where I was doing a little relaxing with Ray and a couple seed dealers. Around ten the local Ford dealer joined our party and started insisting he was going to sell me a car right then and there.

"Well, that was one time when being a lightweight drinker sure paid off. When this fellow started talking, I was still nursing my second beer, so as soon as he described the car he had and quoted me a price, I was clear-headed enough to say 'Yeah, I'll take it.' Either that dealer had way too much to drink or he desperately needed to move some inventory because the next morning I was signing the papers and writing a check. About a week later I was back in Montana with Frances to pick up my brand new Ford station wagon. It had their biggest V-Eight, a three speed stick, and, believe me, it was fast! I'd hit one hundred and ten before I was out of second gear.

"That turned out to be the year a pickup truck stopped being my personal mode of transportation. By then our farming operation had grown to the point where we had a number of full time men and a fleet that included at least ten pickups, so I didn't need to be driving one of my own all the time. Plus, in terms of our overall budget, a car wasn't a major expense. The fifties and sixties were the decades of fine American luxury cars, and I'd end up driving some real dandies."

"I hadn't been back home with that Ford for a full month before I was in with all the Basin's other car nuts. We'd go out to an empty stretch of blacktop highway on Sunday afternoons and drag race, guys stationed at the starting line, others to check us out at a finishing point. Every week it seemed like another new fellow with a hot car would hear about me and want to see what that Ford could do.

"My pal Bud Balch was a big Chrysler fan and loved speed as much as I did. He was always buying something with a bigger engine, a new rear end, or a different gear ratio. Then he'd call me and say 'Chum, I've got a new Chrysler that's going to blow that tin can Ford right off the road!' The next Sunday he'd be over. We'd go out on this one back road that ended in a tee, and Bud would demand at least a half dozen races before he was convinced he couldn't beat me. At times we'd get going so fast we couldn't stop before we hit the tee, then fly off over the barrow ditch on the other side and bounce out across a flat field. Just imagine! Two grown men with huge responsibilities out there drag racing on a gravel road like a couple of school boys! It's amazing that we didn't flip one of those lightweight overpowered cars. Bud never won a single race, but he always went home happy and ready to look for his next car.

"I did that local stuff for about a year, then bought a '58 Chevy Impala with three two barrel carburetors, a fine auto, even hotter than my Ford. I started entering regular drag races in Ellensburg and Deer Park. That's when my racing finally became a real family event with Mom, Pop, Frances, my daughters, even Vic and his family, all coming along to cheer me on. My two girls really started looking forward to their racetrack weekends.

"Pretty soon I had a Seattle car club gunning for me, always putting their fastest cars against me in the prelims, trying to wear me down. Those boys all had Impalas too, and they all were deadly serious. But for me drag racing was just fun, not that I didn't get a real kick out of winning week after week, especially when I could see how much it bothered my competition. Finally the Seattle guys were so frustrated that they lodged a protest with the Ellensburg officials, claiming I'd put a special rear end in my car. In our stock division this was against the rules. Everything had to be strictly factory. A protest meant that my car had to be torn down and checked it out.

"At first I got mad, but then realized the whole thing was funny. I wasn't spending a tenth as much time fine-tuning that

Impala as most of those drivers, and I sure wasn't about to tamper with its rear end. I knew I'd be cleared, which meant the Seattle club would have to pay for the tearing down and rebuilding. Then I planned to make them forfeit all the prize money they'd win while I was out of the races. Unfortunately one of those fellows must have caught me smirking. They withdrew their protest before the tear-down ever started."

Thirty

A MAJOR MOVE INTO THE PACKING INDUSTRY

D rag racing was a welcome but very minor diversion from the whirlwind growth of the Yoshino Brothers farms and packing sheds. The windfall profits of 1952 had been George's springboard to increased acreages, purchasing whenever he could, leasing when this was his only practical option. Before many years passed, he had their farming enterprise spread out from Othello, twenty-five miles south of Moses Lake, to Quincy, forty miles to the northwest, and his interest in packing sheds continued to grow.

"By 1956 I wanted to find out more about how California sheds were set up because I'd read where they were way ahead of our facilities in the Northwest," he recalls, "so I worked out a deal with a friend, Ike Edgeman, a former Air Force pilot who owned a Piper Cub. Ike would fly me down to California in that tiny plane, landing at the smallest airports.

"Once we had to make a fuel stop at Chico, but their asphalt runway was radiating so much heat that our little Piper Cub would catch a hot air draft and float above it when Ike tried to land.

Three times we sailed in and kept right on sailing. Finally Ike had to power down, a pretty scary landing technique because you're never sure how much power to use or if that draft is still going to be there. As long as we didn't crack up, though, that Piper Cub was much quicker than an auto tour of all those packing sheds."

When he felt his knowledge was adequate and the time was right, George met with a couple of Quincy area farmers to discuss a packing shed partnership. After establishing a preliminary plan, they invited four more farmers to join them.

"These were all solid potato farmers, so I definitely felt that this was a project worth pursuing," George states. "We were able to buy a shed from an older gentleman who had moved to Colorado. But then when it came time to put up equal amounts of cash to get our new operation rolling, the other six guys were all short. Finally I proposed that they each put in what they could, I'd match their funds, and we'd allocate shares based on each man's investment.

"As a result, I ended up with fifty percent of our new company, Columbia Growers, Inc., and the six of them split up the rest. Owning half automatically put me in charge, even though I didn't really know how to run a big potato packing shed like that, and I still had to operate our farms and onion sheds. At Columbia Growers, we started off by taking out a $35,000 Small Business Administration loan, the first one in the whole state of Washington that was ever paid off.

"My two biggest problems were that we were starting a brand new business from scratch, and we hadn't finished putting the deal together until the first of June. To handle that year's potato crop, we'd have to be up and running by July. Fortunately I was able to hire a Quincy woman named Jean Lust, who several year's earlier had worked for Ray Young. Jean was a beautiful woman, almost a replica of Maureen O'Hara, but with a better figure. Best of all she had excellent bookkeeping and managerial skills and knew the potato industry. Despite her help, I faced major obstacles.

"When you take over an established company, even if it has a lot wrong with it, at least you start with some established procedures and generally with a marketing base. Then the key to making it profitable is to quickly discover its problems and make the right modifications. With this brand new operation we had to figure out every step, from who to hire for what position to lining up customers for our product, decisions that all fell in my lap. I found myself going into totally new territory, completely cold turkey. I knew building a customer base was vital, so the first thing I did was latch onto a Blue Book and a Red Book, the marketer's twin Bibles in the fruits and vegetables industries. These two books list every company that has a P.A.C.A., a federal perishable commodities license.

"More importantly, they document a company's overall ratings, based on net worth, cash flow, business ethics, all the things you need to know before committing hundreds of thousands of dollars worth of your product to someone you don't know. For instance, one company might have a high net worth, based on the owner's overall assets, but then you discover they're always having cash flow problems. That's a real red flag. Sell potatoes to an outfit like that and at the very least their payments are going to be slow, giving you your own cash flow problems. The books rated P.A.C.A. holders as One-X, Two-X, Three-X or Four-X, with four being tops. If a company didn't have at least a Three-X rating, I avoided them. The ones and twos were way too shaky, often fly-by-night outfits that were manipulating the market for a quick buck.

"My next step was to get on the phone, making sales to distributors all over the country. By the time the potato harvest rolled around and our shed was up and running, we had close to sixty employees, so between payroll and our other expenses, I was under a lot of pressure to make sales. Even when I knew a company's blue book ratings, I had to be careful, to find out everything else I could. For instance, Ike Edgeman was just starting out as a potato broker, and suddenly he had a huge order for us from an outfit in Chicago called Dakota Chief. They'd take fifty rail cars of our potatoes, with a signed contract and all.

"This order was so large and Ike knew so little about this organization that I was more than a little nervous about the whole deal. Dakota Chief checked out in the red and blue books okay, but still I started making phone calls, trying to figure out just who

I was dealing with and how to protect my new company. What I finally discovered was that this outfit had alleged Mafia ties. It was part of what back then was called the Siegle group, and had a reputation for not paying off on its contracts. Instead they'd bribe a federal inspector in Chicago to 'kick every carload over,' to certify that the potatoes had failed to make grade. That way Dakota Chief could pay off the contract with a few cents on the dollar, then turn around and sell perfectly good spuds at their market price. It was a scam they'd been pulling on packing sheds all across the country, breaking a number of small operators.

"If it hadn't been for my friendship with Ike, I'd have backed away from that deal. It just had too many pitfalls. But as long as I knew who I was dealing with, I figured I could go ahead and sign that contract, carefully covering my flanks. First I talked our local inspectors into writing 'Suitable Shipping Conditions' on the paperwork of each carload. When that got back to our state's main office in Olympia, it created a real stir. Federal agents came all the way out to Quincy, just to tell me I couldn't do that. But I pulled out their own rule book and showed them exactly why I could. Those feds were so mad and so corrupt that they fired our inspectors, two men who hadn't done a thing wrong.

"That suitable shipping conditions label might have protected us, but I'd also taken the precaution of shipping every one of those fifty carloads through Kansas City, where I knew they'd have to be diverted to Chicago. Government regulations stated that diversion meant a shipment is both sold and accepted. Dakota Chief's brass could squeal all they wanted, but they knew I had them. They didn't get the chance to kick over a single carload and paid off every dime of that contract. But I also made sure I never dealt with that outfit again because they weren't going to let me outflank them twice. I'm sure those gangsters changed their operation as soon as they realized what I'd done to them."

Being in charge of that first big potato shed forced George to rapidly develop his skill as a marketer, a skill that would become a major asset in the years to come. Every working day he was on the phone, saying yes or no to big dollar deals. If time and motion were his watch words in farming and packing, time alone dictated his marketing decisions.

"If you get a call from a trustworthy buyer at eight in the morning, offering you a thirty carload deal on potatoes, say for delivery in three months, you can't tell him 'I'll get back to you,' and then take a couple hours to study the deal," he explains. "By the time you call him back, someone else will have that order. Decisions have to be made right now. It's a tough, nerve-wracking business when you do it day in and day out, but it fit my temperament perfectly. I thoroughly enjoyed making quick mental calculations and giving instant yes or no answers, when so much was riding on being right.

"And it didn't take long to see the real advantage I had over the straight packing sheds because we were both packers and growers. For instance, if a Vancouver, B.C., buyer called me three months before harvest and made me a good offer on a dozen carloads for late fall delivery, I could say yes because I knew we'd have our own potatoes to cover his order. I also knew what it cost us to raise and pack those spuds, so as long as his offer covered these and gave us a decent profit besides, I'd take it. There were days when I could make $50,000 with just a single phone call.

"But if a packing shed owner who wasn't a grower said yes to that same deal, he was gambling on the late fall market. If potato prices fell, he was going to make money, but if they skyrocketed, he'd really get burned, paying far more for his spuds than the contract paid him, and he'd have to eat all of his packing and shipping costs besides. A single wrong decision could mean bankruptcy for a small packer.

"Sure I was risking the possibility of losing the higher profits of an up market, but I always felt that the trade-off was more than worth it. Those early contracts guaranteed we'd do okay both as growers and packers even if the market plummeted. Any time you can lock in sizable profit in the volatile and high-cost potato industry, it just makes sense to do it."

Again, rapid expansion was the name of the game. The Quincy shed could handle his own and his partners' potatoes in that area, but George needed more space for all the produce that he could raise and contract for in the Othello-Warden area. In 1958 he leased a building in Warden and started a second packing shed. After two years he added another one in Othello. Three years later he bought out his Columbia Growers partners and changed the name of the Quincy operation to Yoshino Western.

"That new name has a funny little history," George relates. "Merrin Cravens, a huge potato distribution house in Atlanta, at first gave us a couple of small orders, but when they saw the consistent quality of our Basin spuds, they started ordering more and more. Finally our potatoes were such a big part of their business that their buyer told me that we should change our name to Yoshino Western, and they'd change theirs to Yoshino Southern. This was just a little inside joke for a while, but when we bought out our Columbia Growers partners, I thought why not?

"By 1962 it was time to restructure everything, at least on paper. Our Quincy facility became Yoshino Western. We closed down in Warden and opened a more modern shed in the tiny town of Bruce, renaming it and our Othello shed Yoshino Produce, Inc., our lands as the Yoshino Brothers Farms. These different names were strictly for tax purposes, making them separate entities with different fiscal year endings. When you're running a big, diverse operation, it's really important to plan out your tax strategy and to be able to legally juggle profit and loss statements between your various companies.

"The way we had this set up, say if we had a bad year in farming and a good one in marketing, I could transfer some of our packing shed profits. The real advantage to making the farms look more profitable is that tax laws allow farmers to use part of their profits to invest in machinery, seed and fertilizer for the next year instead of declaring them all as taxable income. If you keep having profitable years, eventually this is all going to catch up to you, but in the meantime you have the legal use of your tax dollars. It's a strategy you have to employ, or on a high-profit year the tax boys will come in and drain you."

Thirty-one

HIGH RISK, HIGH PROFIT INNOVATIONS

As the majority owner and president of three large and profitable packing sheds, George could again study each process, searching for greater efficiency. At first it was simply a matter of taking care of little things, taking small steps to improve an operation. However, within a year he would embark on a far bigger and riskier innovation. A Portland paper products expert came to Quincy specifically to convince George that cardboard cartons were more suitable for shipping fresh potatoes than the traditional burlap sacks.

Rectangular boxes not only stacked more efficiently than the bulkier sacks, thus drastically reducing shipping costs, but they inflicted far less damage on his product.

The rap on cartons had always been that because fresh potatoes gave off a certain amount of moisture, the cardboard would get so wet that it could weaken and collapse, sometimes destroying entire stacks. George's solution: use two-piece boxes, an inner box to soak up all the moisture and an outer box that telescoped down over the top of the first. This second box would remain dry, thus retaining its strength and shape.

"This wasn't totally new," George admits, "but for some reason our industry hadn't embraced the idea, even though government studies showed that burlap sacks resulted in twenty percent damage before the potatoes even reached their terminal markets, and it sure didn't end there. Add in the higher freight bills for shipping sacks, and the savings were going to be tremendous. I was so convinced these boxes were the way to go that I put together a nice little brochure, explaining the government's findings and all the other data I'd uncovered and mailed it to produce outlets across the country. Then I just sat back and waited for the orders to pour in, completely convinced that buyers would soon be beating my door down, begging me to start shipping them my beautiful new cartons.

"At first I was dumbfounded when they totally ignored that brochure as well as my follow-up phone calls. Finally I recognized my problem. Most people resist change, even when it might be profitable. Produce houses were used to sacked spuds and most outfits had been profitably handling them for years. They simply distrusted anything so new.

Still, I believed in those cartons so strongly that I took a drastic step. I started shipping out fresh potatoes in new boxes to buyers all over the country, all at my own expense. Retailers may have distrusted anything new, but they weren't going to turn their backs on free spuds. That year I gave away several thousand fifty pound boxes.

"Well, in the spring of '58 we again had our big national produce convention in San Francisco. An executive for the Super Value grocery chain, a fellow from St. Paul, gave one of the main speeches, and he went on and on about our new telescoping cartons, all about how they caused less damage, resulted in higher profits, everything I'd been trying to get across. But now this same information was coming from an important exec., not from some shipper who had a new product he was trying to market. Suddenly no one was shy about buying our telescoping boxes. Orders poured in from across the country. Until 1962, when Pacific Fruit of Othello finally started using cartons for potatoes, we had that whole market all to ourselves and could up-charge three to four dollars per hundred weight."

By the time George took the chance on telescoping boxes and made other costly innovations, he admits that he had the advantage of owning a fairly large operation with a strong financial base. A small start-up operator couldn't have taken the same risks.

"Yes, when you're small, you almost have to stick to convention, to follow the pack. Oh, you can make minor changes, do the little things to increase your profits, but If you're going to really step away, to try turning a new idea into reality, you'd better have the economic strength to weather the storm. Like I saw when I first promoted those cartons, even good ideas don't catch on overnight, and you're always going to incur big start-up costs."

In the early sixties a business association that had turned into a close friendship led to George's next innovation. Jim Ward, who owned Seattle's El Gaucho Restaurant and several other big steak houses across the state, had been coming to the Quincy shed with Harry Blackfield to buy potatoes. But Jim didn't want field run. He had built his thriving restaurant trade on the simple premise of always giving his patrons big portions of everything. This included eighteen to twenty-ounce baked potatoes, so he and Harry would stand next to the sorting table and carefully select the best big spuds.

"A problem for restaurants had always been that a box or sack of potatoes right out of any packing shed contained everything from twenty-four-ounce giants to tiny four-ouncers," George relates. "This didn't matter if they were going to mash or fry them, but when it came to bakers, they wanted more uniformity so they didn't have to serve one client a nice hefty spud and the guy sitting next to him a shriveled up runt. Of course we couldn't afford to hand-sort like Jim and Harry were doing, so it was time to do a little research. In California I located a machine that sized oranges. With just a couple simple modifications it worked great on our potatoes.

"Now we could start designating each box according to the number of uniform-sized potatoes it took to fill it, then label that carton accordingly. A box of huge spuds was a thirty-count, then forty, fifty, sixty and so on. This was a perfect system for any food vendor who needed that kind of consistency, and once again, because we were able to give our customers something they really wanted, it allowed us to charge a premium."

With his innovations and his marketing abilities, both potatoes and onions were selling well, but George still wanted to branch out. He kept probing for a foreign market. Finally he felt he had a ready-made inroad when a friend, Ray Kiyohara, who was working for Mitsui, a large Japanese trading company, showed up in Quincy early on a Saturday morning. Ray needed 10,000 sacks of onions for immediate shipment to Japan, with strong emphasis on that word immediate. The entire shipment had to be on the Seattle dock by the following Tuesday because the ship was about to pull out.

"Well, I had the crew and I had the trucks, so I said fine." George recalls. "But first I negotiated a pretty good price. It would take twelve semi-truck loads to move that many sacks of onions, and both Ray and I knew that nobody else had the equipment or the manpower to handle a rush order of that size. But better yet, this would be the first shipment of onions from the U. S. to Japan, and I couldn't help thinking, man, what a sweet deal! A little overtime for my loaders and drivers, a nice profit for me, and this is the ice breaker I need. Once Mitsui knows that they can count on me, I'm bound to get many more and far bigger orders. I had visions of sending out weekly shipments of both onions and potatoes.

"Then three weeks later a nasty piece of reality set in. That morning I received a call from a Mitsui officer in Seattle asking me to come over and look at my onions. This fellow thought they were starting to go bad. My first words were 'What onions? Mine were shipped three weeks ago! By now they're probably being unloaded in a Japanese harbor.' I couldn't have been more wrong. For some reason those 10,000 sacks hadn't gone out on that first ship and were now scheduled to be loaded on a second one, supposedly sometime that week.

"When I reached the Seattle dock, I found all of my onions still sitting in a big terminal warehouse, with the fog rolling in so thick that at first I had a hard time finding the stacks. And stacks they were! Longshoremen had piled our pallets of sacked onions five high, something you simply can't do with fresh produce. The pallet boards dig into the sacks they're sitting on, and all that weight crushes the bottom tiers. I'd never seen fresh onions stored under worse conditions. No wonder they were breaking down.

"By law I could have told Mitsui it's your problem and walked away. From the time I made delivery, they only had twenty-four hours to accept or reject my shipment, and I had the signed and dated bills of lading. Legally those badly abused onions now belonged to the buyer. But of course I was thinking of all that future business, so I agreed to re-sort. That's when they told me that this had to be done immediately because the ship was only a few days from leaving port. Longshoremen were already waiting to load.

"I quickly called my Quincy office, told my foreman to assemble an eight man crew, to load a small sorter table and plenty of extra sacks on a truck. Then I jumped in my car and headed across the pass. Everything was set when I pulled up to our packing shed, so all I did was take on passengers, turn my car around and lead our little parade back to Seattle.

"When we hit that dock, I was still dressed in my business suit, French cufflinks and all, but I wasn't about to stand idly by while my men tackled that awful job. It was going to be long steady hours and hours of emptying sacks on our little sorting table, dumping the bad, resacking and restacking the good. We'd end up working for two days, almost straight through, and we'd discard half that shipment.

"What did I get out of all of this? Well, besides a ruined suit and a whole lot of respect for those eight men of mine, I did get one more order from Mitsui. Japanese trading companies would buy from you once, then if they saw that you were getting all or part of your produce from other sheds, they'd get hold of their names and start going direct, trying to cut out the costs of a middle man. In theory, that sounds like good business. In practice these trading companies were cutting their financial throats. As soon as they'd walk into a packing shed, many times with their expensive cameras dangling from their necks, the owner or manager would realize, 'Aha, the Japanese are entering the onion market!' and prices immediately shot up. The word spread throughout the industry, and everywhere they went, they were going to pay a premium.

"If they'd given me their order, I'd have had the whole ship-ment bought and shipped out before anyone had a clue where it was going. Sure, I'd make a profit as a middleman, but it wouldn't be anywhere close to the thousands of dollars I'd save them. Time and time again I've tried to explain this to their buyers. Even without their cameras, they're going to immediately be picked out whenever they walk into an American business, just as I was picked out when I made a business trip to Japan a few years later. People would come up to me on the street and start practicing their English, even before they'd heard me speak. My clothes, my walk, something other than my race gave me away."

Thirty-two

A WORLD'S
FAIR FIASCO

By the early sixties Harry Blackfield's many political and
business connections west of the mountains were opening
doors for George, but not every business deal that resulted
from these connections turned out to be profitable. In early 1962
Seattle businessmen and politicians were busy gearing up for
Century 21, their big World's Fair Exposition, and of course Harry
was in the thick of things. Through him, George was able to make
the right food vendor connections and was given a contract to
supply them with the tons of fresh onions they'd need to garnish
the thousands of hamburgers and hot dogs that would be sold each
day.

"When we were negotiating, there was a lot of talk about
quality," George recalls, "and we agreed to do everything just
right. So in the late winter, I gathered up all the Walla Walla
Sweet Onions root stock I could find. Then in the early spring I
had my crews plant two hundred acres. Walla Wallas all had to
be set out by hand, sticking each root stock into the ground indi-
vidually, so of course planting was time consuming and costly.

But I had a good contract, and I wanted to deliver a real class product.

"Then suddenly it was April, the fair was set to open, and I realized that my onions were better than a month and a half away from being harvestable. I had a hasty meeting with the vendors, explained my situation and then suggested that I supply them with dehydrated onions, the kind that come in cans, all grated and ready to serve as soon as you mix in water. Some of the vendors were a little cool to this idea because it was a big step down from the quality onions they'd been expecting, but they finally all agreed.

"But by the time my Walla Wallas were ready, there wasn't a single food vendor on those fair grounds who wasn't more than satisfied with this dehydrated stuff. When I told them that I was ready to start delivering the Walla Wallas, their first question was 'Where are we going to put 'em? Looking around their crowded little stands, I could easily understand this question. Dehys in cans not only took up much less room than sacks, but they were lightweight and easy to stack. Plus, serving them didn't entail all that peeling, chopping and getting rid of the refuse. Just open a can, mix the contents with the right amount of water, and they were ready to glop on a hamburger bun.

"The real kicker was that those vendors had quickly realized that serving a gourmet hamburger wasn't a real priority. In fact, they'd totally backed away from their earlier talk about quality. 'These are one-shot customers, here today, gone tomorrow,' one guy told me. 'We're into big volume and turnover here, not repeat business.'

"Well, for those vendors I had to admit this made economic sense, but it was going to end up costing me a hefty chunk of cash, somewhere around $200,000. By the time my onions were ready, the market was way down, so I held back the harvest a few weeks, which turned out to be my second big mistake. When their tops start drooping, Walla Wallas have to be harvested. They simply won't store in the ground. A little later the sweet onion market went up, but by then mine were already starting to break down. I had to dump the whole lot.

"What really hurts is that I could have simply started those vendors off with sacks of fresh onions I could have bought out of

Texas or California, then moved them naturally into my better tasting Walla Walla Sweets. Instead, I'd introduced them to dehys, creating the monster that reached up and bit me hard, right in my wallet. Only one good thing came out of that particular mistake. I was officially designated a Century 21 trader and allowed to use that as one of my fresh pack labels. Years later I'd use it again when I started a new packing shed. Still, two hundred grand seems like a pretty steep price for a logo."

Thirty-three

LOYALTY AND
THE LITTLE GUYS

L uckily, by 1962 profits from his farms and packing sheds
could absorb this loss. In fact, Yoshino Western Fresh Pack
was growing so fast that George had to be constantly
expanding his customer base. But instead of always seeking out
this country's biggest produce accounts, he concentrated on dealing with the little guys, buyers who served the independent grocery stores and restaurants.

"Working with the little guys was actually a two-part deal,"
he now says. "First, after all the help I'd been given when I started
out, I had a hard time turning small operators down. It was a bit
risky, but if I felt they knew what they were doing and were sincere, I did business with them, extending them credit so they
could get started. But helping these newcomers wasn't simply an
altruistic act. Sure, a couple of times I misjudged a man and got
stung, but the vast majority of these young fellows didn't let me
down. They settled their debts and almost every guy who eventually prospered stayed with me. As a group, they turned into my
best customers.

"And, as long as I had plenty of them, I quickly came to believe in my small accounts for another reason. From the late fifties on, I saw too many packers who concentrated on satisfying just one huge account, such as the giant Safeway grocery chain, sail along fine for a while, then get shut off suddenly, and they were out of business. Besides, the small guys weren't speculating like most of the big guys were, and they couldn't afford to stock up on potatoes or onions and then hold out whenever market conditions weren't right. Instead they had to constantly sell produce just to make it, so even in a poor market they needed supplies. As long as they kept rolling along, I'd be moving produce.

"The best thing about the little guys was that they weren't as dishonest as too many of the high flyers. A small buyer wasn't always looking for a way to beat you, like kicking your shipment over so he could get it for next to nothing. I've always maintained that a packing shed could ship me a load of potatoes or onions that only had to travel across the street and I could figure out a way to show that they didn't make grade. If you really want to cheat in this business, it's not that difficult. No, it was a whole lot nicer having a bunch of small accounts with guys I could trust than it was dealing with a single big buyer or two where I'd always have to watch my backside.

"I made sure, though, that a little guy's honesty became a two way street. Two fellows, Harry Myers and Harry Cooper, owners of Produce Supply in Spokane, would send their truck for a load every working day without any orders. Usually I knew what they needed, but sometimes I'd have to call just to make sure. They'd never ask for a price before we loaded. They'd simply take my produce and the invoice and pay the tab at the end of each month. When people trust you that much, then you'd better go out of your way to be a little more than fair. Maybe the two Harrys understood this. By not haggling, they were actually saving a few dollars, as well as always getting top quality produce."

The pleasant memories of these smaller accounts become even better when George remembers his early dealings with a few of the larger corporations.

"Associated Grocers was one of the worst," he recalls. "We were packing both onions and potatoes in our Quincy shed, two products they always needed, so I figured we'd get plenty of their business. Instead, they'd buy almost a whole truckload of potatoes from our competitor, then come over to our shed and want us to fill it out with maybe fifty sacks of onions. That was bad enough, but they'd balk at paying our 'Less than Truckload' price, something every packer has to have to come out on small orders. This happened time after time until finally I told them not to come back. I sure wasn't in the habit of turning away business, but I hated getting shoved around by the big guys."

Another 'big guy' that tried to do some shoving was the Monsanto Corporation. By 1962 George had a fertilizer and chemical dealer's license, mainly to supply his own farms, but also to help out all of his packing shed's growers. That year he had three hundred acres of onions near Quincy and asked Monsanto to check out his ground, to see if it was suitable for applications of Randox, one of their chemicals that was used to control weeds.

"I'd checked this product out with Idaho and Oregon farmers the year before" George explains. "It worked fine on their heavier ground. But I wanted assurances that it was safe for our lighter soil as well. A week later word came back from Monsanto that they'd tested our ground, and there were no problems, so I went ahead and applied it to my whole three hundred acres. The other farmers put it on smaller plots, but every single one of us ended up with undersized onions, no more than twenty-five percent of our normal yield. Obviously we had chemical damage, and Randox had to be the culprit. Then that fall the fresh onion market shot up to seven bucks a sack, making our losses even more significant.

"As a dealer I was sure that I could talk to Monsanto and get them to acknowledge the problem and make a settlement. But all they'd do is stonewall. They wouldn't even discuss the matter. Finally I saw no other recourse. We'd have to take them to court. To represent us, I hired a fellow named John Moore, a top-notch Yakima attorney who specialized in crop damage litigation to represent us. Cases like this are never settled in a hurry because big companies drag them out, hoping you'll give up in frustration. But with John's expertise we had a judgment in just two years. My share alone came to just over $800,000. Monsanto knew they were in the wrong. They didn't even attempt an appeal.

"When you get involved in as many business deals as I did, sooner or later you're going to end up in court, so keeping good records just makes sense. Early on I started taking careful notes of every significant telephone conversation. I'd use a ruled tablet and write down a line by line account, a thorough 'he said, I said' transcript, making sure my writing was so tight that nothing could be added later, and then I'd date each statement. In court this practice really paid off. When I went in front of a judge, I had a carefully dated record to back me up, and most of the time my opposition was left sorting through his memory or at best a few scattered and sloppy notes he'd scribbled down long after the fact.

"My biggest lawsuit headaches were with a couple of Wenatchee attorneys who'd always be around my farms, talking to my weeders and harvest crews, trying to convince them that the slightest injury could mean extra money in their pocket. Pretty soon we had a rash of claims, everything from cuts that didn't require stitches to backs that were suddenly overtaxed. Those were the days of private disability insurance instead of a state policy like everyone has now, and the two Wenatchee attorneys had quickly caught onto the fact that my insurance company didn't like to go into court. I had absolutely nothing against taking good care of an injured worker, but a couple of times I wanted to let a judge and jury decide, just because the claims were so ridiculous."

Thirty-four

THE DOWN SIDES
OF A WORKAHOLIC

Lawsuits, land acquisitions, big packing sheds, farming thousands of acres, altogether they led to constant pressure and a work schedule that included too many round-the-clock days. By the early sixties this mix was putting a serious strain on George's health. Besides the excess tensions, he had developed a few very bad habits.

"When I started farming on my own, I'd trained myself to go without sleep," he recalls, "but eventually this turned into a serious sleep disorder, one I've battled ever since. Whenever the pressure was on, I'd work round the clock, mainly living on cigarettes and coffee, eating a real meal only once a day. Finally my disorder got so bad I started using prescription sleeping pills. One doctor put me on a drug called Placidyl, assuring me that it wasn't habit-forming. I started out taking a single pill, then kept working up until I was taking four at a time. Yeah, I know now that I was overdosing, but even then I could only sleep a few hours at a time.

"One morning I was so wide awake by three that I jumped in my car and went to have breakfast at Quincy's all-night cafe.

Unfortunately the effects of all that Placidyl hadn't worn off. When I walked into the cafe, I felt woozy and couldn't control my movements, staggering around the place, bumping against the tables and booths. Our two night cops were in there on a coffee break and immediately concluded that I'd been drinking. These guys both knew me. In fact we were pretty good friends, so instead of hauling me off to the station, they offered to give me a ride home where I could sleep off the booze.

"At first I argued, telling them I hadn't touched a drop, that what they were seeing was the effects of my sleeping pills. But it really didn't matter. Too much of that drug was every bit as bad as too much booze. Those two cops knew I was in no shape to be driving. After a few minutes of giving them my lame excuses and listening to their rationale, I admitted they were right. That's when I knew that my doctor was wrong. Placidyl was more than habit forming. It was plain addictive and I was hooked. Without it I couldn't sleep at all. With it I'd crash for a couple of hours, then walk around rummy for half a day. And I knew if I kept taking that stuff I couldn't depend on Quincy's early morning empty streets and the help of a couple of good cops to make me a safe driver.

"Fortunately Harry Blackfield and another Seattle pal, Bill Ruff, were heading to Hawaii, and I went along, leaving all my sleeping pills back home. It took thirteen practically sleepless days and nights, going completely cold turkey, before I could finally say I'd beaten that terrible drug. On the flight home I suddenly had a stewardess shaking me, asking if I wanted a glass of orange juice. I'd actually fallen into a sound sleep on an airplane, something I'd never been able to do before. Harry and Bill thought this was pretty funny because they both knew I needed sleep, not orange juice. But I couldn't get mad at that stewardess. I just felt too good."

Placidyl became just a bad memory, but George still had more than his share of bad habits. He's now quick to acknowledge that smoking four packs of cigarettes a day wasn't the best thing for his health, but he believes that for a time his sporadic eating habits were even more detrimental. By the late fifties he'd started having so many demands on his time that whenever he needed to meet with an individual or a small group, he'd quickly say 'Let's have lunch,' figuring that way a meeting wouldn't cut into the rest of his hectic schedule.

"Yeah, I thought I was pretty clever, killing two birds with one stone, but most of these meetings were critical to one or more of my enterprises, so of course they were packed with stress. Plus, that big lunch might be the only real meal I ate the entire day. Well, this all caught up to me in the fall of 1962. I was in Deer Lodge with a produce broker from Texas and my old buddy, Wild Bill. One night Bill took us to Anaconda for a fancy steak dinner. Halfway through that meal I suddenly couldn't swallow right and started choking on a piece of meat. I finally dislodged it, but my throat absolutely ached all night.

"I didn't start really worrying about it until the next morning when I discovered that besides the steady pain, I couldn't swallow a thing, not even liquids. All I could think about was getting home, so I said my goodbyes and caught the first train heading west. That was one long miserable trip. Finally I choked a little water down, but I couldn't eat a thing, not even a small bowl of broth they brought me.

"At home I wasn't much better. Some days I could eat a little solid food, but mostly I was living on liquids and only small amounts of those. A month and four trips to Seattle's Virginia Mason hospital later, I was down thirty pounds to a skeletal one-twenty. The doctors had found no physical cause for my problem and concluded this eating disorder was all stress related. They put me on Librium, a strong tranquilizer. Gradually, I was able to eat regular meals again and pick up a little weight, but after what I'd been through with Placidyl, I sure didn't want to stick to those tranquilizers too long.

"I wish I could say that nasty little episode acted as a total wake-up call, that I immediately gave up cigarettes and coffee, started eating three square meals a day and cut back on my work schedule. None of that happened, but at least I was smart enough to eliminate most of those lunch meetings that were messing up my digestive system, and I did force myself to eat a little more regularly."

Cutting back on his work schedule seemed out of the question for a man who by then was responsible for three thriving produce sheds and who was still expanding his diversified farm operation. By 1963, when a Seattle banker asked for a tour of all the ground the Yoshino brothers were farming, it turned into a two day auto trip. George started out by showing him every crop they were raising near Quincy, then moved south and east. By the time they'd covered the Moses Lake acreages and were surveying the Warden area farms, the sun had already hit the horizon. They spent that night in an Othello motel and finished their tour the next morning.

"By then our crops were so extensive and the distances between some of them so great that I bought a Cessna 175 in partnership with a fellow named Harry White, who owned an air strip and spray plane service outside Quincy," George states. "I'd taken enough lessons to obtain a private pilot's license, so now I could get out early each morning and make a fly-over of all our crops, checking for dry spots, weed infestations, anything that looked like a potential problem. Then the rest of the day I'd use our two-way radios to tell our regular crews where they had to head and what they had to do.

"The real drawback was that although I had the right operator's license, Harry hated to let me solo. He was a real professional aviator himself and he'd look at me and say, 'George, you shouldn't be going up by yourself. You take way too many chances, and your mind's always on your crops, never on your flying!' As young and daring as I still was back in the sixties, I guess I knew Harry was right, but I didn't let that stop me. Too often I'd be sailing along less than a hundred feet above the ground, just so I could get a better view. Then when I really needed to check a situation out, I'd land on a handy gravel road, which was both dangerous and illegal.

"One morning I was in such a hurry to get airborne that I forgot to open the plane's fuel valve before take-off, so when I kicked over that Cessna's engine, all I had to run on was the gas in the line. Luckily I made a long taxi that morning and just before I was ready to lift off my engine sputtered and died. That's when I remembered that fuel valve and did the 'uh oh' bit. Another half pint of gas in my line or a bit more tail wind to cut down on my taxi time, and that little mental lapse could have led to catastrophe.

"A terrible irony in all this was that despite my carelessness I was okay, and Harry, who was an excellent pilot, always conscientious, always planning ahead, would be killed in a tragic mishap the very next year. Spraying crops is a dangerous profession where even outstanding pilots have accidents. When Harry's widow called me and said she'd have to sell the airstrip, I told her to go ahead and sell the Cessna as well. Without that airstrip and Harry around to maintain our airplane, I knew I was pretty much out of the flying business, which for my own longevity was undoubtedly a good thing. Low-level flights and landing on back roads would have been dangerous for the best pilot. When you're a rookie and have at least a dozen big dollar deals on your mind, it's downright foolhardy."

Thirty-five

A BIGGER AND BIGGER FARMING OPERATION

H e may have no longer had a super fast way to survey his crops, but George wasn't about to quit expanding his holdings. His single biggest land acquisition would come in early 1964, the year when an imaginative Coeur de Alene, Idaho, realtor named Elmer Drexel worked out an elaborate three-way trade, enabling George to sell a Moses Lake farm and acquire a thousand-acre place southwest of Quincy.

"It was known back then as the Spearmint Farm because it was mainly planted to mint, had a big mint still and all the other necessary equipment, trucks, harvesters, everything. This place had a beautiful big home we moved into, plus five other nice smaller houses that I could use for my full-time crew and their families. Because it was so much more valuable than the farm I gave up, this deal enabled me to get an additional $250,000 loan from the mortgage company, which let me go ahead with even more expansion. As I've said, that kind of debt never bothered me because I always felt our crops would pay it off. In fact, in the next two years our profits could have paid off that loan and everything else we owed if I hadn't put the money into additional land purchases."

By this time the Yoshino Brothers owned another 600 acres near Quincy, 650 acres close to Othello and still had a 200-acre parcel by Moses Lake. Add in the leased ground, and their total farming operation topped 6500 acres. Not only did they have tremendous potato and onion production and 1200 acres in mint, but they had become the biggest single supplier of beets to the sugar mill in Moses Lake. Plus, George continued to experiment with a wide variety of exotics, from alfalfa and radish seed to parsnips, peppers and lettuce, raising up to two dozen different crops during his peak seasons.

"Like Pop, I was a strong believer in diversifying, so I kept looking for paying alternatives. Because it had such a high profit potential, lettuce appealed to me, but in our area we couldn't raise the popular Iceberg variety. When one of our high warm winds of summer hit, it would burn an entire crop in less than two hours. We could do real well with a more rugged type called Great Lakes, and William's Brothers of Tacoma was willing to market it for me. But Great Lakes wasn't as delicate as Iceberg in either texture or flavor, so on a year-in and year-out basis it couldn't compete. In a season when California had lettuce crop failures, we did fine, but any time there was plenty of Iceberg, ours just didn't sell."

Although he never set out to break a world production records with any of his crops, in the summer of 1964 George ended up with one. Gaines, a variety of soft white wheat seed, was new on the market, and it grew abundantly in the warm, irrigated Columbia Basin. That summer growing conditions were ideal, so all the wheat crops were thriving, but a two-hundred-acre field near Quincy looked fantastic. As harvest time neared, everyone from the state university experts to seed company personnel came out for a look.

"Those fellows knew that crop was something special, but it wasn't until they all watched that thick stream of wheat kernels start pouring into our combine hoppers that a few of the experts actually started talking world record," George says. "That field tallied an incredible one-hundred-seventy bushels to the acre, a record that stood for fifteen years and would only get toppled when the statistics keepers started accepting averages from little ten acre plots that were specifically aimed at breaking the old standard."

Thirty-six

PARENTAL DILEMMAS

H is record wheat crop came the same year that George had moved his family onto the Spearmint Farm, at a time when his girls were already in school and had two little brothers. The older, Michael Stanton, was an aggressive little five-year-old. His baby brother, Harry Walter, nicknamed Wally, was just a year-old toddler. Meanwhile both Jean Frances and Franki Jo were establishing themselves as top students, studious, but still with ample time to do all the kid things that a small town offered. Their musical talents showed up early and would continue to be a major part of their lives. A few years earlier, one whole summer had been spent in San Francisco so that Jean could attend the Julliard Conservatory and further her early expertise on the piano. George drove his family down, set them up in a comfortable apartment, then flew home to get back to work.

"Less than a month later Frances called me, all in a panic," he says. "She immediately blurted out how she'd left the four kids in the car while she ran into a grocery store, just for a minute. Michael, who was always our live wire, getting into about everything a kid his age could get into, had slid behind the wheel and then somehow pulled the emergency brake free. That heavy Chrysler rolled down a little hill, hopped a curb, then smashed right through the big plate glass window of that Safeway store. Our car was pretty beat up, but luckily the kids were all okay, and no one in that store had been injured."

Reflecting back to his children's growing-up years, George is pleased that all four established solid work ethics. However, he also remembers having a short stint of early reservations about his two girls. A few years after that smashed window episode, Jean and Franki Jo decided that they wanted to make money weeding and thinning their father's beets.

"The girls both seemed pretty serious about taking this on," George now laughs, "mainly because they figured it was easy spending money. Well, I put them to work, but right away they showed more interest in chatting with any adult that came within ear-shot than they were about swinging a hoe. Not getting their own work done was bad enough, but I could see they were distracting the rest of my crew. A day came when their beet rows went untouched. They'd sneaked a deck of cards out of the house, then spent the morning sitting way out in the middle of the field, playing one game after another, broke for lunch, and resumed their little escapade until quitting time. Both girls really thought they'd pulled a fast one, that I'd never hear about this, but of course I was told. No, I never let on, but I did let them know I expected them to get their work done.

"Coming from Dad, they figured this was just talk. Finally I had to fire them. Almost the next day they both had jobs working for my neighbor, Howard Morgan. Later he'd delight in telling me how the two of them did a heck of a job for him, better than many of his adult weeders. I guess my girls thought that working for their daddy gave them special privileges. Then as soon as they knew that they had a 'real boss' they decided it was time to get serious about earning a paycheck."

"This was a small incident, but it sure backed up something I'd already been leaning toward. Now I was convinced that working for someone else, at least for a couple of months here and there, was going be the best thing for all my kids. Part of this was because I knew I'd never be as demanding as Pop was with Vic and me, but more important, it's always good for teenagers to spend at least a few years of their lives working away from home, simply to gain a broader perspective. Hoeing onions for my Uncle Takejiro gave me my first insights into what it meant to work for someone besides Pop, and even those terrible experiences I had in Wyoming and Milton added important dimensions to my life. Once you've gone through something like that, you'll always appreciate the decent employers in this world.

"No, I sure don't regret the fact that I wasn't destined to spend many of my best years working for wages, but I'm glad I did some of this when I was young. If I'd gone straight from Pop's farm to running my own, I'd have been ready to work hard, but I'd have missed out on what I like to call 'people training.' A bad boss like Heidenreich, a good one like Percy Driggs, they were both part of my people training.

After reflecting for a couple minutes George went on. "But sometimes I still wonder if I shouldn't have trusted my kids more and given them greater responsibilities, just like Pop did for me. Oh, I don't mean I should have had all four of them driving a vehicle at six, but when they were ten or eleven, I could have taken each of them into any of our big open fields, given them a few basic lessons and then turned them loose on a tractor or in a pickup. But I never had that same confidence in my children. I was afraid something bad might happen. And the first time I tried giving one of them more leeway, something did. It was a warm summer Sunday morning in early June. I'd picked up Jean and Franki Jo from church and was only about a quarter of a mile from home when I spotted one of my tractor drivers having problems with his cultivator. Right away I wanted to find out what was wrong and see if I could help, but I knew if I walked out in that field, I'd be tied up for a while, and I didn't want my girls waiting in that hot car.

"We had a new Pontiac with an automatic transmission, an easy car to handle, and Jean was eleven, so I thought, why not, she's a big girl, she can handle this short run. She'd done a little back road driving, mainly on my lap, so this wouldn't be too different. As soon as I asked if she could handle it, Jean was all smiles and was already sliding behind the wheel. So I explained how to move the stick from park down to drive, how to touch the gas lightly and go slowly until she could turn into our yard where all she'd have to do was apply the brake, push the stick back up to park, then switch off the ignition.

"Well, my girls took off, and as I stood there watching, Jean was doing just fine. She glided slowly down the road, made a nice easy turn and started rolling into our yard. That's when she spotted her mother and grandmother standing together in our garden. Right away Jean was waving, yelling, doing whatever it took to make sure they both saw that she could drive. Jean was so thrilled by all the attention she was getting that when it came time for her to step on the brake, she missed it completely, jamming her foot down on the gas pedal instead. That Pontiac shot across our yard and didn't stop until it slammed into a light pole. Franki Jo's head hit the dash, the car was wrecked, and Mom and Grandma were both close to hysterics.

"Right away I realized I shouldn't have allowed Jean to drive, not because she was too young, but because she'd had no real experience running machines on her own. If I'd given her a few chances out in a wide open field, that little run would have turned out fine. Now I was just glad she could walk away with no more than a bruised ego and that Franki Jo only sported a little lump on her forehead."

Of course there were practical reasons why this new generation of Yoshinos didn't get the same early start on machines or even as day laborers that their father and uncle received. Unlike their grandfather's truck garden farm, their father's huge agricultural enterprise didn't have a need for child labor, and of course the financial circumstances were vastly different. Still, George was pleased when both his daughters and sons showed an interest in farm work and had definite ideas on where they should start.

"When Michael was around six, he liked riding around in the car with me when I'd go out in the mornings to look over our crops," George recalls. "As we'd drive around, he'd listen carefully whenever I'd talk on the two-way radio. I'd be giving out orders, sending different men to different jobs, checking to see if anyone had mechanical or other problems. One day I'd just turned off the radio when Mike suddenly piped up, 'This is what I want to do when I grow up. I want to drive around in a big car like this and talk on the radio and tell everyone what to do!'

"I had to smile over his enthusiasm, but then I pointed to an onion field we were passing and explained, 'No, you're going to start out there, with a hoe in your hands, spending long days chopping out weeds. After a few summers of that, you can work your way up, step by step, just the way I did when I started. Maybe eventually you can drive the big car and give the orders, but only after you've spent a whole lot of years doing every hard job that's out there.' Michael wasn't too impressed with that idea, but I meant what I said. I'd seen too many young men take over their dad's business without knowing what it was all about and lose the whole thing in a tenth the time it had taken the old man to build it up. There's just no substitute for learning a business from the ground up, whether it's farming, marketing, banking or running a gas station.

"I didn't try explaining this to Michael, but the reason I could drive my car by a field of onions or wheat at high speed and pick out a dry patch or a weed infestation was because I'd spent all those years working the land, seeing how different crops came on. That taught me to always be looking for trouble spots and what to watch for. The same was true of all of our farm equipment. Even when our operation was far too big for me to be out in the fields running the newest carrot seeder or onion harvester, I still understood how those machines functioned, and I could spot a problem. I was no longer the guy out there making the adjustments, but I could usually tell one of our mechanics what had to be done.

"But what I really wanted my kids to understand before they took charge is what the guy out there hoeing your onions or the woman standing all day at your sorting table is doing for you. The boss should know what his workers have to put up with day in and day out, and that's knowledge you only get by spending years in the trenches. Too often guys who start out near the top think they can simply plug their workers in when they need them and turn them off like a bunch of light bulbs when they don't. Then they're mad when suddenly they have labor problems. Sure, over the years I had to get rid of a few bad employees, but I always tried to do right by my good ones. And yes, I was definitely hoping that one or more of my kids would follow in my footsteps, but if they did, I wanted them to know that the people they hired weren't part of their machinery."

Thirty-seven

VERTICAL INTEGRATION: THE NEXT STEP

Despite his ever-expanding and profitable farming and pack-ing enterprises, by the late fifties George started to see marketing problems on the horizon. In 1959 his three packing sheds were handling half the fresh potatoes in the state, but he realized he was competing in a shrinking rather than an expanding market.

"When you're controlling that much of the total produce, you get a much clearer picture of the national and even the inter-national situation," he states. "I could see that our potato markets were definitely shrinking, and it wasn't because we were losing out to our fresh pack competition. Processed products, French fries, tater tots, au gratins, potato flakes, potatoes in t.v. dinners, all these were becoming the rage, taking a bigger and bigger share of our consumer market. Every year fewer and fewer housewives were revolving their daily dinners around the baked potato or peeling and mashing their own spuds.

"And with three packing sheds, I was constantly faced with another real dilemma, how to dispose of tons and tons of cull potatoes. As cattle feed, these culls only brought three dollars a ton, which barely paid for our delivery costs. Worse yet, most of the time we couldn't sell them at all and had to haul them out and dump them in a land fill. That just went against everything Pop had always preached and I'd come to believe in. Back in Kennewick, we had a saying, 'Sell the best and eat the rest!' I literally grew up on culled vegetables, everything from the too short and too long spears of asparagus to slightly overripe strawberries. It was all good food or Mom wouldn't have fed it to us. It just wasn't attractive enough to be marketed. Even the vegetables that were too ripe or too withered for us to eat, Pop fed to his hogs, along with all our other refuse. Nothing was wasted. Now here I was, responsible for dumping truckloads and truckloads of usable food stuffs, mainly potatoes but also tons and tons of culled onions and even too many carrots. There had to be a better way.

"The first thing I considered was getting into cattle, setting up a big feeding operation on some barren ground we owned outside Quincy. This piece of land had the right drainage slope and had more than enough acreage to accommodate thousands of cattle. Of course, I was no cattleman and sure didn't have the time to first learn everything I'd have to know and then run a feed lot, so I started looking for the right manager, someone who could run the entire operation. I quickly discovered that guys like that were pretty rare. Several fellows I interviewed had plenty of expertise when it came to cattle, but they didn't have any real business or marketing background. The few all around managers were either already employed by solid outfits or tied up with their own cattle ventures.

"Plus, cattle feeding didn't solve another problem I was facing. I wanted to branch out into bigger crops of carrots, peppers, asparagus and parsnips, again so I'd be more diversified. But I knew that if I was going to go into these other crops in a really big way, I'd have to find my own markets. Setting up fresh pack sheds for them was one option, but because of the national trend towards easily prepared foods, a processing plant started looking like the way to go.

"Working through my friends, Wilbur Hallauer and Wally Miller, I'd already been selling a few of our vegetables to Valley

Evaporating. Wilbur and his brothers owned this company, which had several small dehydration plants spread out in Central Washington's apple districts because dehydrated fruits were their mainstay. Wally was their aggressive manager in Chelan Falls, about seventy miles northwest of Quincy. In the late fifties he'd heard about some of the things I was doing and drove over to the Basin to talk business, and before long I was shipping him truck loads of our produce, mainly carrots and asparagus, but also smaller quantities of peppers and parsnips. This went okay until one time we tried onions, an experiment we'd later refer to as the 'Miller Debacle.'

"Our onions dehydrated okay on their wooden trays. Their finished product sure wasn't top quality, but it was saleable. The 'Miller Debacle' part came shortly afterwards when their company ran $50,000 worth of apples on those same trays and came out with a beautiful looking product that absolutely reeked of onions. Wally not only had to dump all those dried apples, but then he discovered he'd have to destroy his expensive wooden trays because there was simply no way to get that onion smell out of them.

"But onions were the exception. On everything else I made a decent profit, and Wally said their sales were fairly lucrative. The drawback was that their plants weren't set up for the kind of volume I had in mind. Valley Evaporating did what we called a batch operation, first using steam cookers, then drying fruits and vegetables on those trays. This system worked as long as they stuck to the small specialty markets, but it sure wasn't designed for turning out tons and tons of product. If I had shipped them all the carrots or asparagus I could easily have raised just around Quincy, I'd have totally overwhelmed them."

More and more the only logical solution seemed to be having his own processing plant, to take that next big step toward vertical integration. If the nation and the world's consumers were moving more towards French fries and T.V. dinners, it was time for George to move with them. The right kind of plant would make use of every potato and onion that came through his sheds, and it would provide a market for everything else he wanted to raise.

But first he had to decide what kind of processing would best meet his needs. Although what his friends were doing with dehydration was intriguing, he didn't want to limit his options. A dehydrating plant was certainly a strong possibility, but he had to consider moving into frozen foods or freeze drying. To make his decision, he first had to find out which of the three had the best future on the world market. For five years he would fly all over the west, looking at frozen food and dehydration plants in Idaho, Oregon and California, carefully weighing the pros and cons of each process. He contacted well over a hundred different people, everyone from government experts to plant managers.

"Once again Wally Miller turned out to be a real friend and ally," George says. "He'd been making trips to the U.S.D.A. offices in Albany, California, and offered to take me along and introduce me to all the experts he'd already contacted. I ended up making repeated trips to Albany during the next five years, many times listening to and quizzing these experts, but even more often spending my days scouring through their literature.

"Harry Blackfield was another real asset. By the time I was getting serious about a processing plant, he was out of the bakery business, had plenty of free time on his hands, and was fascinated by what he saw me doing. He was always ready to accompany me, whether I was heading down to Albany or just going over to Idaho to study a processing plant. I'd pay his expenses, but other than that Harry wasn't earning a dime. He was simply content to ride along, and once again he became my ice breaker. All his political and business contacts, as well as his fantastic ability to walk into an entirely new situation and immediately make friends, opened more than a few doors for me."

Harry or no Harry, though, George quickly discovered that checking out someone's processing plant wasn't at all like the good old days of talking to the Basin's friendly farmers. Processing plants were highly competitive and their top personnel tried hard to keep any specialized technology they had developed from potential competitors, setting up all kinds of systems to safeguard their trade secrets. As soon as a plant owner or his manager realized that George was one of these potential competitors, they weren't about to give him any answers or allow him to walk freely through their facilities. Most didn't object as long as they thought he was just a casual visitor, but once they realized that he was only there to figure out what they were doing, right and wrong, their doors closed in a hurry.

"Yeah, I ended up getting kicked out of more than one plant," George now admits, grinning broadly over his recollections. "The biggest operation that ended up showing me the door was called Fresh Pack of Idaho. Carl Doud had worked for Fresh Pack a few years earlier and had no problem introducing me to the owner and getting me a tour of that facility. At first this owner was really pleasant, showed me all around, even answered my questions. But after I'd come back a few times, he started getting suspicious. I was asking way too many questions, and by that time rumors were flying. This guy seemed to like me, but he'd been hearing stories about my travels and my long-range goals. Finally he pulled me into his office and asked about my intentions. Right away I admitted I was considering building my own plant. He wasn't exactly mean about it, but it's hard to be real polite when you're telling a fellow to get out and never come back.

"It was a nasty business, all this secretive snooping. Still, I felt that I had to know everything I could before I took that next huge step. Sometimes I'd get to know a plant's personnel, anyone from their production manager to a line foreman. I'd take these guys out to dinner, quizzing them as much as I dared without totally tipping my hand. If one of them really seemed to be sharp, I'd test the waters, find out how satisfied he was with his present employment. The disgruntled ones were always my best sources of information, and I made mental notes to contact them if I ever needed men with their skills."

Gradually George felt that he was getting a better handle on the whole processing industry. He hadn't wanted to rule anything out, but it soon became clear that for a real high volume operation, the only kind that he was considering, he would have to choose between building a frozen foods and a dehydration plant. Freeze-dried foods were a niche market, and by then the canned goods market was on a sustained downhill slide.

"A frozen foods plant had real advantages," he recalls, "but right from the beginning I found dehydration far more fascinating. It's actually the oldest form of preserving vegetables. By the time I was studying them in the early sixties, dehy plants were thriving all over Europe, but for some reason, they hadn't caught on in our country. California had a couple of small plants that dehydrated carrots and a few other vegetables, and Idaho's Rogers Brothers dehydrated all of their own cull potatoes, but that was about it.

Still, I wasn't about to make a decision based on what I found the most fascinating. I had to study the data, talk to the experts, then make my decision based on sound economics, to build the plant that would be best for our operation."

By 1963 George's research also had him leaning toward dehydration, but he was still trying to make up his mind when a chance meeting in Albany tipped the scales. For over two hours he talked to his new acquaintance, a New Zealander who had been all over world studying food processing.

"That evening we had dinner together," George recalls, "and suddenly this guy pointed out the restaurant window and asked, 'What do you see?' What I saw were the city's towering apartment buildings. 'Exactly,' the man said, 'apartments with tiny little freezer compartments built into their refrigerators. In the rest of the world apartment dwellers and even most homeowners don't have that! What they do have are shelves and cupboards with enough space to store tins or sacks of dehydrated vegetables. Yes, frozen foods are going to have their own niche, but there's just no way they're going to catch on in a big way.'

"Then he stressed shipping costs, which even before the oil embargo of the early seventies were becoming a major factor. Dehydration meant you'd be shipping maybe a tenth as much weight, and you wouldn't have to use expensive refrigerated rail cars or trucks. All in all the fellow made a lot of sense and essentially confirmed what I'd already been thinking. I left Albany convinced. I was going home to start planning for my future dehydration plant. Of course it turned out that my New Zealand contact was totally wrong about the future of frozen vegetables. Frozen hash browns, fries, carrots, peas, T.V. dinners, they all caught on in a big way, but he was right about dehydration. By then it was coming into its own in this country, and its world market kept right on expanding.

Thirty-eight

EARLY DECISIONS AND THE POLITICAL ARENA

In the planning stage, George had to select the best location for his new plant. Several Basin towns were anxious to bring in a new industry and its resulting payroll and offered incentives, but his home town had two definite advantages. First, it was located in Grant County, which owned the Wanapum and Priest Rapids dams, big hydroelectric facilities on the Columbia River, giving it the world's lowest electrical rates. Dehydration plants demand massive amounts of energy, so these low rates, as well as a natural gas line George was able to bring into that area, gave him guaranteed power at prices well below industry standards.

A second major problem any new processing plant faced was disposal, what to do with all of its wastes, particularly the gallons and gallons of chemical-laden water and the tons and tons of potato peels.

"Back then processing plants near Othello were simply dumping their wastes in a canal that ran out into the scab lands behind their property," George recalls, "but I'd learned enough at the U.S.D.A. lab and had seen what was happening at plants in other parts of the country to know that this practice couldn't continue. Those Othello wastes were already filtering into the nearby creeks and streams and were destined to pollute way too much of our ground water. It was only a matter of time before that practice was outlawed. When the government did crack down just a couple of years later, established processing plants in both Moses Lake and Othello had to purchase additional ground next to their facilities and then build elaborate sprinkler systems as well as create settling ponds. In at least one case their costs topped ten million dollars before the pollution control folks were satisfied."

By seeing this problem early enough, George was able to get elected to the Quincy City Council, where he and other progressive members pushed through an industrial sewer system, a system that would turn out to be a key factor in bringing several more processing plants to the little community. His original plans called for a two-and-a-half-million-dollar facility, but by the time it would be up and running in the fall of 1965, last minute improvements and expansion had pushed the total price tag to just over three-and-a-half-million. The National Bank of Commerce would become his primary money lender, but getting to this point took careful planning.

"You can't approach financing a big project like that by telling your potential creditors what your new plant will do for you," he explains. "Instead you have to show them what it will do for them, why their institution will come out dollars ahead. When you're talking to a bank manager or anyone else who's going to lay big dollars on the line, it's their bottom line that they care about, not yours. And I knew I needed more than the banks on my side if I was going to pull this project off.

"So the first thing I did was a feasibility study for the Great Northern Railroad, showing just what a dehydration plant located right next to their tracks could mean to their business. My study outlined the number of shipments they could expect, their long-range projected revenues, that sort of thing. Great Northern's execs were so pleased with it that they not only agreed to sell me the ground on a long-term contract, but they even financed the construction of our building on a real estate contract. Later one of their vice presidents told me that it was the first time in their history that they'd ever sold any of their ground for a private project or financed one.

"I used the same 'what's in it for you' approach with banks. I had to show them that not only would they have the interest from my loans, but they'd also be doing far more business with the local farmers and other businesses in Quincy, as well as making car and home loans to many of my future employees."

The year before this new dehydration plant was in its final planning stages, Governor Rossellini had told George about a bill he was pushing, designed to give a sales tax break to certain new industries in the state, notably the Intalco Aluminum plant. The original bill was set up to benefit leased and purchased plants exclusively. By the spring of 1965 Rosellini was no longer in office, but his bill had resurfaced. With the strong backing of the new governor, Dan Evans, and several of the state's most powerful senators and congressmen, this time it seemed destined for quick passage.

George understood that if the bill went through as it was written, he would gain nothing, but he could see no reason why it couldn't be amended to give the same tax breaks to a newly con- structed processing plant such as his. Immediately he contacted Sid Flanagan, a Quincy farmer and an influential state congress- man, and his even more influential friend, Senator Wilber Hallauer, chairman of the Ways and Means Committee. He asked both men for their help, then headed for Olympia to do his own lobbying.

"I'd only spent a couple hours talking to people when Governor Evans heard about what I was doing." George recalls. "That evening he called me at my hotel, asking me to back off. Evans was worried that if I threw something new into the mix or stirred up the wrong people with my lobbying, the whole bill might bog down and never get passed, at least during that session, throwing a real roadblock in the path of the Intalco plant. Even Rosellini was upset when I told him what I was doing. They were both so anxious to see that aluminum plant up and running that they didn't want anything to interfere.

"My immediate problem, though, was Dan Evans. Luckily, I knew him pretty well and I'd given him plenty of support during his first run for governor. In fact, right after he was elected, Evans had called me and asked what political appointment I'd like. He offered me a spot on the powerful liquor commission, but I had no interest in anything that would take up that much of my time. Finally I accepted a less demanding one, on the Columbia Basin Commission, where at least I could work on local problems.

"So the governor was willing to listen to my side of things. As soon as I'd explained everything and he understood exactly what changes I was asking for in this bill and why I and other new construction plant owners needed these tax offsets, he was in complete agreement. In fact, before we were off that phone, Evans not only gave me his political blessing, but he promised to personally back the amendment we'd drafted, which I knew just about guaranteed its passage. It was a good thing, too, because that amended bill not only helped me. It was going to be a real shot in the arm for all the processing plants that would be built in the Columbia Basin."

Thirty-nine

A QUALITY WORK FORCE
AND EARLY GLITCHES

nother major challenge George faced was putting together a work force of engineers, mechanics, boiler operators, everyone he would need to first construct and then operate his dehydration plant. These weren't people he could simply get from an employment agency or hire fresh out of college. Dehydration was too new, and it was far too technical, with complicated machinery and methods that still had to be refined. Potato flakes had only been developed a few years earlier. To get his plant up and running on schedule, George needed top-notch employees with hands-on training.

"Basically I stole these fellows from other dehy plants," he readily admits. "It was all I could do. I hired half a dozen specialists away from Rogers Brothers in Idaho Falls, a manager-engineer from General Foods in California. Oh, I didn't have to do anything crooked or even underhanded to get the personnel I needed. Mainly it was just a matter of giving each fellow that I hired the opportunity for quick advancement in a more modern facility. Guys who'd been assistants in their old plant right away saw the chance to be in charge of their specialty and to grow with a brand new company.

"And I sure wasn't always right about who I hired for those top jobs. I finally had to fire the fellow I picked up from General Foods because he just didn't understand costs as they applied to our operation. He wanted to equate everything to what he called 'industry averages' and as long as our production was matching those figures, he was convinced everything was fine and that he was doing his job. That may have worked okay when he was with a huge company like General Foods, but I didn't give a hang about industry averages because if we were going to survive during our first few years, I knew we'd have to do way better than that.

"Fortunately, when we built our facility, my office manager and accountant convinced me that we'd need computers. This was still the early days of that technology, and I'd heard some real horror stories about computer breakdowns that totally disrupted a company's records, sometimes lasting for months. So before we ever started I told those two, okay, but I want that thing up and running from day one. I don't want to be a month into production and then hear that the computer's not spitting out the necessary information.

"I gave the computer salesmen and techs that came around that same lecture. They all kept telling me that they'd get it right the first time. Finally, we decided to have a company called National Cash Register install our computers and built a computer room, completely windowless, all concrete, with carpeted floors, as sound proof, dust proof and vibration proof as we could make it. Once everything was installed, we hired two key punch operators to run the data.

"Despite all those early assurances I'd kept hearing, those computers definitely had their idiosyncrasies, bugs that NCR's technicians had a hard time finding. For the first three months I couldn't even get a bank balance. It was driving me crazy. But as soon as the problems were corrected, I had unbelievable daily fact sheets. Each morning I had a complete analysis of our costs, our projected revenues, how much product we'd turned out, everything I needed to see how we were doing.

"Right away I could see that our potato slices and dices production costs were outstripping our projected revenues from
those products. I let this go for a few days because I felt I had to
give my plant manager the chance to correct this problem. After
all, this fellow had access to those computer read-outs, and it was
his job to make sure our plant was running efficiently enough to
turn a profit. But when he didn't act, I had to go to him and lay
this all out. That's when he hit me with his industrial averages
explanation. For some reason the fact that our slices and dices
were going to lose money unless we made some major changes
just didn't seem to register. I had no choice but to fire him."

Another significant problem that first plant manager had
been ignoring was on their potato flakes line. For a time, too
high a percentage of the finished product was coming out with
tiny defects, failing to make grade. As the flakes came off the
line, the women who did the final inspection were spotting these
defects, little flecks of dark potato among all the white, and
picking them out, but this was proving far too costly. As each
black speck was removed, too much of the good product went
with it.

"Losing product wasn't good, but our real problem was that
all this picking out defects was way too slow," George recounts.
"It took too many women far too long to make certain we got
every last one out, slowing down our entire operation. The computer read-outs showed me that we were again losing money. I
had to find a better way and decided to try a simple solution first.

"Instead of waiting until they're all processed, why not get rid
of the bad potatoes right away? Why not put a few more women
up on our sorting table, with instructions to pull every imperfect
spud and cut out its blemishes before it ever hit our processing
lines? I called in my manager and explained: 'Get two dozen of our
skinniest women up on that sorting table, and if you have to hire
a few more, do it, but make sure they're thin!' I wasn't trying to
discriminate against heavier women, but that table only had so
much space. If we were going to pack that many sorters around it,
they'd have to be on the slender side. And my little innovation
couldn't have worked out better. Once the potatoes were going
onto the dehydration line as a close to perfect raw product, we had

no further problems making grade, production shot up, and our costs dropped to acceptable levels."

"I made a real mistake when I hired that fellow from General Foods, but overall I ended up with a fine crew, men and women who were both hardworking and capable. Getting a first-rate quality control person right away was maybe the most critical, and I was real fortunate to hire a dedicated young man named Nelson Perry away from Rogers Brothers. Nelson was still in his early twenties back then, but he definitely knew his job, and he sure wasn't afraid to put in long hours.

"You're always going to have problems with a start-up operation, so whenever Nelson felt he had to, he stayed right on the job, many times right through the night. He even brought along his own pillow so that when he had everything running smoothly, he could catch a few hours sleep on his office couch. At the slightest sign of another production glitch, our foreman had orders to wake him, and he'd get right on it."

Forty

UNION HARASSMENT
AND WORKER LOYALTY

A s his plant was getting started, George also knew that he didn't want any labor problems and did everything he could to avoid them. In 1966 the Teamsters moved into the Columbia Basin and started a major recruiting campaign in the food processing industry. Workers at the big Lamb Weston frozen foods plant right next to George's facility immediately voted to unionize, but his crew rejected their overtures.

"It was a good thing, too," George firmly states, "because in those first couple of years we had to do things differently than the more established plants. For instance, I knew from the outset that I had to make every promotion based strictly on a person's ability, not on any type of seniority system as the union would have demanded, and this wasn't simply a matter of making my plant a bit more efficient. It was a matter of survival. I had to find the right people, hard workers who caught on fast, and quickly move them into our critical positions. One young fellow who started out right at the bottom, pushing a broom, became a shift foreman in less than six months simply because he had what it took.

"Plus, to avoid waste, dehydration plants need to run continuously, twenty-four hours a day, seven days a week, holidays and all. To accomplish this we put our full-time workers on varied schedules, working seven-and-a-half-hour days, six days a week. We had this all programmed out, with different lunch breaks, crews overlapping a little, everything we needed to do to keep our dehydrating machines up and running, turning out our product around the clock. My crew understood why we had to do this and accepted it. In fact, the majority of our people really liked their varied schedules because they could take care of things like banking and doctor's appointments during their breaks. But a big union would have fought me all the way on this, particularly running straight through the holidays.

"Looking back, I'm convinced that being a comparatively small operation was a real factor in avoiding early labor problems. It gave me and my managers far better rapport with all our workers. Almost every day my crews would see me around the plant, working on problems or just checking to make sure everything was running right. And once again, Ray Young and Harry Blackfield were real assets. One or the other always seemed to be around, willing to talk to workers who were a bit down, sometimes simply lifting their spirits, sometimes helping them understand our long-range goals.

"It helped too that I was always ready to listen to suggestions from anyone working on our line, no matter what their status, and I didn't do this just to make them feel good. Too often the guys at the top of an organization only want to listen to each other or maybe to a foreman or two, but it's your hands-on people who first spot a problem, and just about as often they can recommend a practical solution. They're the people who are with the machines day after day, and even if they don't have the engineering or mechanical skills to understand everything or make the right changes, they're often blessed with real common sense. Oh, sometimes a guy would get all fired up about an idea he was sure was going to revolutionize our entire production, and it turned out to be critically flawed, but it wasn't hard for my engineers to separate the wheat from the chaff.

"And it sure helped to have a few trusted employees like Ray Young, who would come to me when they saw that something wasn't quite right. In the early sixties Ray's drinking had cost him

his marriage, and I'd had to buy his farm or see him lose it to creditors, but a year or two later he joined Alcoholics Anonymous and
straightened himself out. Plus he still knew potatoes, so I'd made
him my raw product procurement man. Besides handling his own
job, the guy had so many close friends both in and out of our plant
that he'd usually hear about a potential employee-management
problem long before it became a full-blown confrontation. Then
he'd quietly let me know what to expect, and I'd figure out the
best way to head it off.

"A couple of people claimed that Ray was acting as my
informant, and maybe he was, but neither of us ever had any kind
of vendetta. I never felt that I had to be on the lookout for trou-
blemakers, or anything like that. In fact, in every case Ray's information helped me deal more openly with my crew. Together we'd
work through their problems.

"The only time I did have a group of workers vote to go
union was at our fresh packing shed, mainly because a couple of
my foremen were sexually harassing some of our female line workers, and they'd both hired their girl friends, then put them into
supervisory jobs, promoting them ahead of more qualified women.
Right about then, I was too tied up with my dehy plant to spend
any time there, and somehow Ray never heard about it.
Unfortunately, no one else came forward to tell me what was
going on until after that union vote. By then I'm sure those
women thought unionizing was their only protection, but if I'd
known in time, those two guys would have been long gone, and
everyone in that packing shed would have understood that harassment and favoritism of any kind weren't going to be tolerated.

"Harry Blackfield was another mainstay. As soon as we
started building our plant, he and Ray were always around, ready
to help out. If either one heard about a critical piece of equipment
or even a part that we needed, immediately he'd be trying to
locate it. Or they were making the right contacts or checking out
our sub-contractors, even though neither one was on the payroll
yet. They simply wanted to be involved, to see this new plant
grow and prosper.

"Harry was so eager to help that at times I had to be careful
about what I told him because as soon as he heard that I needed

something, he'd work for days trying to get it for me. I remember one day when he suddenly disappeared. Somehow he'd found out that we were missing a critical machine part, had made a few phone calls and located it in a little town better than a hundred miles away, then jumped in his car and drove over there to pick it up. This kind of loyalty was great, but I sure didn't want to take advantage of it.

"Once we were up and running, I hired Harry as my sales rep at large. Other salesmen had regular routes, but on the spur of the moment I'd send Harry wherever he was needed. By then he wasn't tied to a family, so he was always ready to go. He'd get a new assignment, pack his bags, and the next day be in Los Angeles, Chicago, Atlanta, anyplace where we had potential customers, using that old Blackfield charm to get us new accounts. His only problem was that over the years he'd become a bit too footloose, always ready to move on to the next town. I'd send him to some place like Los Angeles, where I expected him to stay for a week, and after three days I'd discover he'd moved on, maybe to Dallas, Houston or even Chicago.

"Harry always had a reason why he'd left the last place, though the truth was he'd developed too much of a restless streak. He thoroughly enjoyed being on the go, but this was one little pleasure of his I finally had to curtail. With all their flying around, my reps were a major business expense, anyway, so I had to make Harry understand that he had to stay in a city until he'd worked on every possible transaction."

Guys like Nelson Perry, Ray and Harry might have been the most involved in George's new plant, but today he feels that almost his entire crew saw themselves as a team, where everyone had a job to do, and they all wanted to make the new enterprise go. They weren't part of a giant corporation, where the owners and the directors were just names on the paper work, and many of the laborers showed up only when they absolutely had to and then did the bare minimum to collect their paychecks.

"I've always felt good about those two union rejections," George recounts. "Sure, maybe we could have survived becoming a union shop, but it would have set us back. More importantly, those no votes showed the kind of loyalty you only get when you treat your workers right.

"The teamsters always targeted management as unfair, but many of their own tactics were downright ruthless. They'd sneak into our plant at night when everyone was busy and throw a wire cleaning brush into the shredder, sending tiny fragments all through our line, contaminating an entire batch of potatoes. Running any foreign object like this through the line not only meant dumping tons of product, but we'd have to shut down for hours and completely clean every piece of equipment. Another night a union goon would throw a handful of nuts and bolts into our cutters to break them, anything to mess us up.

"As the plant owner, the union brass would drag me over to Moses Lake for meetings with the Federal Relations Board, supposedly for negotiations. But all they did was rehash the same old themes, wasting my time. They knew as well as I did that all this was pointless, that I wasn't about to swing over to their line of thinking. The feds were supposed to mediate, but the ones that came over to Moses Lake were nothing but another arm of the union. In their eyes an employer was always in the wrong, the union always right. Those meetings were just a different form of harassment, a way of disrupting my busy schedule and hopefully breaking down my resolve. But as long as I had a crew that voted to stay non-union, I wasn't about to give in."

Forty-one

MACHINES AND
COMMON SENSE

Just as he had always done in his farming and packing operations, George now started looking at each process of dehydration, asking himself and then his engineers why it couldn't be done differently, more efficiently. Whenever he felt as if he had a possible answer, he first ran it past his engineers, then put it to the test.

"I sure couldn't make any of these changes myself," he acknowledges. "That's why I'd assembled top notch engineers and mechanics. But when I was convinced a change was in order, I'd explain what I wanted, then stand back and let the skill guys take over. I still think that's the best thing about being the person in charge. You get to put your ideas into practice and make final decisions. Of course the real downside is that you'd better not be wrong too many times. In the business world you'll hear the expression 'You'd better be right sixty percent of the time.' It's a good saying, but from what I've seen, I'd raise that on-the-plus-side figure by at least ten points."

An early right decision had come when George ordered the plant's equipment. Anticipating future expansion, he oversized everything, purchasing bigger boilers, cookers and coolers than other dehydration plants were using. Immediately these oversized items gave his operation an unexpected advantage. Larger equipment meant that his crew had more time to cook and cool the raw product, so they could slice potatoes a third thicker than the industry standard, resulting in far less cell breakage.

At the time almost all of the Basin's crop land was rill irri-. gated. This, coupled with the region's long hot growing season, created a much denser potato than those grown by George's Idaho competitors. Dehydrated solids, what is left of a potato after the water is removed, averaged twenty-four percent in that part of Washington, compared to Idaho's nineteen to twenty percent. This meant that the new plant would get about one-fifth more finished product out of every processed ton.

"I'd hired Myles Willard as a consultant, a fellow who'd essentially invented the potato flake when he was with the U.S.D.A.," George recalls. "Myles knew we had a good thing with our high solids. But he'd also theorized that the consumer would have to add less liquid to rehydrate our product because we'd be taking less out of the raw potato. That made sense to me. Right away, though, our own cooking tests quickly debunked this theory. Instead we discovered that even when we added a normal amount of water or milk, our cooked mashed potatoes came out way too dry. It turned out that with so much less cell breakage, our dehydrated potatoes were far more absorbent than anyone else's.

"To get a decent taste, we had to add more liquid, not less, to rehydrate, adding that much more bulk to the cooked product. This simply meant that a consumer was going to get more servings from a pound of our product than he'd get from a pound of our competitors'. We were absolutely astounded. As soon as we started putting on demonstrations, so was everyone else who understood food service costs.

"Immediately I had bags printed up stating 'Guaranteed 10% More Servings.' Actually the added liquid boosted it to around fifteen percent, but I didn't feel I could guarantee that so I dropped it back a bit. Still, those bags were going to be a real hit. An extra ten percent may or may not mean that much to the average housewife, but home use wasn't our big market. We had to sell to

SPIRIT OF THE SON 249

the institutional buyers such as schools, prisons, hospitals, the restaurant and big lunchroom suppliers, anyone who had to think in terms of the overall cost of feeding hundreds of people every day. Getting a guaranteed ten percent more servings for their dollars was going to be very popular with these people. When they discovered they could easily beat our figure, they were even more impressed.

"Some states that had previously specified 'Rogers Brothers Quality or Better' when they were ready to accept bids changed this to 'Yoshino Western Quality or Better.' This gave us guaranteed sales because at the time there wasn't another processor in the country that could meet these specs. Orders started pouring in."

Despite his jubilance at discovering this early advantage, George knew that he still had other problems to solve. Before his potatoes could be sliced, diced and dehydrated, they had to have their peels removed. Processors across the country were accomplishing this by first running the raw spuds through huge vats of boiling water mixed with high concentrates of a caustic acid, then running them onto screens and using a pressurized hot water spray to knock the skins off.

"From day one we were running into several major problems with this," George says, his recollections creating a slight grimace. "First, up to thirty-five percent of every potato we processed was getting washed away with its peel, a loss we simply couldn't afford. Second, all the caustic acid we had to use just to break down those peels was expensive, besides being dangerous to handle and a real environmental hazard. That acid was the main reason processing plants needed those big industrial sewage lines.

"I knew that if I could come up with a better method, it was going to be a real win-win situation. Cutting back on that acid was both the right thing to do, and it made economic sense. Besides saving big dollars on the acid itself, I wouldn't be running as much risk of the government eventually stepping in with new rules that forced us to make changes. I've rarely seen a government regulation that wasn't less effective and more costly than a good common sense decision.

"My first idea was to run our potatoes through a pair of warm water tanks, each containing a small amount of acid, but that had

a few drawbacks. Then it hit me! Why not put them on a retention belt and run them very slowly through a single tank with a
much lighter acid mixture? This would give the acid more time to
sink in. My idea seemed so simple and I was so sure it would work
that I couldn't understand why it wasn't already in practice.

"Immediately I called in my engineers, explained my concept, took all their input and then had our mechanics set up the
machinery. We had to do a fair amount of experimenting, making
little modifications at every step. What we finally came up with
was putting a small amount of acid in a first tank, moving all our
potatoes slowly through it on a wide retention belt, then letting
them sit out in the open air for exactly one minute before moving
them into a second tank, this one filled with nothing but hot
water. After that we could quickly and easily remove the skins
with a fine hot water spray.

"Once we had this all in place, our new system still had a few
bugs, but when we worked these out, we cut our acid use by seventy-five percent, and our product loss dropped all the way from
thirty-five down to ten percent, far better on both counts than
anyone else in our industry. In fact when the U.S.D.A fellows
came up and inspected our new process and went over our data,
they couldn't have been more pleased, particularly with our caustic wastes reduction. Before ten years had elapsed, they'd get
potato processors all across the country to adapt our methods. Too
bad I didn't patent that idea."

Forty-two

FROM INTEGRITY
TO PAYOLA

To make it in the increasingly competitive dehydrated foods industry, technological breakthroughs were significant, but getting into bigger and better markets was every bit as vital. His sales reps made some early progress, but the new plant's first big coup came when George landed a contract to be General Mills' sole supplier of dehydrated potato slices, to be used in their Betty Crocker brand au gratins.

"Harry Blackfield made our first contact with General Mills, and he did it with a flair," he recounts. "A Northwest Airlines pilot was one of his many friends, so Harry got this guy to pick up a fresh king salmon in Seattle and fly it to Minneapolis, where he presented it to G. J. Westberg, their number one man in charge of purchasing. It was a small gift, the only kind General Mills personnel ever accepted, but it was a good introduction, a real ice breaker. Westberg was more impressed by the fact that Harry could deliver a fresh salmon that far inland than he was with the gift itself.

"Anyway, General Mills started us out with a small order. Just to make sure that we did everything right, I sent Nelson Perry to their plant to observe and find out exactly what they needed, then come back and tell us if we had to make any changes. When Westberg heard about Nelson's mission, he was definitely pleased that we were trying so hard, but he was even more impressed with the quality of that first small shipment of potato slices. Apparently Nelson had really done his job, and the guys back at our plant had done theirs because right away General Mills designated us their sole supplier.

"Later Mr. Westberg told me they'd never done that before with a first year firm, but he and their other corporate heads really believed in our product. Naturally, I was thrilled to hear that and more determined than ever to never let them down. General Mills people were good to work with but real sticklers for quality. As long as you gave them that, everything was fine. If they started getting a flawed product, they'd cut you off in a second.

"I sure enjoyed dealing with Westberg, who'd grown up in Tacoma and still had strong ties to our state. The best thing about him was his own sense of honor. He never once asked for a kick-back or even hinted that he should receive a large present or two. In fact, he was very careful about accepting small favors. One summer he was in our state anyway, so he came to Quincy to look over our plant and brought his wife and kids along.

"It turned out that they were all much more excited about my farming operation than about watching our dehydrating machines operate. Everything from how we irrigated to the large variety of crops we were raising just seemed to fascinate them. Naturally I had to give the whole family the grand auto tour. Late that morning we were checking out a field not too far from my home when I realized that it was almost noon. So I radioed Frances and asked if she'd fix us all a little lunch, nothing elaborate, just soup and sandwiches.

"I guess the family enjoyed that little lunch a whole lot more than another restaurant meal because a week later Frances picked up our mail and there was a nice thank you note and a fairly expensive gift, just for her. I'm sure it was their way of saying thanks, but Westberg was also making sure that even that simple meal couldn't be construed as some sort of payoff. A little friendship was fine, but he also wanted it clearly understood that all of his business decisions were going to be based on what was best for his company. Like I said, he was a very honorable man. In fact, so was everyone else that I ever dealt with from General Mills."

George's relationship with this giant corporation was so comfortable that when one of his men suggested that he should use General Mills' Big G label on his own product, he was willing to go to them for permission.

"If Carl Doud hadn't tagged me with that moniker a few years earlier, none of us would have ever thought of trying this," he now grins, "and at first I just laughed at the idea. But after we kicked it around, I thought, well, it's a great label, and it sure won't hurt to ask.

"When I approached them, the folks at General Mills were nice about it and said they'd discuss it and let me know. Finally they decided we could use Big G on our fresh product bags and boxes, but not on any of our processed foods. So that's what we did, using Big G as our premium label in fresh pack. Western Maiden, C-21 and Century 21 became the main labels for our dehy packaging."

George was about to discover that these General Mills folks were a real exception in the processed foods arena. Honorable men didn't exactly flourish in this high stakes industry. He hired three sales representatives, experienced men who he counted on to meet the buyers in all the major cities and pick up new orders.

"I guess I was more than a little naive when I started out," he now admits, "because right from the start my salesmen were running into big account buyers who insisted on a meeting with the plant owner. It turned out that they all had the same message for me. Simply put, it said, 'If you want my company's business, first take good care of its buyer!' Oh, there were a few honest ones still out there, but most of the fellows who could swing a million pound contract your way expected more than a new television set or a free trip to Hawaii in return. They figured that they had a hefty under-the-table commission coming, and they weren't at all shy about asking for it. Sure, it was only a tiny percentage of our overall contract, but it was a good chunk of cash nonetheless. That's where I came in. The buyers knew that my reps didn't have the authority to make these payoffs.

"Before long I had a regular schedule, flying to thirteen cities in six days, all over the U.S. A buyer would meet me anywhere that had a little privacy, maybe an executive room at the airport or a nearby motel suite, and right away he'd have his hand out. It was either give these guys what they wanted or forget doing business with their companies. I'd never faced anything like this in the fresh potato markets. These were a different breed, high stakes players who knew how much we needed their big orders, and they were more than ready to take advantage of their positions.

"I wish I could say I rejected all these shakedown artists and only did business with the few honest buyers, but the truth is I had a plant to run. Kickbacks for the contracts we depended on were so pervasive that it was either ante up or go under. In a couple of cases their superiors had to know this was going on because it was so open. Some of the bosses might have been in on it, taking their own cuts. A fellow in St. Louis, a buyer for Banquet T.V. Dinners, was so blatant with his demands and so sure he was untouchable that when I told him I didn't have that much cash along, he offered to take my personal check. He's one guy I did walk away from."

Forty-three

GOVERNMENT
REGULATORS,
A COSTLY LABEL

This new plant also meant that George had to become a member of the national Dry Foods Association and attend their meetings in Chicago. Pillsbury, General Mills, General Foods, Kelloggs, Simplot, and all the other major players in the processed foods industry were all represented. Critical issues were always on the table, including pending government regulations. George would show up alone, but the big companies brought along their high-powered attorneys. Government watchdog groups were always around, trying to make sure there was no collusion between companies, no price setting or anything else that fell under the anti-trust laws.

"Those government folks were the main reason for all those attorneys," George states. "If an attorney saw that a discussion was heading in a dangerous direction, leading to anything the feds could possibly construe as violating anti-trust, they'd quickly step in and shut it off. Without my own attorney, I had to learn in a hurry what I could and couldn't say and early on spent most of those meetings keeping my mouth shut. In this industry you had to be careful. You didn't even have the right to socialize with your competitors because you never knew who might be listening to what you said, and if anything you talked over could be misconstrued, you never knew who might turn you in. It was a nerve-wracking game, totally different than the fresh potato shippers and growers meetings I'd attended, where we'd openly discuss everything in our meetings, including pricing. Then we'd go out for a night of socializing and end up talking business 'til they closed the cocktail lounges."

The processed foods industry had other little nuances that George had to learn to live with. For instance, his sales representative in New York who handled the whole Eastern seaboard, suddenly called him, all in a panic. One of their best East Coast brokers was being pressured to quit dealing with them by two very important Jewish organizations.

"They'd discovered that our packages didn't carry a kosher product symbol," George recalls. "To set things right we needed to do whatever it took to receive one of two seals, either a K. from one of these groups or an O.U. from the other, symbols we could print on our packages to prove our product was kosher and had their seal of approval. Well, I sure didn't want to lose that broker, and when I looked into this problem further, I discovered that we weren't going to survive on the East Coast and probably not in the Midwest without one of those two seals.

"Naturally I turned to my Mr. Diplomat, Harry Blackfield. That same afternoon I had Harry on a plane to New York with orders to check this all out and do whatever it took to get into everyone's good graces. A few days later Harry called me and explained the deal he'd made. I'd pay all expenses for a rabbi to fly out, to bless our plant and do whatever else was necessary. Then all I had to do was write this rabbi a $2,500 check for his troubles and send him on his way. I don't know what I'd been expecting, but if the rabbi's tab had been $10,000, I'd have willingly paid it. A mere $2500, the price of a first class plane ticket and three or four hundred more for related expenses! This all seemed too good to be true.

"The rabbi and Harry arrived in Quincy just before lunch, so the first thing I did was take them both to our local restaurant.

Right away the rabbi insisted he couldn't eat off the restaurant's porcelain because it might be contaminated with traces of pork grease. His dishes all had to be glass, and he'd only take liquids, soup broth and juices. In a little Northwestern town like Quincy, this became quite a show. Before we left the place, he had that whole restaurant in a turmoil. After that I took him to our plant and turned him loose. In less than an hour he was back in my office. Everything was checked out and blessed, he explained. So I gave him his $2,500 check and we said our goodbyes. At first I was thrilled, but then I remember thinking, 'Man, this was just way too easy, way too inexpensive. The other shoe just has to drop!' It sure did, with a real resounding thud.

"It wasn't two weeks later that I discovered our real costs. There was one additive called Myverol that we had to use to make dehydrated potato flakes, a type of lubricant that keeps the cells from rupturing as they go through processing. Eastman Kodak was the lone supplier of this additive, and suddenly they informed us that they'd now only sell us their kosher product, which they said had to be made off a separate purified line, with absolutely no belts so there'd be no chance of pork grease contamination.

"I had no problem with that, but the real kicker was that this kosher additive would cost us three times as much as we'd been paying for the non-koshered Myverol. There was no way a slightly altered process could increase their production costs by three times, so here's where the big bucks were going to be made. Either Eastman Kodak was on a real gravy train, or they were filtering a whole lot of dollars back to those K. and U.O. organizations. Still, I had no realistic options. We needed pounds and pounds of Myverol every year, and all I could do was fork over the extra bucks. Conservatively, I figured it was going to cost us an extra $40,000 annually."

Fortunately the dehy plant had the kind of early successes to handle added costs, and good things kept happening. That first year they were also dehydrating carrots and soon discovered they had another fine product. Their only real competition was from a plant in California, a company that turned out tons and tons of dehydrated carrots. But its raw product always had a large yellow core, a color that showed up in the finished product.

"Our Washington carrots didn't have a yellow core, so our dehys retained that nice red carrot color," George explains. "In fact, after dehydration they were still so bright that our competitors accused us of adding artificial coloring, which was totally baseless. We had a naturally good raw product, and we sure weren't about to tamper with it. Anyway, Knorr Soup, a German company and a division of Corn Products, was so impressed that right away they offered to sign a contract to purchase all the carrots we could dehydrate. I wanted to hold a small percentage back to distribute to other soup and T.V. dinner companies, just to build a better base for years to come, but Knorr insisted on taking it all and set a price I couldn't reject."

Forty-four

GOLDEN MOMENTS AND
A PROMISE BROKEN

The new dehydration plant's first two years of operation paralleled several pleasant events in the lives of Frank and Kazuye. After leaving the farm with its four acre orchard and moving into a Moses Lake home his son bought for him, Frank continued to garden, planting a half dozen new fruit trees, a small plot of vegetables and bed after bed of beautiful flowers. In his little greenhouse he could nurture seedlings and experiment with new flowers and vegetables. Best of all, he glowed with pride over his son's latest project.

"Yeah, I think the dehy plant meant as much to Pop as it did to me," George muses. "Of course I didn't burden him with my headaches. I just kept him informed about our successes and long-range plans. He didn't come out to see the plant that much. All that noisy machinery was way beyond his comprehension, so it wasn't a place where he wanted to hang out, but just talking about it sure brightened his smile."

Ground breaking for Yoshino Western Dehy had barely been underway in early 1965 when George had given his parents their own special day, a Golden Wedding Anniversary party. He had rented Elmer's Restaurant in Moses Lake, invited all his and his parent's friends, then got his old pals, Harry Blackfield and Jim Ward, to bring in special dinners, catered from the El Gaucho Restaurant in Seattle. Ward absolutely refused payment for his food or his services, and of course Harry was only too glad to do this for his number-one friend.

"It was a great day in all our lives," George now fondly recalls. "By then Pop was eighty-five, Mom sixty-seven. Many of their friends were even older, but they came anyway, from Kennewick, Seattle, all the way up from California, bringing gold plated gifts in honor of that special day. As I looked at all those old people, so happy to be there, I couldn't help feeling that it was a real testament to the strength of Mom and Pop's many friendships.

"I was so caught up in the spirit of the day that I broke away from my normal reserve and sang for Mom, belting out a couple of her favorites, 'Impossible Dream' and 'Moonlight Becomes You.' She'd always liked my voice, ever since I'd made a recording for her way back when I was in high school, a recording she kept her whole life. On that big anniversary day she literally beamed when I was going through my songs. As soon as I'd finished, she hugged me and told me that I sang beautifully. She was a fine mother but, as one of my pals snidely pointed out, maybe she wasn't the world's foremost voice critic."

Less than a year later, when the dehydration plant was up and running, Frank was to be given an even greater honor. From 1960 on he and Kazuye had made yearly trips to Japan, mainly to visit family and friends. Now he had been invited to an audience with Emperor Hirohito, to be presented with the prestigious 'The Order of the Sacred Treasure' medal, recognizing his efforts to cement cultural and economic relations between the two nations. Once again he and Kazuye would make this long trip together, this time as their homeland's honored guests.

"Before Pop left, I spent a few hours briefing him on our export problems with Japan," George recalls. "We had to use chemicals designated B.H.A. and B.H.T. in our dehydrated potatoes to prevent rancidness, chemicals that were U.S.D.A approved and had been accepted by most foreign countries as totally safe for consumers. Japan had imposed sanctions, not because of any genuine safety issues, but only because of the protectionist pressures they were getting from their own agricultural industry. We had substitutes we could use, but until we knew what they'd accept, we couldn't move ahead.

"Before the medal ceremony, Pop was given a long private audience with both the Emperor and Prime Minister Saito where he had the chance to explain all of this. He told me later that they both listened very intently, agreed that their trade barriers had to be lowered, and they promised to look into the matter. As things turned out, our plant would never benefit from these talks, but I've always felt that Pop did important legwork for our entire food processing industry and was a real ambassador of goodwill for this country. It sure helped that he went over there as a man of real stature and was fluent in the language. No, things didn't change overnight, but a few years later these sanctions were removed.

"Mom told me later that when Pop sat next to the Emperor at their big banquet, all he talked about was me, my accomplishments, my future, how we were going to rapidly expand our dehydration plant. She said his voice was so deep and so loud that before long everyone in that big room stopped their own conversations and started listening to what he had to say. That's always made me feel good. In a way Pop was returning to his homeland once again feeling like a real man, a man with authority. Maybe now it was because of his son's accomplishments rather than his own, but that was okay with Pop. After all, for him too, it was always all about family.

"And as Mom was telling me this, I could picture Pop, his deep voice resonating through that entire room, and I understood how thrilled he must have been to be my representative, to speak to all those important people on my behalf. I'll always be glad that I helped give Pop his grand moment. Maybe it partially made up for everything he'd gone through and everything he'd lost."

Unfortunately a painful negative memory mars George's otherwise pleasant recollections of his parent's trip. He wasn't with them. Originally he had been scheduled to join Governor Dan Evans and several other prominent Washington politicians and industry leaders on a ten day goodwill tour of Japan, a tour that would have coincided with part of his parents' stay. He would have been present at his father's medal ceremony, certainly an important moment and one he regretted missing. However, his real regret is that by canceling his trip, he broke a promise he had made four years earlier to the man he considered his second father, Uncle Takejiro.

"This really goes back to right after the war," George sadly reflects. "While he was stationed in Japan, Elmer had looked up our cousins and discovered that during all the years Uncle Takijero was in America, his sons had been receiving his military pension. I guess it was only the weak son who'd come to America because these were honorable young men. They'd used every bit of their father's pension to invest in land, all of it in his name.

Elmer explained this to the old man, telling Uncle that he'd even been shown his holdings, and that a couple of them now had tremendous value. One of the bigger parcels had already been turned into a first-class golf course. Elmer tried to convince him that if he'd go back, he'd be well off and treated with great respect. His sons, anxious to have their aging father back in their family again, had sworn to this. But Uncle Takejiro would simply shake his head, repeating his old phrase, 'No, there's nothing for me back there,' and then add a new one, 'Everybody is lying!'

"Well, we all let this slide until 1961 when Mom and Pop started putting pressure on Takejiro to go back, not necessarily to stay, but at least to see his children and older relatives who were still alive. To my parents this was vital. If at all possible an aging person should reestablish family ties, ties they considered almost sacred. My uncle refused, as if he feared making this trip, even for a short visit.

"As I've said, Uncle Takejiro and I hadn't spent much time talking after I grew up, but I knew that he still had great respect for me. He was always talking to Pop about all the different crops we were raising, or quizzing him about my latest land or potato shed acquisition, and I knew he'd been almost as thrilled as Pop over all the talk about our new dehy plant. He didn't say much to me about any of this, and it sure wasn't in his makeup to show me or anyone else any outward displays of affection. But I knew that my successes were a real source of pride for him too.

"And from childhood on I'd known that I was my uncle's favorite, the one he liked having around, the one he counted on to become the kind of man he could respect and admire. Over the years I'd become far more of a son to him than the ones he'd left behind or the glib talker who'd followed him to America. Our relationship was a quiet one, based more on mutual respect and trust than on a whole lot of words, but now I felt it was time for me to go to him and do some talking, to see if I could convince him to make this journey, or at least to find out why he was so set against it.

"It turned out to be the best talk we'd had in years. We covered the past, the future, why I thought a trip back to Japan might be best for him, what returning to his native land and his family could mean in his final years. For once my uncle was very responsive, far more open than he'd been with anyone else. He even told me a little about his fears and why he doubted these stories about all the land he owned and the reception that awaited him. I knew that he always worried about running low on funds and getting stuck somewhere, and despite all of my reassuring talk I could see that he still had grave doubts about returning to Japan. So finally I told him, 'Look, you go, and if you need money or anything else, I'll be there for you. If the stories about the land you own aren't true, if your sons aren't respectful, or if for any reason you feel mistreated or simply don't like it in Japan, all you have to do is write or call me, and I will personally come for you.'

"As soon as I'd said all this, I could see the old man changing his stance. When I gave him my pledge, Uncle Takejiro trusted me because he knew I'd always been a man of my word. It was my promise that finally convinced him to make the journey that for so many years he'd dreaded. He went to Japan with my folks, and after spending time with his children and our other relatives and seeing the property he actually did own, he chose to stay. Of course I figured everything was better than just all right.

"But when he heard that my folks were coming for their big ceremony, Uncle Takejiro immediately wrote to Mom and said, 'Please tell George to come too. I need to see him.' By then I already had my passport and my airline tickets. All the arrangements had been made through the governor's office. Then the week before we were scheduled to leave was the week when I fired that plant manager. The very next day my production manager quit because I wouldn't promote him into that position, throwing my entire operation into a real turmoil. Without these two latest problems, I'd been worrying sick about being away from this new plant for three long weeks. Now my back was against the wall. From a businessman's standpoint, I simply couldn't leave.

"When I canceled that trip, I quickly rationalized. I told myself I'd break away in a few months and go to my uncle on a fast plane. But of course the demands of a new plant and everything else I was doing weren't about to let up, so that was never going to happen. When he found out that I wasn't along on that first trip, Mom told me Uncle Takejiro was very disappointed, but he never would tell either her or Pop why he needed to see me.

"My uncle died less than two years later. Had he simply wanted to tell me goodbye? Was he being mistreated and needed me to get him out of Japan? I have no way of knowing, but it must have been something very important or he wouldn't have said that he needed to see me. And I do know this: when my uncle asked me to come to him, I should have gone, just as I'd promised, no matter what had to be left behind. Once again, I put my business first. I broke my word."

Forty-five

A BROTHER'S NEW PROBLEMS BECOME INSURMOUNTABLE

Temporary management problems may have caused George to break his word to his uncle, an act that to this day hurts him deeply, but these personnel problems turned out to be minor glitches in his dehydration plant's remarkable early success. When he was rid of his less than competent plant manager, he personally stepped into that position and made the necessary changes. Rapid expansion seemed right on the horizon. George envisioned a facility that would be five times the size of this start-up operation, one that would dehydrate larger quantities of potatoes and carrots, plus asparagus, peas and peppers. Onions would require a separate processing plant, a facility he already had on the drawing board.

Once again, though, his favorite brother was becoming a major concern. Vic was still the same willing worker, but suddenly he was going through an alarming personality change, switching from George's comparatively laid-back cooperative partner to an aggressive, even belligerent adversary.

"There was simply no way I could have predicted what was about to happen," George sadly reflects. "Vic and I had just gone through a fourteen-year partnership without a single significant problem, nothing but years of hard work and total cooperation. We were again the best of brothers, a relationship built on mutual admiration, trust and caring. As I've said, in some ways Vic knew more about the farming end of our operation than I did, and he'd always been more than willing to put his efforts into that, letting me handle the land acquisitions, the marketing, anything that involved more communication skills or got into complicated financing. By nature Vic wasn't aggressive enough to get into these arenas but seemed pleased and proud when he saw what I could do. Mutual friends would tell me how Vic bragged about me, saying I was the best marketing man in the whole country.

"Our problems surfaced in the mid-sixties, but later I'd realize that Vic's personality changes, the real cause of our problems, had much earlier beginnings. They'd started with my brother's poorly diagnosed and poorly treated health problems in the late summer of '61. We had a company policy back then that said everyone in management had to have yearly flu shots, but Vic hated needles so much he'd ignored this. Suddenly he was down with a real nasty bout, one of those dreaded Asian varieties that had swept the country. Vic started seeing the local doctors, but never getting any better.

"Early that fall I was in Montana, hunting deer and antelope with Ray Young, Bill Anderson and a couple other guys when Vic's wife Betty called me, in a complete state of panic. Vic's condition had taken a severe turn for the worse. Betty actually believed he might die. But sick as he was, Vic swore he wouldn't go to any hospital unless I was there to go with him. I barely took the time to tell my host what the problem was before I was in my car and burning up the highway. When I walked into his bedroom and saw my brother, I sure understood his wife's fears. Vic was in horrible shape, burning with fever. He'd lost so much weight, and now coughing spells wracked his thin body.

"No more local doctors for him," I immediately swore. "Vic's going to Virginia Mason Hospital. As fast as Betty could get him ready, I had him in the back seat of my car and was speeding towards Seattle. Within a day the Virginia Mason doctors figured out that he had encephalitis, a flu bug that had attacked his brain.

Now it simply had to run its course, they explained, and hospitalization wasn't necessary. So I took my brother home again.

"But once back in Othello, Vic kept running back to his local doctor, getting more and more prescriptions. The first real change I saw in him was that he became very medicine conscious, actually enamored of all those pills, and he loved to show them off. Any time someone he hadn't seen for a while came around, Vic would pull out his big plastic case and show off his pills, going into this long litany of what each one did for him and why he couldn't stop taking it. Then suddenly he was displaying mid-morning drunk symptoms, staggering around, slurring his words, even having occasional blackouts. Right away I ran him back to Virginia Mason. At first the doctors thought he had a tumor or multiple sclerosis, but the tests proved negative.

"The real problem was that Vic wasn't being totally honest with them. They'd ask, but he'd never say a word about all the drugs he was taking, so of course they had no way to diagnose the possible side effects. Finally they just told me to take him home and keep him in bed for a few weeks. When I had Vic back home again, I demanded to know if he was taking Placidyl, the sleeping pill that had messed me up so badly a few years earlier. At first he denied it, but finally he confessed. He swore that taking it was the only way he could get any sleep. I wouldn't argue because I knew how damaging that drug could be. I simply destroyed his supply and warned him to start playing straight with those Seattle specialists. I even tried to get him to stay away from one local doctor, who I was convinced was giving him way too many different drugs. But he wouldn't go along with that. All those pills had become too important to him.

"Getting rid of Placidyl eliminated his drunken symptoms, and it let Vic function again, but by then his personality was changing. For instance, for years I'd been getting invited to all kinds of out-of-town functions by my business and political contacts, gatherings that were a mix of socializing, business and making new contacts. I'd always made sure that Vic knew where I'd be and what I hoped to accomplish, partly so he could get in touch in an emergency, but also to make sure he felt involved. A couple of times I'd invited him along, but he'd just shake his head, smile and say all of that social stuff was my job.

"Then suddenly Vic started showing up at all these gatherings. I sure didn't mind him being there, and neither did anyone else. In fact, if he'd as much as hinted he wanted to go, I'd have brought him with me. But he'd never say a word. He'd just show up. I'd always wonder why, and I think other people did too, because he never had any agenda. In fact, he was always pretty quiet, as if he simply wanted to be part of that crowd.

"Of course this alone was minor, but I guess it was part of the new Vic. His next change was far more disturbing. Suddenly my easy-going brother was becoming aggressive, wanting to make more and more of our company decisions. By 1963 he'd decided he should run our Othello packing shed and started spending his time at that facility. This created a couple of real problems. First, Vic didn't know what it took to run a business like that and he sure didn't understand marketing, so I had to continue to give it guidance, pulling the strings from above. What was worse, he began to seriously interfere with our manager, a fellow who did know his job.

"At the same time Vic was neglecting our Othello farm operation, which had always been his real strength. Then when he did spend a few hours at the farms, he wasn't making good decisions and treated his top men with contempt. This got so bad that Geo Matsumura, who was our Othello farms manager and a long-time friend of Vic's, finally came to me for help, asking me to come over there and straighten that whole mess out. Vic's orders were so contradictory, and he'd get so nasty when anyone tried to talk to him that his men often didn't know what they were supposed to do. I tried, but by then I wasn't getting through to my brother either. A month later Geo quit.

"I felt that part of what Vic was experiencing might be my fault, that as president of our companies I'd been making all the major decisions, and he felt too left out, too unimportant. So in 1964 I set up a five-man board, the three of us brothers, plus our attorney and accountant. We'd meet and discuss every major decision, then each cast one vote, with the majority ruling. Not only would this give Vic the prestige he suddenly craved, but it would bring him and Elmer more into our business loop. I wanted them both to understand our balance sheets and expansion plans.

"The board's first big vote unanimously supported my decision to go ahead with the plans for the dehydration plant. Its second was to reduce our farming and fresh pack operations' capital expenditures budgets to zero, at least for the next two or three years while we took on the enormous costs of getting the plant up and running. This simply meant that we'd be buying no new equipment, which wasn't going to hurt us because we'd been steadily upgrading. Our farm and packing shed machinery were in excellent shape.

"Vic voted for this new budget change, right along with the rest of us. Then the next thing I knew, he'd gone out and spent almost half a million dollars on new farm equipment, tractors, potato harvesters, trucks. At first I just talked to him and tried to get him to see that he was going contrary to the board's decision and that none of us could do this. But reasoning no longer worked. Right away he'd turn belligerent, arguing that we needed to stay modern, that everything he'd purchased was for the good of our farms and that we couldn't let that slide just because I'd built a new plant.

"Because he was a full partner, I couldn't simply order him to stop purchasing this stuff. His name was on a big line of credit contract we had, and when he started becoming irresponsible, there was no way I could get it off. His signature was as good as mine. Canceling that line of credit wasn't an option either, because we needed it to get the new plant started and to run the rest of our operation. My brother could buy and buy until eventually the bankers were going to step in and close us down.

"Unfortunately Vic had started running with a new crowd, guys he thought of as real businessmen and high flyers. I think he liked showing them all that new machinery, as a way of boasting about our accomplishments. Some of these new friends really used him too, borrowing our equipment, letting Vic pick up the tab when they went on expensive trips.

"These new alliances were even a little spooky. In the spring of '65 I was called in by the Intelligence Office of the I.R.S. Apparently Vic and his new buddies had been playing the commodities market over in Yakima, and there were rumors of shady deals.

"No legal proceedings ever came of that, but I was starting to hear real echoes of our Weiser days, only on a much larger scale. And just like in Weiser, Vic became totally committed to this latest set of unsavory pals and dropped everyone he'd been close to earlier. As one of his former close friends told me a few years later, 'It was as if everyone who'd been Vic's friend became his enemy.' This fellow couldn't have said it better. Unfortunately, I'd always been his best friend, so now I became his worst enemy.

"We were able to absorb Vic's first purchases, but then the next year he did the same thing. He even bought an airplane, a fancy twin engine LaBaron and hired a full time pilot, claiming that he was doing this all for me, so I could fly to my many meetings. The truth was he and his new buddies were using that plane to fly all over the west coast. Nothing makes a banker more nervous than a company that suddenly starts purchasing high-priced airplanes they don't need. I explained this to Vic and insisted that the plane had to go back. He wouldn't relent. Everything I said, no matter how I approached the subject, just seemed to deepen his hostilities.

"That fall and right into the following year Vic's belligerence took a different turn. We'd all agreed that our farms and our fresh pack operations would always make sure that our dehy plant had plenty of product, but suddenly he was fighting me on this too. I'd make arrangements to get several loads of potatoes from our Othello packing shed, send the trucks over, and they'd come back empty. Vic had given orders that they weren't to be loaded, claiming that our fresh pack and dehydration operations were completely separate entities and that I hadn't purchased his potatoes. In a few cases he'd already sold the spuds I needed to a third party.

"By the spring of 1966 so many other things were going so well, especially with our new plant, but my problems with my brother had become intolerable. I could no longer trust him to do the right thing. I had to start giving him definite orders. I told him that there would be no new purchases and no more empty trucks coming back from Othello. He had to follow the decisions of our board. His immediate response was 'All right then, I want out!'

"I realized then that Vic's personality had swung one hundred and eighty degrees, and I didn't see any way to swing it back.

In retrospect, maybe I should have done something more for him, perhaps sought out new doctors or therapists. Of course this is real speculation because I doubt if Vic would have gone in for any kind of treatment, especially if I'd had a hand in setting it up, and right then I had absolutely no time for this anyway. I really didn't know what else to do, so I gave Vic his way.

"For his third Vic received the Othello and Bruce packing sheds and the Othello area farmland. As soon as he was on his own, he had to give up the airplane, and with his medical problems he couldn't even manage the farms, to say nothing of those two sheds. In less than two years he'd lost everything and ended up moving to Canada, where he did small scale farming. Finally he became a Canadian citizen, mainly to take part in their socialized medicine program.

"Looking back, I have to wonder if Vic wasn't also suffering from what psychologists now call the 'middle brother syndrome.' I know as kids he deeply resented Elmer, who was far more outgoing. And despite the fact that all three of us were equal partners financially, our whole enterprise revolved around me and had from the beginning. I was the one who made the deals, dealt with the banks, started new enterprises, became politically involved. When we'd grown to the point where newspapers wanted our story, I did the interviews.

"To me it seemed like the natural order of things. Elmer was never knowledgeable enough for any of this and didn't seem to care, and for years Vic had been more than willing to let me lead. Oh, he knew he wasn't simply another hired man because he did have to make many of our farming decisions. In the end, though, maybe this wasn't enough.

"But I'm sure taking all that medicine was bad for Vic and had a lot more to do with those years of open hostility, not just towards me but towards all his old friends. It wouldn't be 'til the late seventies that we'd mend our friendship. By then his aggression had once again passed, and once again he showed real remorse. If Vic's apologies had ever been necessary, that time too had passed. I was willing to accept him back on any terms.

"I was even able to give Vic some work, checking out Canadian farms for me. But by then his health was definitely on a downhill slide. He was taking lots of prednizone and too many other drugs. He told me himself that he'd become very accident prone. Finally his bones were so brittle from all that prednizone that one day his back snapped when all he was doing was lifting a sack of groceries out of his car trunk. After that he had to live in a nursing home, where he died just a few years later.

"I guess I could dwell on what Vic cost me and the rest of our family, first in Weiser and then in the Basin, but I'd rather remember all of his best years. Sure, things went wrong for him, and yes, he lost control and made some terrible mistakes, but the real Vic, the one I really knew, was a loving brother and a devoted friend."

Forty-six

FINANCIAL PRESSURES, A DISASTROUS DECISION

Splitting with his brother had created another immediate dilemma for George. Giving up the two Othello packing sheds and all that farm land significantly reduced his company's assets without decreasing its debt load. As a result the bankers stepped in, insisting that he take on a new partner, one who had significant assets, at least enough to replace what Vic now owned.

"What the bankers were asking for wasn't unreasonable," George acknowledges. "Our new plant was doing well, but because of the expanded facility and equipment we'd added, our initial building costs had topped our first estimates by about a million dollars, and we'd just gone through that real dollar drain that always accompanies a start-up operation. Without the Othello holdings, our assets were spread pretty thin. Personally I wasn't worried about this because I had no doubt that we'd pull out of the red in just a few years. But I couldn't expect the bankers to have my confidence. I understood their position."

With all of his contacts in the food processing industry, George was sure finding a viable partner wouldn't be difficult. As soon as he put out his first feelers, several solid company owners showed a definite interest. The most promising appeared to be John Bez, who along with his father Nick owned Peter Pan Foods, West Coast Airlines and several other significant companies.

"John was another of the guys Harry Blackfield introduced me to," George says. "He was pretty much running their Peter Pan operation by then, and we had one early talk about jointly marketing our products. Then we met to see if we couldn't co-mingle both our rail car and overland truck freight. Peter Pan had been getting hit hard by high shipping costs, and so were we. If John and I could figure out a way to co-mingle, filling out each other's long distance shipments, we'd both come out way ahead. Somewhere during that second discussion I mentioned that I was looking for a partner and gave him a quick sketch of the details. John was definitely interested."

In February of 1967 George was heading to Seattle for an unrelated business meeting, so he tried to set up another meeting, but John had to be out of town that week. 'Why don't you meet with my dad?' he suggested. Nick Bez would have to be in on any final negotiation anyway, so George quickly agreed. This meeting took place in the elder Bez's Seattle office and quickly turned into a disaster. Nick came on as a gruff, tough, demanding tyrant, not at all like his son. Almost before their introductions were finished, he was telling George what his company would do, exactly how they would do it, and what they would expect of him.

"Within five minutes I was completely turned off," George remembers, grimacing, "more by his tone of voice than what he said, though they were both pretty bad. It was as if Nick thought he was talking to an employee, someone he'd had to haul into his office for a good old-fashioned tongue lashing. After a couple hours of his tirades, never getting to say much myself, I walked out of that office thinking, 'Man, there's absolutely no way I'm going into business with this guy.'

"I'd find out too late that I wouldn't have had to deal with Nick because by then his son was running their operation, and from everything I knew then or would discover later, John Bez was a decent fellow, a solid businessman, and a real straight shooter. It's just too bad that single meeting with his father ever took place. By then the bank was really putting pressure on me, and I'd walked out of Nick's office knowing it was time to intensify my search for a viable partner."

That evening, still smarting from his disconcerting afternoon, George met a couple of his Seattle friends for dinner and drinks. Over cocktails at Rosalini's 4-10 Club, a wealthy businessman named Sid Eland joined the group. George already knew Eland slightly, mainly as a friend of friends. They'd met several years earlier when Sid and several of these friends hunted pheasants on the Yoshino Farms. In the course of that evening George talked a little bit about what he'd just gone through and said it looked as if he was still in search of a partner. Sid, who had been quietly taking this all in, suddenly said 'Maybe I'd be interested.' Not much more was said that evening, but the two agreed to meet the next day.

It didn't take George long to find out that this man had the finances to be a viable partner. Sid owned Best Way Motor Freight, Quench Soft Drinks, a Rainier Beer distributor, as well as valuable Seattle real estate and timber and agricultural lands across the state. Their first real meeting resulted in a second, and everything looked good. Sid was personable, his assets would more than satisfy the bank, and the two seemed to have a lot of the same ideas about what a partnership should entail and were quickly able to iron out minor differences. Before long it was time to call in the attorneys and draw up the final papers. Sid would only put $50,000 into the company, but his name would go on all of Yoshino Western's liabilities. For this he'd take over fifty percent ownership of both the fresh pack and dehydration operations but have no percentage of the farms.

"It was a very good deal for Sid," George admits. "I knew I was giving up a lot, but I saw this as a way to not only satisfy the banks but to go into much more rapid expansion than I could have ever done without his tremendous wealth backing me up. If in the next couple of years I could build an onion dehy plant and all the other facilities I had on the drawing board, I'd definitely feel that giving up half had been worth it. That's what Sid said he wanted us to do, and with his assets we'd have no trouble convincing the loan officers. I felt we were really going into a win-win situation."

"By the time we were drawing up the final contracts, I'd been in Seattle for ten days, trying to run the plant, our sheds and farming operation, all with long distance phone calls. Of course the new plant was my biggest concern, but it was also March, the month when so many of our farm crops had to get in the ground. I was getting desperate to get back to the Basin. The last details on the contract were taking forever, even though everything seemed to be in place and all the provisions agreed to. Finally I was so anxious to leave that I instructed my attorney, a fellow named Jim Kendall from Quincy, to finish up the incidentals. Then I signed the contracts and headed for home.

"Well, in my absence Kendall let Sid and his lawyer slip in several last minute changes. These changes were all bad, but by far the worst was a disclaimer, stating that Sid had no responsibility for our company's outstanding debt. Sharing that debt fifty-fifty had been my sole reason for bringing him in as a partner, to free me from all that banker pressure and let me get on with my expansion plans. In our original contract he'd signed on for all this debt, but now his disclaimer negated this.

"When I first saw this, I simply couldn't understand how Kendall could have let this slip in and hoped there was some mistake. Right away I called Sid's attorney, a man named Wally Aikens, and tried to get this taken out. But he said Sid was adamant. The contract was all signed and legal, and he wasn't about to agree to any further alterations. That's when I knew I'd been had. For a lousy $50,000 Sid had purchased half of Yoshino Western Dehy and Fresh Pack.

"Yeah, my attorney really blew that deal. From the beginning I had the feeling that Sid had offered him something, maybe money, maybe a position. Later, enough things fell into place to convince me that Kendall had sold me out, though I'd never be able to prove this. And of course I had to admit that I'd blown it too, first by not investigating Sid more thoroughly before I started our negotiations, and second by relying on Kendall. I should have been more careful and less trusting. Sure, I tried to blame the pressure I was under from the bankers for that first mistake and the stress of having a huge operation to run for the second, but neither excuse worked. I'd made two horrible blunders. Now the whole balance of power had shifted to Sid, and it didn't take long to find out what he had in mind.

"He knew zero about our operation, but he'd carefully gone over our books and he'd seen our tremendous profit potential, particularly in the dehydration plant, and wasn't about to be satisfied with half of all those dollars. Even by 1966 we'd started making money, which was phenomenal in itself for such a new plant, and with our new markets and greater knowledge of how to keep everything running smoothly, 1967 promised to be far better.

"Sid's first strategy was to undermine my authority. Sometimes the way he went about this was just plain stupid. He'd show up in Quincy right after dinner, hit the local bar for three or four hours, then head over to our plant, drunk and belligerent. As soon as he walked through the doors, he'd start railing at the night crew, criticizing me to anyone within earshot. Next he'd go after my night manager, telling him he was incompetent and needed to be replaced. He'd even attack the workers on our lines, putting them down, using the worst profanity, completely disrupting our whole operation.

"The next morning I'd hear all about all this and get absolutely furious. The first time I called Sid into the office and told him, 'Look, nobody, not you, me, absolutely nobody, goes into this plant drunk. That's a policy I've stressed from day one, and it's not about to change.' Right away Sid apologized, agreed that this was a great policy, even blubbered something about how sorry and ashamed he was. In less than two weeks it happened again and then again. He'd always be so contrite afterwards, but that was all a show. The man's apologies were as insincere as his promises.

"Part of Sid's strategy was to convince my managers and other personnel that they'd be better off without me around. He may not have had a shred of ethics, but he was smart and had realized right away that if he did succeed in getting rid of me, he couldn't run the plant without this crew that I'd so carefully put together. When he couldn't win or buy the men's loyalty, he'd switch to intimidation, telling them that he was the plant's real owner, and they'd better get in line.

"Almost every man, from management and quality control to mechanics and boiler operators, stayed loyal to me. Some of the real key ones, like my top quality control man, told Sid flat out to take a hike when he tried buying or threatening them. These were not only men of integrity, but also guys with real knowledge and skills in this new food processing industry. They all knew that they didn't have to pander to a man like that. After seeing him in action, they wanted no part of any plant he was going to be running.

"Only one of my key people turned against me. My office manager threw in with Sid right from the start, maybe because he believed Sid's line about being the real owner, maybe because he was bribed. Either way, he gave the man everything he asked for and torpedoed me in every way he could.

"The bankers were another grim story. Our major accounts were with the National Bank of Commerce in Seattle. We dealt primarily with a couple of their vice presidents, Walter Funk and Bob Matthews, two men who had very little integrity. They knew that I was the only one signing on our liabilities, and they were equally aware of Sid's tremendous wealth. In their eyes he'd become the new power, and they gave him everything he wanted, even if it was bad for the plant and ultimately endangered their own bank loans. Give any man total control of an operation's finances, and he can start calling all the shots.

"I sure wasn't ready to give up, hoping desperately that I could keep everything together until I'd get a break. But by then I was caught in an unwinnable war. My time had to be spent running the operation because even as I watched our problems magnify, I still believed in the future of that plant. I'd assembled a fine crew, brought in top-of-the-line equipment, made the right modifications, and had strong and growing markets. Throw in our high density potatoes and the potential for dehydrating more and more specialty products, and what more could you ask for? It was just a beautiful operation.

"Oh, like any big business we made mistakes along the way. For instance, in the fall of '67 I was at a meeting in New York and had a hotel suite so that I could entertain our numerous clients. Suddenly, though, it wasn't just our regular clients I was seeing. Different buyers kept coming by the suite or calling me on the phone. All the T.V. dinner people and everyone else in the industry suddenly wanted to buy our product. I was being besieged with orders. At first I was thrilled, but then I started thinking, 'Man, this is way too easy, something's just not right here.' I called Sid, told him what was happening, and said I was flying home so we could assess the situation.

"Back at our Seattle bank, it only took half a dozen quick phone calls to discover what all the panic buying was about. Idaho's potato crop had suffered a hard freeze. Everyone was speculating that very few of their potatoes would be usable for anything. As soon as they heard this, Sid and the bankers quickly agreed that we should quit taking orders and start building up our inventories. They, along with almost everyone else in the industry, expected our late fall and winter prices to go right through the roof.

"But instead, those tons and tons of partially frozen Idaho potatoes were worthless only for the fresh market and the frozen foods processors. Most of them were still salvageable for dehydration, allowing our Idaho competitors to get all the raw product they wanted for practically nothing, in most cases just for hauling it out of storage. Of course the bottom fell out of the dehy market, sticking us with that huge inventory. Sid and the bankers immediately blamed me for making a bad decision, when in fact they had ordered me to hold out for a higher market. If I'd been strictly on my own, I never would have totally cut off sales like that. Sure, I would have held some of my inventory in reserve just in case those early predictions proved accurate, but the philosophy I'd always lived by was that a fixed profit is better than huge speculation.

"Taking the heat for this one big financial setback was minor compared to my real problems with Sid and his banking cronies. The whole time I was working day and night to make things go, he was working almost as hard against me, devising new ways to get rid of me, even if that meant first bringing our whole operation to its knees. Despite hitting the bars and cocktail lounges every single day, he remained clever, always plotting.

"His next tactic was to close down our entire line of credit, for no reason except to put more pressure on me. And this sure worked. We operated under the Lawrence Warehouse System, which was set up to regulate inventories. Lawrence personnel were assigned to our plant, and they used a system of receipts to show everything that was coming in and everything that was going out. This was all turned over to the bank so that we could get our accounts receivable and inventory financing.

"Then suddenly the bank, no doubt at Sid's urging, froze our whole inventory. I had all these outstanding orders, and now I couldn't even fill them. If we'd been on a rising market, we'd have immediately been sued by our customers. Because the market was flat, these accounts just went elsewhere, and I was faced with running a plant with no line of credit and with a frozen inventory. With absolutely no money coming in, it was no time before our payroll checks started bouncing, and I couldn't pay our big power bills. Sid and the bankers refused to budge. My whole operation was quickly collapsing around me.

"When payroll checks bounce in a little town like Quincy, it doesn't take long for everyone to get worked up. I'd get angry calls from business people who were suddenly holding those checks. Most of them were simply scared or angry, but one tavern owner, and I really didn't know this guy, tried to help out, telling my workers, 'Bring your checks to me, I'll cover them.'

"Finally I managed to scrape together enough dollars to cover those payroll checks, but of course this couldn't last. I had four hundred and fifty employees at our fresh pack and dehy plant and another two hundred doing farm-related work. Without a two-way cash flow, we were finished. I had to cease operations, laying everyone off, closing down both the plant and our sheds. This was going to ripple across the entire Basin, but you can imagine what it did to a small town like Quincy. A couple of our town's merchants told me that their sales were cut in half as soon as I closed everything down.

"Sid's next move was to have his attorney call me and say they wanted to file Chapter Eleven bankruptcy. Sid was a clever man, always thinking ahead to his next move. He knew if he could get the plant into bankruptcy court, he could buy it back, pennies on the dollar, and I'd be history. But without my signature, he couldn't file, and there was no way I was going to give him that.

"Instead I started scrambling for someone who'd buy Sid out and right away had several viable offers. Rob Rose, the C.E.O. of Idaho's Rogers Brothers, and a couple of his board members made the trip over and went through everything with me. These guys were willing to buy out Sid's half or purchase the whole plant as long as I'd sign a five-year-contract to stay on as its manager. By that point I was ready to go either way, to do anything it took to get that plant up and running again.

"My friend Ole Bardahl, who owned Bardahl Oil in Seattle, was also ready to step in, and he too definitely had the necessary finances. Even a couple of our local businessmen, Orville Duby of Nexus Chemical and Arlis Aikens who owned the local super-market in Quincy, felt that they could finance a buy-out. General Mills liked our product so much that they were willing to either buy the plant or loan me the money to purchase Sid's half. There were many ways to refinance, but you had to have a willing seller, and again Eland wouldn't budge. Even when he had to realize that not selling meant the whole operation could permanently collapse and he'd lose his investment, he wouldn't hear of it.

"At the time I had a hard time understanding his belliger-ence, but later I realized that a big part of Sid's problem was that every offer we had was contingent on me staying on, either as part owner or at least as the manager, with a long-term contract to run the plant. The way his mind worked, that would have meant he'd lost and I'd won, and Sid hated losing. I'm sure it was something he'd had little experience with in his entire adult life. In fact, for him winning was what this was all about. If he couldn't have that whole operation for himself, he was more than willing to let it go under, even if that cost him a few hundred thousand. With his for-tune that was just a drop in the bucket anyway. Of course, his losses were going to be nothing like mine because by then all my profits from years of farming, packing, and processing were tied up in that dehy plant.

"Before 1968 was over I was forced into involuntary bank-ruptcy. Cliff Collins, an Ephrata attorney who'd sided with Sid from the very beginning, came over with court papers and kicked me out of my office. That was definitely a grim day, maybe as bad as I've ever had in the business world. But I still wasn't ready to give up. I kept looking for the right buyer or a different way to refi-nance, anything I could use to break Eland's stranglehold."

A DREAM DISINTEGRATES

This was definitely a time when George found out who his real friends were. Several people who he had helped and who he had counted on to remain loyal baled out immediately when his financial woes began. Others stepped forward just as quickly, offering their financial or moral support, willing to do whatever they could to help him through this terrible mess.

"A few people really surprised me," he reflects, "because I hadn't known much about them before I was in trouble. Our district's congresswoman, Catherine May, first called me to see if her office could do anything to help get our plant restarted. Then she got in touch with Joshua Green at People's Bank. Green came out and was ready to loan me the money for a buy-out, but here again Sid blocked us.

"Maybe the guy who surprised me the most was John R. Lewis, a well known Moses Lake attorney. Jack was a boisterous, blustering fellow, who'd won his share of big cases and made his share of enemies along the way. In fact, just a few years earlier I'd been in a real shouting match with him myself. But as soon as he heard about the troubles I was having, Jack was on the phone, asking me what he could do to help. And this was no idle offer. In the next couple of years he'd do hours and hours of legal work for me and never charge a dime."

Even with this competent legal help, George was finding it impossible to get past the Eland juggernaut. In about the middle of 1968 Sid called and asked him to come to Seattle. He claimed he was ready to work everything out, to get the operation rolling again. George made the trip, accompanied by his new attorney.

"The truth was all my key employees were ready to come back to work for me but not for him," George states, "and he was totally clueless about putting together a new crew. Sid had finally realized that without me there was no way he could restart that plant or get back our big markets. I knew full well, though, that there was absolutely no way I could ever work with him again and only went because I hoped we could convince him to sell.

"But we weren't in that office half an hour when both Jack and I saw that this meeting was going nowhere and we started to walk out. As soon as Jack cleared the doorway, Sid jumped up from his desk, grabbed my arm, and pleaded 'Don't you go! Let him go but you stay. We'll work this out!' All I could say is 'Just how stupid do you think I am? Do you really think I'm going to let you put me through another two or three years of hell?'

"If I'd thought for a minute there was any chance that things would be different, I'd have listened to his proposal because right then there was nothing I wanted more than to see that plant and my sheds operating again. But I knew that Sid would always be Sid. His mind would always be a one-way street, always searching for new ways to beat you. A renewed partnership would simply have led to more misery on my part, and it would have ended up the same way."

"Yeah, I made some mistakes early on in my career, but as my enterprises grew, I'd tried hard to be aware of and ready for any man who totally lacked scruples," he now sadly reflects, "and until I ran up against Sid, I'd always done a fairly good job of spotting the real shysters. Just this once I hadn't been wary enough, a single mistake that was going to wipe out twenty years of incredibly hard work and planning, and would take paychecks away from hundreds of fine people. Ever since I've wrestled with all those nasty 'why' questions everyone always asks after a major mistake. Why hadn't I checked Sid out, why hadn't I looked carefully into his background and discovered exactly how he'd come into such enormous wealth? Why had I signed that contract and trusted its final details to others?

"I guess part of the answer is that Sid seemed to be a friend of so many friends of mine, so I didn't start out with all my normal suspicions. During our early negotiations, I'd talked to at least a dozen guys who knew the man, and not a single fellow as much as hinted that I could run into problems. Only after it was much too late did I start hearing horror stories about Sid's earlier takeovers, how he'd ruined other people in almost the same way. But for some reason none of my good friends stepped forward and warned me early on. Reflecting back I'm sure this had a lot to do with the kind of man he was. Sid was both smooth and powerful. In any social situation or at the beginning of a new business deal, the guy definitely knew how to talk, how to lull you into believing that he was one of the good guys. In the cocktail lounges, he was always surrounded by people, sometimes negotiating other big-money deals but always buying rounds for his crowd.

"In most cases Sid could simply con a potential adversary. Others he'd terrify with his powerful financial connections. Besides his enormous personal wealth, he sat on the directory boards of several of Seattle's biggest banks, and he wasn't above using these positions to ruin someone he thought had crossed him. I sure wish someone had stepped forward and warned me, but I do understand that anyone who felt forced to deal with this man directly or knew he could harm them indirectly certainly had every reason to fear him. He was totally vicious. It meant nothing to him whether he destroyed one individual or closed down an entire plant and left hundreds of families without a paycheck.

"By the time I knew him, Sid was well past sixty and already one of the wealthiest men in the Northwest. Still, all he thought about was grabbing more, no matter how many people he hurt along the way. I'd already been exposed to plenty of con men and crooks, but I'd never run into anyone like him before, and I haven't since. The man was pure evil, pure greed."

As it turned out, George may have held onto his dream of restarting his dehydration plant and his packing sheds for too long, ultimately costing him his farms. In the spring of 1968 his many problems had at first made it impossible to get farm loans. When U & I Sugar finally agreed to finance his beet crop, it was planted too late, resulting in poor yields. By 1969 he was so absorbed in trying to find new financing that he turned too many of the important farming decisions over to his oldest brother.

"Elmer understood that we were in trouble and he really tried," George acknowledges. "Unfortunately he just wasn't a real farmer or a decision maker. He could never figure out ways to get a job done without incurring tremendous labor and machinery costs. Despite having decent crops, we kept heading down towards zero until we lost our farms too. Jack Lewis was the court-appointed trustee looking into our financial problems, and he finally had to ask me to declare bankruptcy. It was really all I could do to salvage anything."

Certainly George had seen his dehydration plant in terms of mega-bucks, the huge profits it would return to him in the very near future. But it had represented much more. It was his creation, that next giant step toward fulfilling his vision of a complete agribusiness empire built on his long cherished idea of vertical integration. Giving up on this vision was not going to come easy.

Forty-eight

A SHORT SOJOURN
TO JAPAN

All through 1968 and well into 1969 George kept up his search for start-up funds, making long trips, talking to anyone he thought might be able to help. It was a search that took a couple of bizarre turns that began when a friend introduced him to a man named Ed Desareau.

"Desareau had worked as an official for the Organization of American States," George recalls, "and he claimed he had plenty of contacts back in Washington D.C., all with important bureaucrats who could set me up with a fifteen million dollar government loan, more than enough capital to revive my entire operation. Of course, he'd be looking for a pretty healthy commission out of all of this, but I figured that if he could get me the kind of loan he was talking about, he'd have it coming. We took several trips back to D.C., Desareau paying for everything, and each time we met with different people, sometimes in their offices, more often in our hotel suite. But I was never sure these were the right contacts, the ones who could pull the financial strings. At any rate, my big loan never materialized."

About a year later Desareau asked George to join him on a trip he'd lined up to meet with the big trading companies in Japan, this time as a paid consultant. George agreed, mainly because once again he hoped to make the right contacts to revive his operation.

This time, though, Ed Desareau had his own major agenda. While he had been with O.A.S., he had discovered and laid legal claim to a large atoll in the Pacific, almost straight south of Catalina Island.

Now he had grandiose plans to turn this pile of rock into his own island nation, with upscale resorts, gambling casinos, condos, yachting berths, a protective sea wall that traveled all the way around the island, everything that would attract the rich and famous. He'd already hired engineers, architects, accountants, even a community planner, and he was armed with dozens of preliminary drafts. Financing was to come from wealthy European investors.

But before it could be turned into an island nation covered with posh resorts, this barren atoll had to be further expanded, then made fit for human habitation. Under Desareau's scheme this meant hauling in millions of tons of boulders and soil from Mexico. That's where the big Japanese trading companies would come in. These company's owned the huge barges and cranes that would be necessary for this massive undertaking, and Desareau hoped that George could convince them to be part of this project.

"When we finally met with all those executives, they asked if I could negotiate in Japanese." George recalls. "Well, I agreed to try, but the Japanese language has two very distinct voices, the masculine and feminine. Unfortunately, I only knew how to speak in the feminine voice, the only one that Mom had taught us in her language classes. Of course these gentlemen all spoke a masculine form, a form I could neither speak nor follow. I don't know which was worse, my embarrassment or my confusion. When I explained my dilemma, these gentlemen quickly agreed to negotiate in English.

"But Mom had really helped me out in a different way. She'd contacted all her relatives, not only to tell them I was coming, but what I'd be doing. One day a Mr. Arata, who was my distant cousin and highly placed in the government, showed up at our meeting with another important official. When these two walked in, I was the only one in that room who didn't recognize them, and all those big executives immediately stood up and bowed, showing respect for their positions. Then both Mr. Arata and his companion walked over to me and they immediately bowed, showing me this same respect. My cousin had even brought me several gifts.

"Immediately I saw a change in how those executives viewed me. Suddenly I wasn't just another foreign negotiator who was trying to get something from them. Now I was a man of importance, a man to be taken far more seriously. Unfortunately even my new prestige wasn't enough to get Desareau's island deal to go through, mainly because he couldn't get enough financial backing out of Europe or anywhere else, but it did allow me to make valuable contacts that helped me a few years later."

If high-powered negotiations and long-term contacts were the catalysts for this trip, it was a side journey to Chigasaki, his father's old home town, that would have the most profound effect on George. Several of his cousins met him at the train station and immediately took him to their family's ancestral graveyard. In its center stood a towering figure, the Yoshino statue. Around it were the graves of George's ancestors.

"My cousins treated that place with great reverence, and as I stood there, looking at those manicured grounds and the tombstones of my grandfathers and great grandfathers, I understood why," George quietly reflects. "I'd never known a single grandparent, either on my father's or my mother's side. They were all in these graves before I was born. As I stood there, my emotions deepened. For me this became a special place, even a spiritual place, where for the first time in my life I felt connected to my father's past and to my own."

Since childhood George had been aware of the Japanese custom of bowing to one's superiors, but when he visited his relative's homes, this custom took on surprising and even disturbing dimensions. Women would lower themselves before him, at times lying flat on the floor, and never rise.

"I knew this was their custom, a big part of their culture and class system," George acknowledges, "but all that bowing really made me uncomfortable. I didn't know what to do or what to say. I just wanted these women to stand up, to face me, to treat me as their equal, not someone far above them. But I guess that would have been as foreign and incomprehensible to my cousins as all this was to me."

Forty-nine

IN SEARCH OF
FINANCES, MEXICO
TO GUATEMALA

Once back in Washington the strange twists of the Desareau
saga soon took its first really bizarre turn. This started
when the man's continued pursuit of his island nation
dream brought him and George into contact with an official from
Mexico, a connection that would lead directly to two intriguing
ventures.

"For the life of me, I can't remember the man's last name,"
George explains. "His first name was Carlos, and he held a cabi-
net post in the Mexican government. I first met him when he
came up to Seattle to make a deal on the millions of tons of rock
and soil that Desareau needed for his island resort. Our meeting
wasn't supposed to involve anything else. But somehow the topic
of Mexico's problems with their perishable commodities exports
came up. Essentially they were losing most of their U.S. and
Canadian vegetables and fruits trade because they had virtually no
quality control. Mexico's prices could compete with anyone's, but
an American buyer just never knew what he was going to get
when he sent an order to one of their brokers. One time he'd get

decent quality, the next time he'd end up with nothing but junk, stuff that was so bad he'd have to dump it.

"Quality control was something I definitely understood, so I explained to Carlos what their problem was, and I gave him a basic outline of what had to be done to fix it. Mexico needed a solid quality control organization that would oversee and certify each shipment before it left the country, kicking over anything that didn't make grade. Suddenly his face lit up. 'Then let's do it,' he almost shouted. 'Let's set up our own quality control company with complete authority over every shipment that leaves my nation.' The idea immediately fascinated both Desareau and me. Here we had something Mexican produce exporters definitely needed, and we had a high official of that country ready to go into business with us. It looked like a no-miss deal with a real silver lining.

"We did a lot more negotiating before a basic plan emerged. Desareau and I were to set up and manage this new company, charging a commission for every shipment we inspected. This commission would be a very small percentage of a cargo's value, but because of the fantastic volume we'd be inspecting, our revenues were going to be huge.

"Initially, Desareau and I were to get fifty percent for running the operation, Carlos and other officials, including, they kept hinting, their president, would split the other half. I know this sounds pretty corrupt, but it was their way of doing business, and it was the only way our new company could get set up or have enough clout to impose quality standards.

"We made five or six trips to Mexico City, always dealing with Carlos and his political cronies. At first everything looked promising, but then we started to see the entangling web of Mexico's politics. Sometimes it was simply disruptive and irritatingly slow. We might have a nine o'clock meeting set up with their customs officials, and these guys would show up at two, without offering any explanations, excuses or apologies. Punctuality meant nothing to them. In the meantime, we'd sit around waiting, drinking that strong chicory coffee they kept bringing us. I drank a lot of coffee in those days, but this stuff would get me absolutely wired.

"Carlos himself tried hard to keep us interested. Whenever we'd fly down, he'd meet us at the airport, drive us to our hotel and all our meetings in this big Cadillac of his, the only one I ever saw in Mexico City. Those rides were a real adventure. We'd go tearing along the busiest streets, scattering the pedestrians who were constantly risking life and limb by darting across in front of us. At least a dozen times I was sure we'd clip someone. I'd cringe, tense up, then say a silent prayer when I didn't feel the expected thump.

"But whenever I'd say anything to Carlos, he'd just shrug his shoulders, make a disgusted grimace and reply, 'Well, they'd better get out of my way. Cars have the right-of-way in my country. That's our law.' Then I swear he'd hit the next intersection even faster just to show me he could. Before too long I learned to cringe in silence.

"Wild rides and disrupted schedules we could have lived with, but then Carlos and his cronies kept bringing in more and more people, new officials who they said had to be involved. Each time a new man came on board, we'd have to start all our negotiations over from the beginning. Plus, every new bureaucrat demanded a cut of those future commissions, and Ed and I kept watching our own percentage shrink. By itself this wouldn't have been tragic because even twenty-percent of the potential revenue would have made us both wealthy, but we didn't know where or when this was going to end.

"Carlos kept telling us how much he and the president both wanted this new organization, and I really think that by then at least he understood why his country needed this, but still we couldn't make any headway. Our expenses just kept mounting as their bureaucratic quagmire became deeper and deeper. Finally we just had to give it up."

Shortly before George and Desareau decided to cut their losses, Carlos introduced them to Guatemala's vice president, Clemente Rojas, an introduction that led into an even more intriguing adventure. Rojas was very popular in his own country and was ready to run for president, but Guatemala was so entangled with U.S. interests and communist insurgences that he couldn't win that office unless he had the backing of America's Central Intelligence Agency.

"Desareau was a smooth operator, and when he started talking about his O.A.S. and Washington D.C. connections, right away Mr. Rojas figured that he was just the man to help him establish the ties he needed with our C.I.A.," George relates, "so he flew him down there, and I caught a plane back to Seattle, figuring my time spent on his affairs had come to an end. But about two weeks later Desareau called me from Guatemala, desperate, begging me to come down there immediately. He'd had a serious heart attack and was laid up in a Guatemala City hospital. If I'd agree to make the trip, Rojas would take care of travel arrangements and pay for everything. All I had to do was agree to take over Ed's role. I didn't know what I was getting into, but Ed was so panicky that I said yes. If nothing else, I figured I could help a very sick man get back to his home.

"When I landed at the Guatemala City airport, Mr. Rojas and his entourage were waiting for me with their full red carpet treatment, a big limousine, a motorcade, the whole works. It was as if I was the important American ambassador who was going to take care of their problems. I didn't even have to go through customs. The countryside literally crawled with communist guerrilla bands, so every road toward the city had barricades manned by armed guards, but these didn't slow our big motorcade down. We'd drive up and immediately get waved right through.

"After a quick stop at my hotel suite, it was on to the hospital to see Desareau. I was a little shocked when I saw the man. He looked far worse than he'd sounded on the phone. Ten days later the authorities shipped him back to Washington and he wound up in a Spokane hospital, where he'd recover just enough for a short release. A few months later he had a fatal relapse.

"Back then Guatemala was torn by constant civil war. While I was still in my hotel room the next morning, right in the very heart of Guatemala City, rifle shots suddenly rang out from the street below. Soldiers and communists were doing battle less than a block away. I could actually look out my window and watch the troop movements, but pressing your face against a pane of glass for too long wasn't highly recommended. That whole country was faced with this, snipings and running gun battles going on every day. Despite all this I never felt seriously threatened myself because my political connections had me very well protected. Guards were stationed on my hotel floor, and when we traveled, always with that motorcade, we had plenty of well armed soldiers surrounding us.

"The second day I was down there, Rojas took me out into the countryside and showed me a huge banana and coffee plantation with a beautiful big home and maybe two dozen smaller houses, the worker's quarters. It was all mine, he said. All I had to do was arrange C.I.A. backing, the key to his political future. He was one of the richest men in all of Guatemala, apparently very popular among his people, and he was willing to do whatever it took to be their next president. He told me he was ready to make a big campaign contribution to any American politician I could get to help him.

"I'd met our state's Henry Jackson, a powerful U.S. senator on the Ways and Means Committee, so right away I gave him a call, explained who Desareau and I were promoting, the potential campaign payoffs, everything. Jackson agreed to thoroughly look into all of this and said he'd get back to me as soon as possible. A few days later the senator made good on his promise. Unfortunately it had only taken him that long to find out that Rojas was okay, but Desareau was being investigated by both the C.I.A. and F.B.I. Jackson didn't know exactly why, but his advice was succinct: 'George, get out of this thing, or they'll tie you in with him.' I quickly heeded his advice.

"Even when I was back home, Mr. Rojas called me several times, begging me to simply drop Desareau if his background was clouded, then come back to Guatemala and work the deal out all on my own. In retrospect maybe I should have. From everything I'd heard, Rojas was a good man, deeply committed to his people's long-term welfare.

"Plus, it was an exciting world I'd entered down there, and the potential payoff could have been fabulous. If I'd gone it alone, I think I could have brought it off, but by then it really bothered me to suddenly dump Desareau, particularly when he was so sick. Plus, this whole thing, from the communist insurgents to possible F.B.I. investigations, had made me more than a little nervous. It was time to back away and head in a different direction."

Fifty

TRAGEDY
COMPOUNDED

Putting aside the intriguing prospects of a Latin American banana and coffee plantation and once again concentrating on his home front was by now a daunting task. As if 1969 hadn't been traumatic enough for the entire Yoshino family, early that fall Frank's asthma became much worse, weakening his already congested lungs. Then just as the harsh November weather arrived, he came down with a severe cold. By Thanksgiving his condition was critical. On November 29th this fine family patriarch died, a few week's shy of his eighty-ninth birthday. His funeral would once again bring hundreds of his friends and relatives from all over the west to Moses Lake.

"I'd never told Pop what forced me into bankruptcy," George somberly recalls. "And he'd never said a word to me about it. No, he never criticized me in any way or asked for an explanation. He'd reveled in my successes, but he was far above saying anything negative about my failure. But I knew my collapse had hurt Pop badly. So much of what I'd accomplished, all that he'd watched me build up and had taken such pride in, was suddenly gone. For

294

him, it must have seemed like the internment years all over again, with our family enterprise suddenly yanked away.

"Before his funeral I wrote him a note, apologizing for letting him down. Then I added a few lines, just to let Pop know what he'd meant to me. I never was any good at saying 'I love you,' even on paper, but in my own way that's what I was trying to get across. When I stood by that open casket for the last time, I quietly slipped my little note into his pocket."

In today's world, with all of its emphasis on direct and open communication, there are many who would say that this was a note that came too late, that all these words should have been spoken while his father was still alive. George disagrees.

"During those miserable years when I was fighting to keep my plant alive, I never once went to anyone with my problems," he states. "Even after it closed, I never tried to explain to a single friend or relative what I'd gone through or what I was feeling at the time. Lengthy confessions, pouring out your feelings of either guilt or affection, that was never my way. It wasn't Pop's either. Just as he'd silently endured internment and everything that had cost him, he'd have expected me to endure my losses in silence, and then to use all of my abilities to make a comeback. And any open profession of my feelings for him would have embarrassed us both. I hope Pop knew. I think he did. But verbalizing those kinds of feelings, well, that was never our way."

Kazuye was so devastated by her husband's death that she found it almost impossible to stay in the home that she and Frank had enjoyed so much. Her family rallied around her, each of them spending more time taking her places, getting her to spend her days and many of her nights in their homes. Still, in less than a year Kazuye's own health started to fail. She had the first of a series of minor heart attacks.

When the Yoshinos farming operation had ceased, Elmer had been forced to find other work. He landed a job in Los Angeles, working for an old college friend who imported nuts and bolts. George was helping him and his family make the move to California when they received word.

"Life has its own little ways of catching you off guard," he now reflects. "I'd offered to drive Elmer's U-Haul truck to Los

Angeles so he could go with his family in their sedan. Driving that miserable rented truck wasn't exactly what I'd call a fun trip, but my long-time buddy, Tom Hayashi, had flown up to Washington to help me drive, and our journey south turned into a real trek. In a way, Tom's companionship and our little misadventures were just what I needed right about then to get my mind off my real troubles, at least for a few days.

"The U-Haul we'd rented was many miles past its prime. It's steering was so bad that I had to do all the driving, but I was sure glad to have Tom along riding shotgun and reminiscing. I had to constantly fight that wheel with both hands, just to make sure we stayed on the road. Whenever we'd hit a wind gust, I'd have to redouble my efforts. Then just as we were heading through a long barren stretch near the Oregon-California border, our alternator started going bad. As darkness came on, it was dead, and our battery began draining down rapidly. After only a few miles we were losing our headlights. But I hated to just pull off the road and spend a miserable long night in that cab, then have to hunt for help in the morning.

"Finally our lights were completely gone, so Tom had to stick his head and shoulders all the way out his side window and shine a flashlight on the road ahead, a beam that was slightly better than nothing. I could kind of make out the center lines, and with no other traffic on that road, I kept inching that crate along, wondering when our engine was going to die. We'd barely crested the last hill before we hit Ukiah and were moving towards its bright lights when that's exactly what happened. I quickly jammed in the clutch and let that old truck roll, right down into the city and onto, of all things, a U-Haul Rentals parking lot.

"Across the street sat a decent little motel with an all-night restaurant right next to it. After hours of fighting that beast of a truck and figuring we'd be stuck out on the highway, either trying to hitch-hike our way in or spending a miserable night in that cab, we couldn't believe our good luck. Now we could get a meal, take much needed showers, sleep on real beds, and in the morning get those U-Haul people to fix their miserable piece of equipment.

"Tom and I were still laughing over our good fortune the next day as we headed into Los Angeles, that is until we pulled up in front of the house Elmer was buying. Immediately we spotted a note pinned to its door. It was from the local police, telling us to call home immediately. I didn't have to find a phone to know it was Mom. Pop's death, then Elmer moving back to California, the combination was just too much for her. Though Vic was still over in Othello and Louise was living right there in Moses Lake, I'm sure Mom felt she was witnessing the final breakup of her family, something she'd always prayed would never happen. That's what had sapped her will to live and brought on those earlier heart attacks. Now she'd had another, a stronger seizure. This one proved fatal."

Fifty-one

SIFTING THROUGH
THE WRECKAGE,
PICKING UP THE PIECES

A s the decade that had started with so much promise and ended in such misery was drawing to a close, even George started to understand it was time to move on. Shortly before his father's death, he had taken an apartment in Seattle, temporarily leaving Frances and their children in Quincy. Using his wide web of business world connections and his agricultural marketing expertise, George opened a consulting office, lining up financing for business connections, working as a purchasing agent for various corporations, always on commission. Fred Yasunaga, a fellow George had known since his internment camp days, was now a title company agent in Seattle with dozens of contacts, from real estate and banking to the big foreign trading companies, and he was more than willing to help his friend meet the right people.

"I did what I had to to make a living," George now says, "but except for meeting new people with Fred, this sure wasn't what I enjoyed doing or what I planned to settle into for the rest of my life. Consulting pays fairly well, but it's a tough business. You're always trying to straighten out someone else's problems. I'd get hired to find out why a company wasn't as productive or as profitable as it should be, then after a month or more of looking into every aspect of its production and marketing practices, I'd discover that the man who hired me was the real weak link in that organization.

"How do you go to a company's president and say 'You're the problem! Hire someone who's competent to run this place, then get out of his way!' That's not exactly what a man who's worked his way to the top and has a pretty high opinion of his managing skills wants to hear. In fact, it's almost a guaranteed way to get the consulting fees that you're depending on to pay your own bills withheld."

However distasteful, this new career was a very minor part of George's real problems. These still centered around the closure of his plant and his deep sense of guilt and his bitter hatred toward the man he held responsible, a hatred that was starting to engulf him. Work became only a few hours of partial escape. His long evenings were spent in cocktail lounges, drinking himself into a stupor.

"Yeah, that first year in Seattle I became the classic example of a man trying to drown his sorrows," He readily admits, shaking his head sadly. "Oh, I guess I could blame part of this on my new ties to the Japanese Trading Companies. If you were going to do business with those guys, they expected you to be out there doing plenty of heavy drinking with them too. It was all part of their male-dominated culture, but later I'd often wonder how those trading companies could remain so successful when all of their key men were out boozing night after night.

"But for me that wasn't it at all. It was just an excuse. For years I'd been the real lightweight among my drinking buddies, the guy who'd always held back, the one who wanted to keep a clear head for anything that came up that night and who didn't want to spend the next day nursing a bad hangover. I could have kept that up.

"Now here I was, sousing myself almost every single evening, partying it up in the cocktail lounges until they closed, then going back to that empty apartment and falling into bed around two a.m.

Most days I'd end up sleeping the whole morning away, then make a noon luncheon with Fred and at least one client. That night I'd be out there again, hitting the booze. It was stupid, I know, but right then I just couldn't get over what had happened. Why didn't I see what that man was going to do to me? How could I have done things differently? I'd ask these questions over and over, never coming up with anything close to a good answer.

"And of course Sid was always right there, at the very center of my thoughts. Yes, I'd known plenty of other dishonest people in my life but never a man like this. I've had real contempt for a few guys I've met, men who were too conniving or just plain cruel. But with Sid my feelings were different, the kind I'd never experienced before. To this day, he's the only person I've ever truly hated.

"For one long year that became my dominant emotion. In fact, I was so full of my own hatred that at times I was dangerously close to being irrational. There were nights and even days when I seriously considered having Sid killed. I'd catch myself thinking, 'A man like that shouldn't be allowed to live.' Then I'd actually entertain ways to get the job done, hiring a hit man, sending a Mafia type after him.

"Fortunately my irrationality never went beyond that 'dangerously close' stage, but never being able to get Sid out of my mind was tough. And running with the crowd I did, I could never get away from hearing about him. One night my pal Harry Blackfield surprised me by mentioning that he'd gone to work for Eland, setting up financing for bars and night clubs. Sid owned a beer and wine distributing company, so what they were doing was strictly illegal, in direct violation of our state's liquor laws. Finally I warned Harry, 'Get the hell away from that guy. He'll use you, then if this thing goes bad, he'll let you take the fall.'

"I know I was right, but I should have kept my mouth shut. Harry kept telling me that he had to make a living, that he knew what he was doing, and that he sure didn't need any advice from me. In no time our argument turned ugly with both of us cursing and shouting, calling each other names. Harry was a good man and for so many years he'd been a wonderful friend, but when he decided a man had wronged him, even if it was just once, he'd set hard against him and he'd never relent. I'd seen this happen before, sometimes over pretty trivial incidents, so I should have guessed what I was in for.

"But we weren't just friends. We were the best of friends. Surely, I thought when I woke up the next morning, he'll let this one bad tirade blow over and I can make my apologies. I was ready to shake hands and forget that whole episode, but Harry wouldn't have it. For weeks I tried. He wouldn't answer my phone calls, and he even quit coming into the 6-10 Club and other spots that I frequented. We haven't spoken since."

If he had to lose one close friend during this time of bitterness, George will always be thankful that he gained another. Back in their Weiser days, Fred Yasanaga had actually been Vic's friend, one of the young Nisei lads who had come out of the Heart Mountain internment camp and ended up hanging around the Yoshinos' farm. Now he had his own family and had become a rock solid business man.

"For me that friendship will always have a special quality because Fred chose to become my friend at the lowest point of my life, and he was sure instrumental in helping me get through it," George says. "He had to have really wondered, perhaps even worried about all my heavy drinking. He was almost always there, especially when I socialized with the trading company guys.

"When it came to alcohol, Fred was even more of a lightweight than I was, so he'd become the real master at only pretending to imbibe, and he knew I was capable of doing the same thing, but he never criticized me or asked me to change. He was just always there for me. We didn't talked about it, but Fred had a pretty clear idea of what I'd just gone through, and I guess he was wise enough to know I needed some time and confident that I'd come out of this on my own.

"Without him and his wonderful wife and daughter, though, I'm not sure if I'd have made it through that miserable year. They had such a warm home, a place where I knew I could simply drop in and I'd always feel welcome, a home that gave a bit of stability to my otherwise rudderless existence. Any time I wasn't totally caught up in the nightclub scene, I'd go to their house, mostly just to spend a few quiet hours, sometimes for an entire evening when I'd get a wonderful home-cooked meal and real camaraderie.

Fred's wife, Gloria, could put any guest at ease, and before long she'd made me feel like part of her family. Their little daughter Lorie started calling me Uncle George. In later years she'd tell people that I was her second dad.

A day finally finally came when George realized that these valuable but sporadic evenings with Fred and his family weren't going to be enough. To get beyond the morass of hatred and self pity he had fallen into, he would have to make major changes, both in his mental state and his lifestyle.

"Maybe a man like Eland deserved my animosity," he now says, "but I knew I had to go back to that old lesson I'd learned early in my teens: 'Dwell too long on what a vicious human being has done to you and he wins. Get beyond him and you do.' No, I couldn't simply say it was over and then sit back and watch all my hatred and bitterness disappear, but no longer would I let it dictate my actions."

In June of 1973 he took another major step towards stabilizing his life. He bought a home in Lake Forest Park, a Seattle suburb, and brought his family over. By this time Jean and Franki Jo were in college, but they would come home in the summers and find office jobs in Seattle. Michael was fifteen and Harry Walter eleven, bright active lads who had no trouble fitting into their new schools.

"Yeah, it was good to have my family around again," he acknowledges. "It helped me get my focus back and made my life a whole lot steadier. Unfortunately, my rough financial times coincided with Jean and Franki Jo's college years. Oh, I still helped them some, but mostly my girls did it on their own, getting academic scholarships, working summers in Seattle and part-time while they were in college, doing whatever it took to make ends meet. Jean graduated with a business degree from Washington State. Franki Jo finished two years at that school, then decided to switch to a dental hygiene program over in Yakima. For ten straight years I'd get to attend Dad's Day at W.S.U., first for the girls, then the boys.

"Considering how much I was gone during all their growing-up years, I fully understood how fortunate I was to have such good kids. All four were top students, and they sure never backed away from taking on a job or seeing it through. In fact, my older son Michael was so determined to make it through Washington State on his own that he wouldn't let me help him even when I could. By the time he hit college I was doing better than in the years right after my crash, so I'd occasionally send him a check, but he'd always send it right back.

"Walter, our youngest, earned enough working in a grocery store and doing all kinds of odd jobs while he was still in high school to buy his own car, and he paid for a lot of his own education too, especially when he was in Pullman. When he went on to a private school to get his chiropractor's license, his costs were pretty steep, more than he could pay for with a summer job and part time work. Fortunately by then I was able to step in and help.

"I'm almost positive that if I'd been able to keep our plant alive, at least one of my sons and maybe a daughter would have followed me into that business. They all have what it takes: quick, inquisitive minds and solid work ethics. If I'd started them out as I intended, working their way up from the bottom so they understood every phase of the operation, I'm sure they'd have done well at it. Just like my father, I'd had real dreams of building up and passing on this family business. For years afterwards I tried not to dwell on that too much. It only added to my bitterness."

Fifty-two

THE U & I YEARS

A t the time his family moved to Seattle, George's income was on the slender side. Consulting jobs were getting harder to come by, and brokering products that ranged from vegetables to timber and cement for the Japanese trading companies had its limits. He knew that he could do a little better than make ends meet if he continued these pursuits, as well as arranging financing for various companies, but he felt it was time to seek out a new career, something that would both pay better and be more in tune with his real strengths, his farming and marketing expertise. His chance came in the fall of 1974 when the Utah & Idaho Sugar Corporation, headquartered in Salt Lake City, first contacted him to do consulting work, then suddenly asked him to bring a complete resume to their initial meeting.

U & I had acquired a huge land holding in southeastern Washington, over 100,000 acres in an area known as the Horse Heaven Hills directly above the Columbia River. Their initial undertaking was to develop several hundred irrigation circles, each one capable of irrigating one hundred and twenty acres.

They planned to raise tremendous crops of potatoes, corn and wheat. After checking George's resume carefully and listening to his ideas, the company brass offered him a full-time position as an Assistant Senior Vice President, working out of their Pasco office.

"I wasn't exactly sure just what that title meant," George reflects, grinning. "The initial pay wasn't all that great, but I'd have a chance to work my way up, and I knew this job would fit me a whole lot better than the consulting work and everything else I'd been doing. At first I was a little cautious about it, though, so I rented a small apartment and left my family in Lake Forest Park. It was a full year before I bought a house in Kennewick and brought Frances and the boys over."

George's first task with U & I was to interview the company's officers and its other key personnel and then do a feasibility study concerning what they could expect as they developed those thousands and thousands of irrigated acres. His first report hit their corporate office like a bombshell.

"My figures clearly showed that if we met our production goals in the next ten years, we'd be harvesting enough potatoes to process a quarter of the nation's total French fries. Anyone at all familiar with our industry would have known there was absolutely no way the existing Washington processing plants could have handled this, to say nothing of what it would have done to our regional and national markets. U & I's top executives would sit in our meetings, scan my report and just shake their heads, asking me questions, trying to find a flaw. But in the end they couldn't deny that report's accuracy. I was using all their own figures to determine our yearly tonnage. The rest of the math was pretty basic.

"Until they saw my figures, those guys had no idea what they'd been heading into. All they'd planned for was huge production, as if profitable potato markets were going to magically appear. Finally I convinced them that there was just no way they could raise that many acres of spuds without first owning a processing plant and establishing viable national and perhaps even international markets."

George would spend four and a half years with this firm, developing markets, working out kinks in their farming operation, being a liaison to the Northwest's processing plants. In 1975 he met with a man named Norm Hyder, who was building a new potato processing plant in Boardman, Oregon, less than sixty miles from U & I's big land holdings.

"I knew Norm back in the early sixties when he was buying potatoes from me," George recalls. "So when he ran into money problems while his plant was still in the building stage, he came over to Pasco and looked me up, hoping I could get my company to either finance him or buy him out. After checking over his blueprints, the state of his facility, his books, everything I thought was pertinent, I put Norm in contact with the right U & I executives.

"Considering what could have happened, our top brass gave Norm an amazingly sweet deal, buying him out on very favorable terms. They not only took over all of his debts. They gave him some cash and a good chunk of stock in the company. They even retained his company name, Gourmet Foods. Unlike what so many big corporations would have done, U & I didn't take advantage of the man when he was down. I know for a fact that there was at least one big company waiting in the wings for Norm to declare bankruptcy so they could take over his plant for next to nothing.

"But being owned by the Mormon Church, U & I couldn't operate like most big corporations. They had to be far more sensitive to negative publicity and at times they were willing to spend some big dollars to avoid it. In this case all that worked out fine for everyone. They pulled Norm out of a real financial bind and ended up with a processing facility they needed."

If his job wasn't perfect, at least George felt that he now had a suitable position, a decent future and a few minor perks. For a couple of years he was able to get his son Michael a good paying summer job, doing manual labor on the company's huge land holdings.

"Yeah, Mike got on because of my position, but once he was working, they sure didn't give him any soft jobs. Much of the time they had him cleaning out their grain bins with a shovel, working a twelve hour shift. That's a dusty, dirty job any time of year, and in our sweltering summers it's miserable. But Mike never complained. He just did his work and used his paychecks to finance his education."

If things had continued to run smoothly, George may have stayed on with U & I for many more years. However, in 1978 life with this big corporation took a nose dive. It all started when the big bosses retained a supposedly high-powered Boston consulting firm to do a three-million-dollar feasibility study of their entire operation. Suddenly George found himself inundated by this firm's personnel, a half dozen men sitting in his office day after day, studying his reports, asking him question after question.

Having these fellows around may have been unpleasant, but they were a minor irritation compared to what the results of their study created. After several months these consultants apparently believed that they had gleaned all of the necessary facts, and they came forward with a single major recommendation: U & I should close down its sugar mills immediately, and then put these plants up for sale.

"To me, that approach was totally absurd," George vigorously states. "Yes, I understood we were having problems with these mills, but one of our biggest assets at that time was our strong markets. U & I had excellent ties with the soft drinks and processed foods buyers, the two groups you have to have if you're going to sell large quantities of sugar in this country. But all of these markets were going elsewhere the minute the company announced we were shutting down our mills, and we'd never get them back. Plus, once our growers were put out of the sugar beet business, they'd have to sell off their machinery and move into different crops, destroying that whole network.

"I pleaded with the top brass to keep those mills running until we could find a suitable buyer. An operating mill with strong retail sales would be very attractive to this nation's big sugar companies. An idle one with no markets and no grower base was going to be next to impossible to restart."

George's arguments would prove to be both ignored and prophetic. U & I closed its sugar mills, lost its markets, and left hundreds of beet farmers stranded with costly and now almost worthless seeding and harvesting machinery. The mills would remain idle for years to come. Almost immediately these closings had a major impact on George. To trim expenses U & I fired his boss, replacing him with a Salt Lake executive, a man who had long been in charge of marketing. Now he would be managing all the irrigated farm units.

"Right off I could see that this wasn't going to work," George recounts. "This fellow might have been okay in sugar marketing, but he knew next to nothing about running a huge farm operation. That sure didn't stop him from making all the important decisions, most of the time without consulting me or anyone else before he gave his orders. Things were sliding rapidly downhill when one day he asked me what I thought my job should be. 'I should have your job,' I immediately told him. 'That's what I'm really qualified to do.'

"I still believe I gave him an honest if not a very tactful answer, but at least I refrained from adding 'and you're not.' Yet, when I saw how my answer visibly upset this guy, it didn't come as a real surprise that he didn't give me what I'd asked for. Instead, he offered to make me the new marketing manager, a job I could have easily handled. I'd already gotten U & I into the better potato markets, but I wanted to be more than someone else's marketer, and with this guy running our entire farm operation, I could see nothing but problems ahead. It was time for me to move on, so I resigned."

Fifty-three

THE END OF
A MARRIAGE

That summer closed out a far bigger chapter in George's life. After almost thirty years of marriage, he and Frances were divorced.

"Actually, I'd moved out of our house the year before and was living in an apartment," he recounts. "It's strange, but when I was working for U & I, I was home far more than I'd ever been during my farming, packing, and processing years. Maybe that was our problem. Suddenly we seemed to fight all the time, over everything from the way we dealt with our kids to throwing out old newspapers. Frances once told me that the worst day of her life was the day I announced I was going to start a dehydration plant. She felt that its demands would be the final step in keeping me away from home, pushing us further apart.

"I guess she was right. During those start-up years I'd often stay at that plant all night, catching a few hours sleep on my office couch only when I was totally exhausted. On Sundays I might be home all day, but by then I'd be so worn out, I'd sleep sixteen hours or more at a single stretch. Yeah, the dehy plant may have

been the final straw for Frances, but I know that our real problems
went back a whole lot farther. From at least 1958 on I'd been
working day and night, getting home way too sporadically. With
the dehy plant I was out of town far more often, but that was the
only major difference.

"I think our single biggest problem was that throughout so
much of our marriage I'd stayed way too distant, never really confiding in her, not keeping her informed of my business dealings.
From at least the late fifties on Frances never even knew how
much land I was farming or what crops I was raising. Whenever I
was working on a big land purchase or getting ready to take on a
potato shed, she was left out of the loop. Oh, when we had time
together, I'd sometimes touch on a few of the good things that
were happening, but I kept all my problems to myself.

"Intricate business deals weren't something I talked about to
anyone, unfortunately not even my wife. After the fact, I'd
explain what I'd accomplished to Pop, mainly because I knew it
delighted him so much, and I kept Vic pretty well informed on a
weekly basis, but that was about it. I always felt I was doing my
family and friends a favor by not laying my business burdens on
them. After all, I'd tell myself, they can't do anything about these
problems anyway. I'm the one who has to come up with a solution,
so why worry or maybe even frustrate them? To this day I tend to
think this way, but maybe I'm wrong. Maybe if I'd shared more
back then, Frances and I wouldn't have grown apart.

"And I know that the years surrounding our plant closure
and the rest of that financial collapse were tough ones on our marriage, again partly because I kept all the details bottled up, but also
because I wasn't a pleasant person to be around right then. The
combination must have been terrible for my wife.

"Again we never really talked about it, but I know our kids
took our divorce real hard. Quite naturally they rallied around
their mother, and I sure can't blame any of them for that. She was
the one who'd been with them while they were growing up, the
parent who took care of their daily needs. Frances might have had
a few of her own problems with our kids, particularly when they
were getting older and started resenting a couple of her stricter
rules, but she was still Mom, the one who'd always been there to

dole out plenty of love along with the discipline they all needed, and the one they'd turn to in a crisis.

"It's hard to say exactly how much resentment my kids felt towards me because that was just one more thing we never talked about, but I know it had to exist. At least in a couple of cases I sure saw the evidence. When Jean was married in 1988 and Mike a few years later, I wasn't invited to their weddings. Each time Frances called me and insisted that I had to be at these ceremonies. My first inclination was to say no, if they don't want me there, I'm going to stay away, but finally I gave in to her arguments. In retrospect, we'd all have been better off if I'd stayed home. Jean's marriage was her second, so maybe she didn't feel any great need to have her dad walk her down the aisle, but she didn't include me in the photo sessions either.

"At Mike's, I not only didn't get into the family photo, but I wasn't even treated as a welcome guest. I ended up sitting up in the church choir loft. I fully understood that he and his sister had plenty of reasons to resent me right about then, but, like I say, if I'd known what I was going to face at those two weddings, I'd have avoided them. My being there simply made life harder for all of us. Later, Jean and I repaired our relationship, and now we do visit back and forth, but unfortunately that hasn't been the case with Mike and me."

Fifty-four

NEW BUSINESS OPPORTUNITIES, AN OLD FRIENDSHIP

Even before his resignation from U & I forced him to seriously start looking for other economic opportunities, George had started dabbling into his own farming ventures. In 1979 he had one partnership with Sas Nakamura and another with a man named Skarperud. He and Sas were farming new ground north of Pasco, a hundred and fifty acres of potatoes, a hundred and twenty in dry red beans. They would have done okay, but a big dirt dam that held back their irrigation water broke in mid-summer, wiping out the entire bean crop. The ground with Skarperud was all in spuds. Market-wise, it wasn't a great year for potatoes either, but they survived.

Despite this poor farming year 1979 turned out to be a major turning point in George's fortunes. That summer he was approached by Fred Spada, primary owner of the Portland- based Spada Corporation. Among his many holdings, Spada had a potato packing shed near Pasco, but he knew it was being badly mismanaged.

"I'd met Spada way back in the late fifties," George recalls, "and for the last two years I'd sold him some of U & I's potatoes. So we had tie-ins, enough that he knew I had managerial and market-ing skills, and his Pasco potato shed definitely needed both. Only the life-support dollars he was pouring into it was keeping that oper-ation alive. Everything was down to zero. It had no product coming in, no growers lined up for the future, and no markets. All that was left were a few salaried employees desperately clinging to their jobs. So Spada made me a tremendous offer. If I'd become his manager, I'd have total control, I'd draw a monthly salary, and at the end of each fiscal year, we'd split all profits fifty-fifty.

"It was exactly the opportunity I'd been looking for. Within a week I was lining up farmers, making marketing calls, refining ware-house procedures. In no time we went from what would have been a no-volume potato shed that season to one that was really hum-ming. That first year we handled more tons of potatoes than any other shed in our state. My good workers loved this. No more long layoffs and wondering if they'd ever have a job to go back to. Now they could depend on a weekly paycheck all year around.

"Naturally Spada was thrilled, and I felt that I was finally back where I belonged, hiring new people, contracting with the region's growers, marketing our product all over the country, making quick decisions every single day, challenges I thoroughly enjoyed. For the first time since the good days of running my own sheds and pro-cessing plant, I couldn't wait to get to work every morning."

Within months George had the Pasco shed turning a profit. By the next year he felt confident enough to purchase his own one-hundred-and-thirty-acre farm near Pasco. Gradually he'd expand this to four hundred acres. Besides the packing operation and man-aging his own land, he started developing more potato-growing partnerships with local farmers, providing them with both financ-ing and a solid market. Eventually these partnerships totaled over four thousand acres annually. Between overseeing so much farm land and his multiple tasks at the packing shed, he was again work-ing day and night. In the banner years, when potatoes went as high as one hundred and thirty dollars a ton, his profits were fantastic. And once again, by having his own marketing arm, he could do bet-ter than barely survive during the down years.

"Being fully in charge of that operation had some nice side benefits, too," he muses. "For instance, it allowed me to once again develop a working liaison with my old pal, Ray Young, who by then had taken control of his life. Ray was still going strong with Alcoholics Anonymous and had remarried. By the time he came to work for me, A.A. was sending him around to schools and other youth groups to give talks on the evils of too much liquor. With his personality and great sense of humor, I have to believe that Ray was a big hit with the younger generations.

"Besides his school runs, Ray and his new wife were spending plenty of time traveling the country with their pickup and fifth wheel camper, so I started using him as my eyes and ears. He'd travel down to California, into Idaho or over to Montana and check out what my seed potato growers were up to. Their product was supposed to be certified, but sometimes a grower would let his crop get infested and still try to pawn it off on you as bug free. All I could pay Ray was a retainer to cover his expenses and once in a while a small commission for buying seed potatoes, but that was okay with him. He was semi-retired, wanted to travel anyway, and was thoroughly enjoying life, out there being the happy warm hearted guy he was meant to be.

"Unfortunately, our rekindled relationship wasn't destined to last many years. In '82 that warm heart of his had been crippled by a major attack, and it hadn't totally responded to his new sobriety and healthier lifestyle. In '88 he was hit by a brain aneurysm he wouldn't survive. I guess like most of us Ray made plenty of mistakes in his life, but he was also a man who picked up hundreds of people with his humor and kindness. When he died, I knew I wasn't all alone in missing this fine friend. I've never met anyone, not even my close friend Harry Blackfield, who total strangers warmed to as fast."

Although the late seventies and the early eighties had their tragic aspects, they were also years of renewed prosperity. Besides his successes in farming and the Spada enterprise, in 1982 George latched on to yet another golden opportunity. A group of area businessmen were planning to start a bank in Kennewick. When they needed someone with an extensive agricultural background, Russ Dean, a local Ford dealer and the bank's first director, gave George a call.

"Russ explained that his group was offering me the chance to become an original major investors and a member of the bank's board of directors," George recalls. "I had questions at our first meeting, but when they gave me positive answers, it didn't take me long to say yes. This was a solid group of businessmen with a good financial plan, and I remembered too clearly a couple of earlier banking opportunities I'd failed to act on.

"Back in the late fifties the National Bank of Commerce asked me to start a small bank in Moses Lake. Then a year or so later they tried to get me to start one over in Othello. National Bank's long range plan was to let me get these banks rolling, then come in and buy me out, giving me a handsome payoff for my time and investment. By law they couldn't start their own new bank, but they could take over an existing one. I turned them down both times, figuring that starting up and then owning a bank even for a few years would be way too time consuming.

"Only later would I realize the mistake I'd made. The potential profits in starting up and then selling those two banks would have been substantial, and I'd known several excellent men back then who would have gladly stepped in as my bank managers and taken care of all the intricate details and the day to day decisions. I'd have had to put in more meeting time than I was already stuck with, but with the right manager even this would have been minimal. No, I'd made two mistakes along this line. I wasn't about to make a third."

Although the new bank, originally the American National Bank of Kennewick, may have had a good plan, it did get off to a bit of a rocky start. A few of the investors had made a written commitment to a builder, but then the directors had the opportunity to take over an existing savings and loan building in an excellent location. They all agreed that they had to back away from that earlier agreement.

"The builder sued us and won, which cost us a bundle, but we were still able to move forward. Right away we hired a fellow named Rich Emery as our C.E.O., and he did a great job for us. Rich thoroughly understood banking, and he knew how to work with people. We couldn't have made a better choice. Our board and various committee meetings did eat up a fair share of my time, especially early on, but getting involved with that bank was sure one of my better business decisions. Between dividends and stock splits it was a highly profitable investment for fourteen years. Then in 1996 we sold out to the First Hawaiian Bank, again for a good profit. A year later they renamed it Bank of the West."

Fifty-five

A FORTUNE LOST,
A BUSINESS GAINED

In those early eighties the packing shed had also continued to do well. In its best years George not only realized sizable dividends, but Spada provided him with a luxury company car, a Cadillac El Dorado, as well as a new pickup. Nothing but solid profits and perks seemed to be on their horizon.

"Yes, our shed was doing great, but by the fall of eighty-five I started to be bothered by what I heard was going on in our corporate offices in Portland," George recalls. "By 1986 these stories seemed to have enough substance to really make me nervous, so I resigned from their board of directors. I felt confident that I could still run their potato warehouse and continue to make that profitable, but I wanted to legally separate myself from the rest of Spada's operation.

"Just a year later Fred's son was involved in a huge onion speculation down in Chile. He ended up contracting for a whole freighter of fresh onions and had them shipped up to Philadelphia. But the U.S. inspectors discovered an insect infestation in the cargo and forced them to dump the whole works in the ocean.

Spada's loss on that single shipment was so great that it wiped out his entire corporation, their Oregon onion plant, everything, and that included our Pasco warehouse. Fred himself was still a wealthy man with plenty of other assets. He simply let his corporation take that fall.

"I could have handled losing that year's Spada profits, but my whole potato crop, everything we'd grown on my own land and the farms I had leased, was already in that warehouse when it went into receivership. We kept the plant operating until April of 1987, and I was able to see that every farmer who'd sent us potatoes was paid. Unfortunately, I couldn't do as much for myself. I wouldn't receive a dime.

"Maybe this was one debacle that wasn't in any way my fault, but right about then, this was no real solace. Spada's crash had hurt me bad! With all my production costs and everything else, I figure I dropped a little over $1,200,000 on that deal, the biggest share of this on my farming operation."

As bleak as his economic picture suddenly looked, George quickly realized that this was no time to become paralyzed by his losses. Right away he hired his old friend and attorney, John R. Lewis, and the two made a deal with U. S. Bank to restart the potato shed. By the first of July George had a signed lease and a verbal understanding with the bank manager that he could purchase the plant if and when it came up for sale. He renamed his new business Century 21 Products Incorporated, a title he could still carry over from his world's fair connections, and he was ready to get back into potato packing.

George knew this meant meeting all the unforeseen glitches that accompany every new business head on. Within a few months glitch number one arrived in the form of a letter, the first of several from the U.S. Dept. of Agriculture. This letter threatened to pull his brand new Century 21 license almost before its ink was dry. This license was issued under the Perishable Commodities Agricultural Act, or PACA, and now its administrators were claiming that George had still been on Spada's board when that company collapsed.

"Anyone who was on that board at the time of the crash would have been painted with the same brush, responsible for forfeiting the company's bond," George carefully explains. "PACA licensing is used to cover all the industry's problems, including not paying farmers or produce houses. The whole food packing and processing industry is built on trust, and if you break that trust and the government can prove it, you're done. In many ways it's a good system because it weeds out disreputable dealers, but sometimes it brands the innocent right along with the guilty.

"If I'd still been on Spada's board, I would have been blacklisted, even though I was personally running a highly profitable packing shed and had nothing to do with their failure. Plus, despite that crash, I'd been able to keep our shed going long enough to market everyone's spuds and make sure all our growers were paid, but as far as those bureaucrats were concerned, none of this would have benefited me in the least. Fortunately, I'd resigned from the Spada board in plenty of time and had the paperwork to prove it. It took dozens of letters and a couple of drawn out meetings to get this point across to them, but finally even those U.S.D.A. bureaucrats understood what I was telling them and were forced to acknowledge that I had the documentation to support my contentions."

Once his license was secure, George quickly realized he faced an even larger obstacle in overcoming the new distrust of many of the Pasco area potato farmers, a distrust that couldn't be erased simply by having the right paperwork. Although he had been the only grower that hadn't received full payment, Spada's sudden collapse had created an atmosphere of panic and doubt.

"I'd been running that potato shed for so long that in the eyes of most of the local farmers I was Spada," he now says. "Its failure was seen as my failure. If Spada couldn't be trusted, then neither could I. It wasn't hard to understand their thinking. My job was to change it. All I could do was go out and start making contacts again, explaining what had happened, how I still had viable national and international markets, and why I could still be trusted to handle their spuds. Essentially, I had to do whatever I could to rebuild grower confidence. It took several years, but gradually most of my regulars came back, and I started pulling in new growers."

Fifty-six

ANOTHER OLD FRIEND
COMES THROUGH

As tough as regaining grower confidence was, for a short time it almost seemed irrelevant. Because People's Bank also thought of him as part of Spada and tied him to that company's bankruptcy, it suddenly announced it was cutting off his entire line of credit. George still owned valuable assets, but his recent losses had created a major cash flow problem. Without this line of credit, he was soon going to have trouble paying his packing shed's operating costs.

"Yeah, the bank's sudden decision left me scrambling," he says, shaking his head. "It would have been bad in any case, but this was 1987, a year when our entire nation's farm economy was in terrible shape. Land prices in the Columbia Basin had plummeted. A piece of irrigated ground that would have sold for $2,000 in 1985 now had a tough time commanding half that price. No wonder those bankers were nervous. Everyone was.

"So when People's Bank pulled my credit line, I couldn't simply walk across the street and get their competitor to quickly take me on. Oh, I was convinced that I could get another bank to

320 SPIRIT OF THE SON

step in because I had a solid company with good markets, and despite the recent crash, my own farming ventures were still sound. But I'd have to first find the right bank and then do some careful convincing. To come out of this, I needed a quick infusion of cash.

"After some real soul searching I first turned to my older son, Michael. Since college he'd been climbing IBM's corporate ladder and a few months earlier had asked me for tax saving advice. I was sure I could figure out a way for him to do this by investing in my plant and farm. This was long before that wedding ceremony embarrassment, but even then I wasn't sure how he'd react. When I reached him by phone and asked for a loan, carefully explaining why I needed it and how we might set it up for his taxes, at first he said he didn't have any money. Then when I pressed him, he finally said 'Well, I'll have to get back to you on this.' But he never did. He never said another word about that loan, and I sure wasn't about to ask for it a second time.

"I was really hurt, partly because my son had given me no explanation, but I think more because it had been so hard for me to swallow my pride and approach him in the first place. The next time I saw him at a family luncheon we had in Seattle, I stayed pretty aloof. I guess Michael felt badly snubbed, We've hardly spoken since. Add in that wedding fiasco a few years later, and our father and son relationship was pretty well destroyed. I keep thinking that somewhere, some time, we'll be able to bridge this thing and become family again, just as Vic and I did. In the meantime Mike has two little girls growing up on the east coast, granddaughters I've never met."

Despite his disappointment and emotional pain, George knew he had to try other avenues for a quick cash fix. Fortunately his next phone call met with far better results. This one was to Los Angeles, to his old friend, Tom Hayashi.

"All Tom said when I told him that I needed a loan was 'How much?' When I answered $50,000, his next words were 'Fine, where do I send it?' The next morning he made the wire transfer to my account, no papers signed, no more questions asked. Less than two months later I was set up with another bank and was again okay, but Tom's $50,000 sure came at a critical time. Because it worked out better for him tax wise, I paid that loan off with interest over a period of several years.

"That loan was an act of pure friendship, one I'll never forget. At that time Tom really knew very little about my financial situation or the future prospects of my company, yet he was just willing to step forward the minute that I needed him without asking for any type of security or even a receipt. For Tom, my word was good enough. But considering the man he is, I can't say I was surprised. It's the kind of bond we've had over the years, like the best of brothers. Now whenever Tom comes to Hawaii, he's our guest. He stays in our condo as often and as long as he wants. I'm just glad I have this little way to say thank you."

Fifty-seven

BACKING AWAY
FROM A NEW VENTURE

lmost as soon as he'd straightened out his problems with the bank, George started looking into the possibility of building another processing plant, this one to turn out frozen hash browns and croquettes. Again he was looking for a better outlet for his lower grade potatoes, everything he couldn't sell on the fresh market. After another lengthy feasibility study, he was convinced a small hash brown and croquette plant had the most promise.

But because of the huge initial investment, he started looking around for a partner. The Japanese trading companies seemed a natural because Japan already had a multi-billion dollar market for croquettes, a patty that's made out of potatoes, meats and other vegetables.

"My proposal was to go partners," George recalls, "setting up this new plant to make both hash browns and croquettes, the latter entirely to their standards, and I'd run the operation. Exporting to Japan would give us a good start, but I also explained that I wanted to start marketing croquettes in this country. With all our new emphasis on microwaved meals, I figured they'd be a natural. Right away the trading companies were interested, but they all wanted me to go ahead and build the plant, then when it was up and running, they'd be willing to buy into it or make some other deal that would get us into bigger croquette production, and they'd help open up the Japanese markets.

"Essentially what these fellows were telling me was to go ahead and take all the early financial risks of high cost construction and start-up. Then they'd be willing to step in when it was much closer to a sure thing. This sure would have been a sweet deal for one of those trading companies, but I wanted no part of it. Maybe if I'd been forty, I'd have tried to line up the financing to swing this deal on my own because I definitely felt it was viable.

"But at sixty I just didn't feel that I could once again risk everything I'd built up. Without the new plant, I already had a sound packing business and enough other good investments for my lifetime. Going it alone on a venture of this magnitude was simply out of the question, and this wasn't all because of the caution that comes with age. When I was on that five year study of processing plants, I'd attended seminars where they'd talked about the high percentage of new businesses that fail. Back then I was still young enough to believe that ultimate failure was something that only happened to others, but now those figures kind of took my breath away."

Financial fears and age may have prevented George from moving forward with this latest plant, but fortunately the city of Pasco was destined to prosper from his initial efforts. Almost as soon as he'd formulated his first plans, George had contacted a man named Dave McDonald, Pasco's Development Director, and explained his future need for an industrial sewer.

"What we'd done in Quincy during the sixties was an excellent example of what Pasco needed to do in the eighties," George states. "I went over everything with Dave, how Quincy handled their bonds, how they obtained the necessary permits and let out contracts, everything he needed to know. Then I had him get hold of the Quincy public works people, and they were more than just helpful. They came right over to Pasco and showed Dave the plans for their system and explained them, point by point.

"Well, the upshot was that Pasco went ahead and put in its own industrial sewer system even after I'd told them that I was giving up on building a hash brown plant. Since then four major processors have come into our town and a fifth is on its way, all bringing good jobs, as well as better markets for area farmers. Without that system, none of these plants would have located here."

Fifty-eight

A NEW LOVE,
A PAINFUL LOSS

For George the late eighties were certainly demanding, but they weren't all about business. They'd also bring a long time friend back into his life. Almost twenty years earlier his good pal, Fred Yasunaga, had introduced him to Marguerite Hilburn, a highly successful real estate woman in Lakewood, a town near Tacoma. He and Marguerite knew many of the same people, and they would often end up at the same social gatherings. They even did a few business transactions together, working out small timber sales. She would handle the sellers, and he would set up the financing and line up buyers.

"I'd always admired Marge and enjoyed being around her," he fondly recalls. "She was a dynamic woman, always involved in her business and raising four children all by herself. But after I left Seattle for Pasco, I didn't see too much of her. On rare occasions, maybe once every three or four years, we'd again meet at a social gathering, maybe a cocktail party or at a dinner with half a dozen or more friends. From time to time I'd hear about her, where she'd been, what real estate deals she was closing, always through Fred.

"Then in 1988 Fred was in Pasco and drove me to Seattle for my daughter Jean's wedding. I was a bit uptight about what I might have to face at that wedding, but I was far more worried about my friend. Fred had a horrible cough that had been hanging on for months. His doctor was treating it as a bad chest infection, but by then Fred had to be concerned that this might be much more serious. As I'd listen to him hack away, then struggle to regain his breath, I was sure wondering.

"I went to my daughter's wedding that night and then took Marguerite to dinner the next, our first actual date. We'd always been pretty comfortable around each other, laughing, chatting, speaking our minds. Marge is naturally way more gregarious than I am and has a way of opening me up, of getting me to talk about things I normally wouldn't. We had a wonderful evening, yet given our hectic work schedules and the distance we lived apart, it's hard to say where our relationship would have gone if I'd returned to Pasco. But despite all the business pressures that demanded my return, I was about to spend an agonizing three months in Seattle.

"It started a couple days later when I went with Fred and Gloria to Swedish Hospital, where he had to see a specialist and undergo a series of tests. We'd only been back in Fred's room a short time when his regular doctor burst in and blurted out, 'Well, you have lung cancer and there's nothing we can do!' Next he was off on a long spiel about moving Fred out of the hospital, getting him tied in with hospice care, letting him die at home.

"I couldn't believe what I was hearing. No forewarning, not the slightest sign of sympathy or compassion in either his voice or expression. What kind of doctor was this? How could he just blurt that out to any man, especially in front of his wife and daughter?

"Even the best bedside manner can't take the sting out of such a grim message, but this guy was beyond crude, using those blunt words and that detached demeanor to hide from his own failure. He'd misdiagnosed Fred for over half a year before finally agreeing to send him to a specialist who'd found the cancer immediately. For six long months that disease had gone untreated. Now it had spread to both lungs and was so pervasive that even the specialist conceded it was beyond treatment.

"All I could do was be there, to talk to my friend when he felt up to it, to stay by his bedside when he didn't, to do whatever I could for Gloria and Lorie. For the three of us, it was a painful time. I can only partially imagine what Fred was going through. Dying would be his release, and it was the only thing that could put the rest of us on the road toward closure. His death came three months after that terrible diagnosis.

"Fred's funeral fell on a very rare Seattle day, when the city was blanketed with more than a foot of snow and temperatures dropped below zero. Still, hundreds of people attended, showing respect for this man who'd done so much for others. Seeing all those people buoyed my spirits, at least a little, because I felt it was a real tribute to my friend."

In those trying months before his friend's death, sometimes Marguerite had accompanied George to the hospital, and the two of them started spending more and more of their late evenings together, gradually growing closer, realizing that they had much to share and a real compatibility of spirit. Friendship soon gave way to romance, and their long talks turned toward a lasting relationship.

"Obviously I couldn't uproot my packing shed and move west," George states, "but Marge could think about coming to Pasco so we could be together. When her mother, Rebecca, came out from New Jersey for a visit, she and I immediately hit it off. Right away I knew this was a class act lady, and I guess she saw enough in me to encourage her daughter to make the move across the Cascades. In fact, Rebecca helped Marge pack up and relocate. A year and a half later, on December 8th, 1990, we were married in Las Vegas. "

As soon as Marguerite became a major part of his life, everyone who really knew George, from his lawyer to his own children, realized they were seeing a different man, a happier man. For the first time in his life he discovered the real thrill of having a child, Marge's little grandson, spend a quiet hour sitting on his lap.

"Yeah, having Marge around sure helped me drop a little of my reserve," George admits, "mainly because she and I could talk so openly, but partly because she could get me to laugh at myself. Once when I was taking my car through the automatic wash, I realized too late my aerial was still up. Without thinking I jumped

out to push it down, it stuck and before I knew it, those big
brushes slathered me with soap while the sprayers drenched me to
the skin. If Marge hadn't been home when I came back dripping
wet, no one would have ever heard that story. But for the next two
months she'd tease me into telling it at every gathering, until I
started enjoying it as much as my listeners. My grandson, Lance,
still figures out clever little ways to work grandpa's car-wash bath
in every time I see him, his own brand of humor that's good for
both of us.

Sixty

A TIME TO
RETHINK PRIORITIES

A new marriage, a thriving business, the nineties were definitely starting off on a high note. Century 21 was again
humming, handling twenty to thirty thousand tons of
potatoes each year. George had regained his growers' confidence,
and he continually used his marketing skills to broaden his base of
outlets. Just when it appeared that little else could go wrong, a
personnel change at U.S. Bank gave him another scare.

"I'd been riding along on the original agreement that I'd made
with their bank manager, always paying my rent on the building on
time" he says, "without a single complaint from anyone. Then suddenly the bank had a real internal shakeup, getting rid of the manager I'd been dealing with as well as several of its other officers.
Almost immediately the new guy they brought in and a woman
show up at my office and announced the bank was ready to sell the
warehouse. I said fine and asked for a few particulars.

"With absolutely no explanation he tossed out a ridiculous
selling price, at least twice what our facility was worth. Then
before I could even react, he walked out. The woman just sat there

for a few minutes, looking as shocked as I was. Finally she mumbled a brief apology and excused herself. The next thing I heard was that the bank had put my building on the market and had already sold it to some Oregon company. I called their realtor and was told it was a done deal and there was nothing I could do. Well, I knew better than that.

"The agreement I'd made with their former manager may have been only verbal, but I had plenty of witnesses. Plus I had certain legal rights because I occupied the building and had a thriving business that depended on it. The bank couldn't simply evict me without giving me the first chance to purchase. I hired a Seattle attorney and prepared to once again end up in court. Fortunately U. S. Bank's attorney was John Moore, the same man who represented us in that big Monsanto chemical case. After all the depositions were in, I think he understood that the bank didn't have much of a case. At any rate they didn't want to get tangled up in the courts, where banks always seem to come out second best, so they dropped it and let me purchase the building at a realistic price."

For the next five years George and Century 21 rocked along nicely together. His hours were long, his schedule demanding, and he wouldn't have had it any other way. At times a little shortness of breath reminded him that he was now well into his sixties, but he rarely entertained thoughts of retirement, though he readily admits he no longer had the drive that had marked his first fifty years. He had enough farm equipment to handle much more ground than the four hundred acres he owned and the four hundred he leased, but he no longer felt up to it. Admitting that he already had enough demands on his time was something brand new for George, but he did it. Still, full time retirement had no appeal.

"Maybe if somewhere along the line I'd picked up a serious hobby or two, I'd have thought differently," George acknowledges. "After Marguerite came into my life, I did take a little more time off for travel, but my work was always right there, always in my thoughts. Even when we left town for a week or two, I'd keep in daily contact with my office. No, getting in a few good holidays and spending more winter days in the Hawaiian sun were fine, but retirement simply wasn't right for me. Why would I want to quit doing something I thoroughly enjoyed?"

Then came June 24th, 1996, a day that would force George to rethink his priorities and realize that it was time to shift his life's pattern. All the way through May and into the first weeks of June, he'd been having chest pains, but that was a busy time of year in farming, so he ignored them, assuming he had angina.

"That morning I was walking out the garage door when it really hit," George recalls. "The pain was awful, much sharper than what I'd been feeling, strong enough to bring on nausea, dizziness, the whole bit. Right away I knew this one was serious. Somehow I made it back into the house to tell Marge. In no time she had me at the emergency room. By the time we made it to Pasco's Lady of Lourdes Hospital, their staff was waiting and they swarmed all over me. They ran tests, gave me medicine, did everything they could to bring me out of this. It sure boosts your morale when you see you're in such competent and concerned hands. Lourdes is a heck of a fine hospital.

"As that day wore on, my pain eased and everything seemed to be under control. Then that evening just as my doctor made his evening rounds, it came roaring back. Immediately the doctor decided I needed to be in Spokane's Sacred Heart Hospital's special care unit and called for a helicopter. Maybe it's exciting to get airlifted a hundred and fifty miles like that, but by then I was in no shape to enjoy the ride."

The Sacred Heart doctor ordered more tests and determined that George had definitely gone through at least one fairly serious heart attack. A major problem was that for years George had dealt with a mild form of adult diabetes, and all the blockage was in the smaller vessels leading to his heart. Bypass surgery wasn't an option. All his doctors could do was put him on blood thinners. He'd start the next morning, June 25th, by celebrating his sixty-eighth birthday in a hospital bed. Marguerite and Tom Hayashi, who'd dropped everything to be there, were at his side. By then the chest pains had abated.

"Yeah, I even felt good enough to eat a little of the birthday cake Marge had brought along," George recalls. "And it was great seeing Tom there. But all I could think about was the work I should be doing, and here I was stuck in Spokane. If the doctors couldn't operate and I was getting the right pills, I could see no reason to lie around in a hospital room. It was time for me to get back to work.

"At first Marge wouldn't hear of it, but finally my heart specialist, Dr. Kavanaugh, agreed. 'He's probably going to be under more stress staying away from that office and worrying about what's happening than he will be if he's up there making the decisions,' he explained to my fretting wife. I guess he understood my mind set pretty well."

George came home and went right to work, but that first heart attack had definitely changed his thinking. He had to admit that his days of running a big operation and putting in long, stress-filled hours month after month had to end. The time to sell out, to turn Century 21 over to younger people, was fast approaching. In less than eight months he would have a second reminder that a change of lifestyles was imminent. He and Marguerite were vacationing in Maui when the chest pains hit. Fortunately he was wearing his heart monitor and could telephone a reading to Dr. Kavanaugh, who ordered immediate hospitalization.

"If I'd known what I was in for, I'd have hopped the first plane to Honolulu instead," George grimaces. "I ended up in the Kahialui hospital, the only one on that island. For five hours I laid on a hard hospital bed in their emergency room, which was so grim it could have doubled for their morgue. The fellow next to me moaned and groaned the whole time, with no one ever coming around to do a thing for him. I was sure the poor guy was dying and maybe exposing me to a couple of infectious diseases before he checked out.

"When that hospital's lone cardiologist finally showed up, about all he did was complain because I was making him miss Engleburt Humperdink's act at a local hotel and then brag about the posh homes he owned in California and there on the island. When you're lying on a rock hard bed in a fourth-rate emergency room with your heart all out of whack, it's tough to sympathize with a fellow whose main problem in life is missing a concert. It's even tougher to be impressed by a detailed description of his precious real estate holdings.

"Finally this doctor called in a nurse and told her that I'd have to spend the night and to put me in a regular hospital room. Her reply was 'I can't. They're all full!' Then she and the doctor left together, apparently to see if they could double or triple up a few more of their patients. About two hours later the nurse returned and wheeled me into this tiny room that must have doubled as a supply closet during slack times. It had totally windowless concrete walls, with bare electrical wires running everywhere.

"The next morning I got zero attention, no tests, no medicine, not even any breakfast, and by this time I hadn't had a thing to eat for twenty-four hours. In fact, that cardiologist never did show up again. Finally I was so disgusted I called Marguerite and told her to come get me. I'd had more than enough of that place. I was checking myself out. We had reservations to fly to Honolulu that day anyway, and I had to believe they'd have better medical facilities than Maui. But someone at the hospital called the airlines as soon I walked out the door, and at first their staff wouldn't let me on the plane. Fortunately, Marguerite had called my kids who in turn got hold of Frances' brother, Roy Tosh Kaku, an E.N.T doctor in Honolulu. When Roy called and agreed to meet my plane and I signed a responsibility waiver, they finally let me board.

"Everything went okay, but when Roy was ready to take me to the hospital, I insisted on making a quick stop. The First Hawaiian Bank people had invited us to their sky box at the Hawaiian Open, and I at least wanted to stop in and say hello. After what I'd just survived in that Maui hospital, I figured this posed no threat. Well, Roy finally said okay, but as soon as he could, he whisked me off to the hospital, where I received first-class treatment. Their cardiologist thoroughly checked me out, then let me fly home. I came out of this episode sure of two things: Getting sick in Maui is a bad idea, and it was definitely time to slow down, to sell out, so that's what I did."

Sixty-one

ALL IN HIS
OWN WORDS

When I first decided that I wanted to have this book written, I didn't really understand what I was getting into. I'd had a number of intriguing experiences, and I definitely wanted my life's story told, but I didn't realize how difficult dredging up parts of my past was going to be. Many of my most poignant memories were deeply and painfully buried. Writing out my own notes and doing hours of interviews forced me to relive some pretty miserable experiences, first with everything that surrounded my family's internment and later with the collapse of my entire agricultural enterprise.

"Being such a private person, I've always internalized both the bad and good experiences that came my way. No one, not my closest friends, not even my family knew what internment meant to me or why my plant closed. For too many years I kept everything that hurt to myself. But if this book was to be written, I finally had to open up.

"Internalizing was part of my old 'Gambatte,' a part of being Frank Yoshino's son and Takijero's nephew. But, as I said, it's a story I definitely wanted told, partly so that my sons, daughters, friends and anyone else who's interested could see what I tried to do with my life and why. And partly because mine is simply one more American story, one more mixture of the good and bad that's happened in this powerful nation. Yes, and I wanted it to be the story of a few of the good and bad people I met along the way, the kind of people who make this nation what it is.

"The two internment camps and the events that surrounded them were by far the hardest for me to recollect because I'd buried them the deepest. But here I don't think I'm much different from the majority of Japanese-Americans who went through that experience. Like I said earlier, internees reacted in two ways, a minority becoming bitter and self-destructive, the majority picking up the pieces and moving on with our lives. Either way, internment wasn't something we talked a lot about, not even among ourselves, and certainly not with our Caucasian friends.

"It was the next generation, the Sansei, who revived all this talk about the camps. By the time they came along, internment simply loomed as something almost inexplicable in our distant past, a disturbing curiosity maybe, but not a painful memory. They wanted to understand exactly what happened and why. It's a good thing too, the Sansei stepping in and getting all this out in the open. In the end nothing good comes out of burying the uglier parts of our lives.

"This later generation felt free to ask all the hard questions about the camps because unlike those of us who lived through them, they've grown up in a world where they've always felt totally secure in their rights as Americans. They've never seen those rights suddenly stripped away, simply because they or their parents had come here from the wrong country. In fact, few among the Sansei have ever been forced to think seriously in terms of their race. They grew up as Americans, went to schools that were racially mixed, and lived in an era when the words 'Japanese-American' were starting to sound archaic.

"My own kids went through grade school, high school, college and on into their professions with little serious concern about their heritage. They were simply Americans. The three married ones all have Caucasian spouses, which now seems perfectly natural, but when I was a teenager and even a young adult, it wouldn't have been readily accepted by either race. Today it's a very different world than the one we faced both during the war and in the hostile climate that lingered afterwards.

"The thing I'll always hate the most about internment is what it did to my parents. Our farm was only the most tangible thing they lost. What they'd always been, strong decision-making people, with stature both in our household and in our community, was irrevocably destroyed. Yes, Mom and Pop had many good years later on, but they never regained their old confidence or decision-making abilities.

"Especially Pop. Until we were shipped off to camp, he was so confident, so forward looking, so ready to move with the changing times. After camp he still wanted us to move forward as a family, but as soon as we hit Weiser and had our own place again, he let me take the lead. That wasn't like my old Pop at all. Before camp he'd been plenty willing to listen, as long as we all understood that he had the final word.

"When I look just at my own life and what internment did to me, well, that's a bit harder to analyze. I do know it shocked me out of what had been a fairly pleasant childhood up to then, and it forced me to come to grips with the dark side of humanity a kid shouldn't have to face. But if I suddenly had to see the worst in people during that painful time, I also saw the best, and was able to internalize a couple of very important values. The worst people I've had to deal with don't need any more print here, but I can never say enough about the good ones, starting in Weiser.

"I'll always be thankful that Mom and Pop fought so hard to keep us kids from sinking into bitterness during those months in the camps, but all their efforts may not have been enough if we'd ended up in the wrong community. I do know that Milton wasn't the only little town in the Northwest that displayed strong hostilities towards Japanese-Americans. Later I realized the restaurant owner who turned on me so viciously in Payette was a real reflection of his town. That little burg was openly racist.

"But somehow most of Weiser's whites, or at least those who mattered in my life, had escaped the worst of this. Maybe they'd been neighbors with enough of the good Issei and Nesei who lived in that valley for so long that common sense had simply prevailed. Or maybe this little town was lucky enough to have a few far-sighted community leaders, folks who didn't tolerate ignorance, who set the right tone. I don't really know, but whatever made Weiser more accepting, it sure made my teen years a whole lot more palatable. I never went anywhere, whether it was to our local cafe or our implement or seed dealer, where I didn't feel welcome. Sports might have helped me personally because before that first football season ended, everyone knew me, but my folks felt just as accepted.

"Both Kennewick and Weiser were such good places to go to school that I still try to hit all their class reunions, just to spend a little time with my old friends. Of course I didn't attend school in Kennewick after the eighth grade, so grads who came after that would wonder who I was when I showed up. But my old classmates let them know in a hurry, and before the first festivities were over, we were all sharing stories.

"I've enjoyed the Weiser reunions so much that when Tom Hayashi invited me to one of his, I jumped at the chance. Arlen Webb, one of my basketball teammates that first year, was Master of Ceremonies. He talked about different grads, what they'd done with their lives, about old times at Weiser High, all the stuff his audience wanted to hear.

"Then suddenly Webb was talking about internment and how wrong it was, but how Tom and I had been able to come out of those camps and fit right into their high school. He talked about how we hadn't let the camps become our permanent road-blocks, but had gone on to lead fulfilling lives. He said he wanted everyone at that reunion to know how much he admired us for not letting this huge injustice destroy us or make us bitter.

"Arlen ended by directing his remarks towards Tom and me. He personally apologized for what we and our families had been subjected to and complimented us for having achieved so much despite all that. It was good to hear this from a man like Webb, a man I've always felt was more than a few cuts above the average in intelligence and compassion. But I could apply those words to quite a few of my old Weiser and Kennewick pals.

"If the ugliest parts of the camps and the racists I had to face in that era taught me anything, it was to never stoop to their level.

Sure, maybe it would have been comforting during internment or after that miserable summer with old Heidenreich to go off on the Anglo-bashing tirades I heard from guys like my old camp buddy, Satoshi Koyama. But as I've said, that mentality has two deadly pitfalls. Right away you're reduced to the level of the racists, and you're cut off from the good people of every color, anyone who's risen above petty bigotry. If I'd fallen into that terrible line of thinking, I'd have become so absorbed in my own hatred, always on guard for that next racial slur, real or imagined, that I couldn't possibly have moved freely and successfully in the business world the way I did.

"And I hate to think of all the close friendships I'd never have made. In this book I've been able to touch on just a few of the most significant, but a real listing of the people I admire and who really meant something to me would go on and on. Getting caught up in the bigotry and racism of those war years not only would have ruled out all the fine white friends I've had over the years, but it would have cut me off from the best people of my own race, fellows like Fred Yasunaga and Tom Hayashi, men who were able to rise way above that kind of thinking.

"Luckily, I went in the right direction and at least tried to deal openly and honestly with the people I met, starting with the thousands of employees I've had over the years. If those months of misery, first on the Wyoming beet farm and then in Milton, were what it took to teach compassion for my own crews, well, they were worth the price. Except for a few genuine shirkers who might still be blaming me for not handing them a free ride, I honestly don't think any of my former employees holds real animosity.

"Plus, in the late fifties and through much of the sixties I was able to assist so many young Basin farmers, sometimes with an early partnership, far more often just by helping them with their finances. A potato grower's two biggest costs are seed and fertilizer. If I provided these, either for a percentage of the crop or a cash payment after harvest, a young farmer could usually handle the rest.

"In choosing who to help and who to reject, I had my own workable system. I wasn't going to back any idiots, but I was far more concerned with a man's energy level, his willingness to take on a task and give it everything he had. If I believed he was a doer, a real man of action, I'd back a guy in a minute. If I felt he was your basic eight-to-fiver or more interested in his time off than the task at hand, I said no. Very few of these young men ever let me down. Oh, a couple times my evaluation of a man was off and he left me holding the financial sack. But all the good ones, the ones who not only paid me back but then went on to become real success stories themselves, more than made up for that occasional deadbeat.

"Two brothers, Koke and John Oda, were prime examples of the good young men I was able to help. When they moved to Quincy from Utah, they had all their worldly possessions in a couple of old beater pickup trucks, but right away I felt they both had the drive and the good sense to make it in farming. In 1956 I took John on as a partner, farming one hundred and fifty acres of potatoes while Koke worked for wages on a neighboring farm, and his wife Ruth did waitress work in a Quincy restaurant. A few years later I formed a second partnership with Koke, raising both potatoes and onions, gradually expanding our acreages. Right around 1960 those two were ready to strike out on their own.

"Years later quite a few of the men I helped looked me up or at least telephoned, just to say thanks and maybe to let me know how they'd done since I'd last seen them. Their first question was always 'Do you remember helping me get started?' The fifties and sixties were busy years for me, so often I didn't remember, but those fellows sure did.

"Without first prospering myself, though, I couldn't have helped anyone, and I'm equally proud of how I accomplished this. I don't remember the author's name, but a few years back I ran across this quote:

> 'The world is full of very competent people who intend to do things tomorrow, or as soon as they can get around to it. Their accomplishments seldom match those with less talent, but with a sense of getting started now. The people who make things move share the same sense of urgency.'

"Those are easy lines for me to believe because they accurately reflect so much of what I've seen. Sure, you first ask plenty of questions and find out as much as you can before plunging into a new venture, but in today's business world the point where you have to act comes in a hurry. Else you'll be watching from the sidelines while someone else is busy capitalizing on your good ideas.

"This sense of urgency must have been instilled in me early because I really can't remember a time when it wasn't there. Whenever I think of the worst periods of my life, the internment camps, those few months in Milton, and particularly the years surrounding the closure of my dehy plant, a big part of my frustration was that I had no control. I wasn't able to call the shots, to make decisions that were going to let me move ahead. Others were pulling the strings, and I simply had to go along with their dictates.

"When I think of the best years of my business life, they all revolve around being a problem solver, making one quick and vitally important decision after another. From way back in the late forties when I was maximizing our profits on that little fifteen-acre onion patch to when I was building up the dehy plant and finally during the years when I was bringing my Century 21 potato shed back from the brink, I was always excited about going to work, always looking forward to what that day might bring. All that pressure took a real toll on my health, but emotionally and mentally I thrived on it. I thoroughly enjoyed a life of taking charge and having the final say.

"And I have to admit to being the classic workaholic. But even with what that cost me in my family relationships, it's hard to completely regret it or honestly say that if given a second chance, I'd do things differently. When you have ideas you believe in, what could be more satisfying than a life spent turning them into reality? Sure, some of my ideas didn't work out, sometimes because they were flawed, sometimes because I was trying to get a little too far ahead of my time.

"For instance, back in the early sixties I spent a fair amount of time and mental energy looking into the fascinating possibilities of using irradiation to stop our onions and potatoes from sprouting once they were in storage. This all started when the Atomic Energy Commission invited Mike McCormick, who was with General

Electric's Hanford Nuclear Division at that time and later would become our district congressman, to a meeting on this subject. McCormick asked Wilbur Hallauer and me to join him. Later the three of us had several meetings on our own, brainstorming the possibilities of setting up a plant to irradiate fruits and vegetables.

"The idea was fascinating, but we were facing two major barriers. First, the public wasn't anywhere close to accepting irradiation, and second, the costs of using it on big volume, low cost produce such as potatoes and onions was prohibitive. Until someone convinced the world's consumers that irradiated foods weren't going to lead to a cancer epidemic or something equally terrible, the entire technology would remain in the lab, and if someday it was accepted, we realized that it would only be practical for more expensive foods, such as meats and higher priced fruits.

"Still I was so intrigued by irradiation that after McCormick and Hallauer gave up on the ideal, I contacted Dr. Pigott, a brilliant University of Washington professor, and worked with him on actual tests. He'd try different amounts of irradiation on a product, seeing exactly how much it took to kill the spores that could grow into sprouts without damaging the vegetable. A bit too much and it altered the taste of potatoes or onions, too little and they still sprouted. Get it just right and irradiation definitely worked.

"Fascinating or not, though, I finally had to give up on any dream of building an irradiation facility. But my ideas that did work, everything from that plow-disk-packer trio I set up in the early fifties to my new telescoping boxes, to the peeling process we developed at the dehy plant, all gave me tremendous satisfaction.

"Back then I had the exuberance and naivete of youth on my side and didn't know how hard it is to make real changes, even for companies with plenty of resources. For instance, in 1965 I was at General Mills when they were taste-testing a new product called Bacos, a substitute bacon bit made from soybeans. The flavor and texture were good, and with all the health scares about real bacon, I figured they'd dominate the market in no time. Well, I guess you can still buy Bacos, but they sure haven't taken over from the real bacon bits, despite General Mills' reputation and tremendous promotional powers. Yeah, major changes in the food industry are always tough, even for the major players.

"When we ended up in Weiser and a few years later in Moses Lake, it seemed only natural that I'd follow Pop into farming. Later I'd discover that my real strengths were in the business world. Oh, I did okay as a farmer, but my biggest profits almost always came because I packed and marketed the potatoes and onions I grew.

"Had I remained strictly a farmer, it's hard to say how I'd have ended up, but I do know this: I wouldn't touch it today if I couldn't also be into marketing or at least have real ties to someone who was. It's one thing to grow a crop. It's entirely another to make it profitable. Combine today's costs of everything from machinery to fertilizer and fuel with market volatility, and it makes sticking seed potatoes or onions in the ground in hopes of respectable harvest time prices only slightly less risky than the Vegas roulette tables. In fact, these two entities work just about the same. Play long enough and you're probably going to end up broke.

"I look at some of the young farmers starting out today, and at times I feel badly for them. All the ambition and ability in the world, and many of these lads have plenty of both, won't save them from the real market downturns that are bound to hit. The big farmers, the ones with their own produce sheds or who have the right alliances, are going to continue to grow. Every year I see more small guys drop out and go into another line of work or hire on with a corporate land holder.

"My biggest regrets? For starters I wish I'd never taken on major partners. I had no trouble with joint ventures, such as in the bank, where there were clear corporation rules and a competent C.E.O. to carry them out. And my small partnerships, mainly growing spuds and onions with various young farmers, had far more pluses than minuses. Even when I partnered up with those six Quincy farmers to start our first big potato shed, that worked out okay, mainly because as majority owner and president, I could assume full control. My biggest business failures always came because I couldn't exercise that same kind of control, and too often it was a partner who made that impossible.

"Plus, In the business world I was at my best when I could quickly analyze a problem, come to a decision, then act immediately. Having a partner made this tougher because I had to keep him informed and get his input. That's okay if you're a big corporation with plenty of resources and able to call many of the shots because of your size, but I was always in a building-up mode, where an enterprise could go forward or backward in a hurry, and quick decisions were essential.

"When I let my brothers become full partners, well, of course that ended up being a huge mistake, but even without the final mess that cost us everything, It was a bad idea. Although Vic and I worked great together in the early years, that partnership had two basic flaws. First, it always put Vic in my shadow, and second, it forced me to rely on and answer for someone else. We'd have both been better off if I'd have simply hired Vic, giving him big bonuses when we had high profit years, and eventually helped him finance his own operation. I still could have helped him market his produce, and Vic would have been concentrating on his real talent. As an independent land owner, he'd have had far greater pride in his accomplishments.

"But I also have to admit that my own disposition created part of my partnership problems. Whenever I felt that I was putting everything I could into making an operation go, I expected my partners to at least hold up their end of our bargain and do what we'd agreed on. When they didn't, I was less than tactful in letting them know about it.

"And I deeply regret losing our dehy plant and everything that went with it. Sure, no one likes losing a potential fortune, but that whole enterprise, especially the plant, meant much more to me. I took such pride in that operation, the crew I'd put together, the quality product we were turning out, our growing reputation in both the national and international markets.

"Now when I look back, I see a real parallel between what happened to me then and what happened to Pop during internment. Our strong beliefs in who we were, authority figures who made important decisions, men who not only took care of our families but also our workers, men with real status in our communities, suddenly all that was taken away. Pop felt he was nothing when internment stripped his authority. I felt the same way the day my plant closed. He lost what was to be his legacy to his children and grandchildren and so did I. The biggest single difference was that when this happened to me, I was still young enough to rebound and only wrong-headed enough to waste a year trying to drink myself into oblivion.

"Yes, I finally came to my senses, moved on, and rebuilt my life, but I'd be lying if I said that I'm completely over that loss. Too much was involved, everything from my self concept to Mom and Pop's happiness to my family's future, to all those people who lost their jobs. No, I don't let myself dwell on that long ago debacle on a daily or even a monthly basis. I haven't done that since the very early seventies. But to this day, in a quiet, reflective moment, it all comes surging back, and once again I'm left asking why.

"And I deeply regret that last split I had with my brother Vic. Maybe it was his actions that set off the chain of events that ended in my bankruptcy, and maybe in my darkest moments I've resented him and harbored a real bitterness, but deep down I know that wasn't Vic. He'd become a very sick man, irrational, turning on all his friends. If it hadn't been for that, I know we could have lived out our lives as the best of brothers, the best of friends.

"What hurts the most is that we didn't get Vic to the right doctors soon enough to cure his problems. We didn't get him back to his old warm-hearted self soon enough to keep both our family enterprise and our friendship intact. Thankfully in his last few years he and I patched things up. During the late seventies and early eighties I was able to help him out financially, but all the prescription drugs he'd consumed cut his life way too short. We sure missed out on a lot of good years.

"Then of course there was my divorce. By the time Frances and I split, we really did have what the legal profession calls 'irreconcilable differences', and I'll sure take most of the blame for those. Still, a dissolved marriage wasn't the way I'd wanted things to go for us. I'd started out sharing my parents' values about the sanctity of marriage and the importance of maintaining a strongly united family. Divorce shattered the first of these and drove huge wedges into the second.

"My greatest inspiration in life? Without a doubt that has to be my father. I've already talked about how his early life in this country inspired me when I was a young farmer, but that same inspiration was going to be with me through every facet of my adult life. Whether I was walking into that big Spokane warehouse and seeing all those sacks of soaked and sprouting onions, mentally dueling with a crooked Chicago brokerage house, flying to thirteen cities in ten days, or starting all over and rebuilding another fresh pack business, Pop's image, what he'd not only endured but conquered, was always in front of me.

"So often I'd recall that long-ago auto trip, when Pop accompanied me on one of my Gila Bend Runs. As he pointed out place after place where he'd been with the railroad, most of them stark, dusty little towns surrounded by miles of arid countryside, I was struck by his excitement and enthusiasm for this land. What could Pop have seen that would have stirred him up and made him willing to sacrifice so much? The only real difference between what we were looking at in the arid parts of Oregon, California and Nevada and the land he eventually settled is that Kennewick had a mighty river running past, and Pop must have fully understood the significance of this seemingly endless supply of irrigation water.

"The man had vision, yes, but his dedication to that vision is what I'll always find inspiring. Everything from an incredible language barrier to his long days running that body-breaking Fresno and hand planting acres of strawberries and asparagus to coming home night after night to that empty shack would have sent a lesser man packing.

"Years later, in my reflective moments, all the 'how' questions would come flooding back. How did Pop learn to farm, to do everything from plant and irrigate to drive a team of horses? How did he find the right equipment and all the root stock and seed he needed or know how to build functional packing sheds? And how did he communicate with his white neighbors when they set up that intricate Kennewick Irrigation District? But most of all, how did he face his loneliness, the years of isolation that simply had to exist before Mom entered his life? How did he endure?

"I began this story by saying that I've finally realized I am very much my father's son, both in my temperament and my mental outlook. But when I really dwell on what Pop faced when he started out, I have to honestly wonder if I would have had the same courage and perseverance. Maybe I could have handled the labor, but throw in his isolation and cultural difficulties, well, I just don't know. Had I been in his place and looked out that shack's lone window on yet another bitterly cold February day when a raw wind was blowing up the Columbia, and thought about once again hitching that heavy logging chain to my team to rip out sagebrush, I might have gathered up my meager personal effects and caught the next boat home, where I'd have dusted off my law degree and led a life of comparative luxury and refinement.

"No, I can't say I inherited every bit of my father's metal, but I guess I did pick up a fair share of his work ethic, his desire to try new ventures and his problem-solving abilities. His unflinching honesty and his vision of what could be? I hope I had just enough of these. At any rate, they were a big part of why Pop's been my inspiration.

"Finally, it all comes back to gambatte, that word Uncle Takejiro explained and Pop exemplified. Recently I've seen it described as 'The Never Say Die Syndrome,' which pretty well summarizes what those two men instilled in me. Always trying to succeed, never satisfied with anything less than being number-one, dedicating yourself to your work, these all have ties to gambatte, and I'm proud of the fact that they became my key tenets.

"Everything in my early life, from sports to the camps to coming out and taking charge when I was only fifteen, definitely reinforced it. Being an adherent of gambatte, the perfect philosophy for any competitor, wasn't a real choice, even by my teens. It's just who I was.

Now it's time to admit that my days of being a real competitor are over. Today the only work I have to look forward to is managing my stock portfolio, which has done very well, but it's just not the same as running a dynamic enterprise and dealing with dozens of people on a daily basis.

"More and more I understand that I'm now in the autumn of my life. Lately I've seen my health slipping fast and I feel strongly that I don't have too many days in front of me. I guess it's this that now makes me spend hours reflecting on all my old friends and the good business associates I've had over the years. Most of them were older than me and are gone now. I miss them more than ever."

Author's Note

Right after Christmas George sent me the notes that comprise his final paragraphs. That week and the week prior, he and I had some of our best conversations, just a few hours when he succinctly clarified some of the main points of this book. On the evening of December 30th, 2000, Marguerite telephoned to let me know that George had passed away that afternoon, succumbing to a final heart attack. It was his time to go off and join those good friends, as well as his beloved father and mother, his brother Vic and his sister Louise. And it is left for us, the friends and family he left behind, to do the missing.